The History of the Origins of Christianity
Christianity
Book I: The Life of Jesus

By Joseph Ernest Renan

Edited by Anthony Uyl

Devoted Publishing

Woodstock, Ontario, 2016

The History of the Origins of Christianity - Book I: The Life of Jesus
By Joseph Ernest Renan
Member of the French Academy
Edited by Anthony Uyl

Originally Published and Printed by:
London: Mathieson & Company

What kind of philosophies do you have? Let us know!

Contact us at: devotedpub@hotmail.com
Visit us on Facebook: @DevotedPublishing
Get more products via our website: www.devotedpublishing.com

Published in Woodstock, Ontario, Canada 2016

For bulk educational rates, please contact us at the email address above.

ISBN: 978-1-988297-69-9

Table of Contents

TO THE PURE SOUL OF MY SISTER HENRIETTA

Who died at Byblus, 24th September, 1861.

FROM the bosom of God, in which thou reposest, dost thou recall those long days at Ghazir, when, alone with thee, I wrote these pages, which were inspired by the places we had visited together? Sitting silently by my side, thou didst read each sheet and copy it as soon as written--the sea, the villages, the ravines, the mountains being meanwhile spread out at our feet. When the overpowering light had given place to the innumerable host of stars, thy delicate and subtly questions, thy discreet doubts, brought me back to the sublime object of our common thoughts. Thou saidst to me one day that thou wouldst love this book, because, first, it had been written in thy presence, and because, also, it was to thine heart. If at times thou didst fear for it the narrow opinions of frivolous men, thou felt always persuaded that truly religious souls would, in the end, take delight in it. While in the midst of these sweet meditations, Death struck us both with his wing; the sleep of fever overtook us at the same hour, and I awoke alone! Thou sleepest now in the land of Adonis, near the holy Byblus and the sacred waters where the women of the ancient mysteries came to mingle their tears. Reveal to me, O good genius!--to me, whom thou lovedst--those truths which conquer death, strip it of fear, and make it almost beloved.

PREFACE TO THE THIRTEENTH EDITION

THE twelve first editions of this work differ only from one another in respect of a few trifling changes. The present edition, on the contrary, has been revised and corrected with the greatest care. During the four years which have elapsed since the book appeared, I have laboured incessantly to improve it. The numerous criticisms to which it has given rise have rendered the task in certain respects an easy one. I have read all those which contain anything important. I believe I can conscientiously affirm that not once have the outrage and the calumny, which have been imported into them, hindered me from deriving profit from the just observations which those criticisms might contain. I have weighed everything, tested everything. If, in certain cases, people should wonder why I have not answered fully the censures which have been made with such extreme assurance, and as if the errors alleged have been proved, it is not that I did not know of these censures, but that it was impossible for me to accept them. In the majority of such cases I have added in a note the texts or the considerations which have deterred me from changing my opinion, or better, by making some slight change of expression, I have endeavoured to show wherein lay the contempt of my critics. These notes, though very brief and containing little more than an indication of the sources at first hand, are sufficient in every case to point out to the intelligent reader the reasonings which have guided me in the composition of my texts.

To attempt to answer in detail all the accusations which have been brought against me, it would have been necessary for me to triple or quadruple this volume: I should have had to repeat things which have already been well said, even in French; it would have been necessary to enter into a religious discussion, a thing that I have absolutely interdicted myself from doing; I should have had to speak of myself, a thing I shall never do. I write for the purpose of promulgating my ideas to those who seek the truth. As for those persons who would have, in the interests of their belief, that I am an ignoramus, an evil genius, or a man of bad faith, I do not pretend to be able to modify their opinions. If such opinions are necessary for the peace of mind of certain pious people, I would make it a veritable scruple to disabuse them of them.

The controversy, moreover, if I had entered upon it, would have led me most frequently to points foreign to historical criticism. The objections which have been directed against me have proceeded from two opposing parties. One set has been addressed to me by freethinkers, who do not believe in the supernatural, nor, consequently, in the inspiration of the sacred books; another set by theologians of the liberal Protestant school, who hold such broad doctrinal views that the rationalists and they can readily understand one another. These, adversaries and I find ourselves on common ground; we start with the same principles; we can discuss according to the rules followed in all questions relating to matters of history, philology, and archæology. As to the refutations of my book (and these are much the most numerous) which have been made by orthodox theologians, both Catholic and Protestant, who believe in the supernatural and in the sacred character of the books of the Old and New Testament, they all involve a fundamental misapprehension. If the miracle has any reality, this book is but a tissue of errors. If the Gospels are inspired books, and true, consequently, to the letter, from beginning to end, I have been guilty of a great wrong in not contenting myself with piecing together the broken fragments of the four texts, like as the Harmonists have done, only to construct thus an ensemble at once most redundant and most contradictory. If, on the contrary, the miracle is an inadmissible thing, then I am right in regarding the books which contain miraculous recitals as histories mixed with fiction, as legends full of inaccuracies, errors, and of systematic expedients. If the Gospels are like other books I am right in treating them in the same manner as the Hellenist, the Arabian, the Hindoo treated the legendary documents which they studied. Criticism does not recognise infallible texts; its first principle is to admit that in the text which is examined there is the possibility of error. Far from being accused of scepticism, I ought to be classed with the moderate critics, since, instead of rejecting en bloc weak documents as so much trash, I essay to extract something historical out of them by means of delicate approximation.

And as no one asserts that to put the question in such a manner implies a petitio principii, seeing we take for granted à priori that which is proved in detail, to wit, that the miracles related by the Gospels have had no reality, that the Gospels are not books written under the inspiration of Divinity. Those two negations are not with us the result of exegesis; they are anterior to exegesis. They are the outcome of an experience which has not been denied. Miracles are things which never happen; only credulous people believe they have seen them; you cannot cite a single one which has taken place in presence of witnesses capable of testing it; no special intervention of the Divinity, whether in the composition of a book, or in any event whatever, has been proved. For this reason alone, when a person admits the supernatural, such a one is without the province of science; he accepts an explanation which is non-scientific, an explanation which is set aside by the astronomer, the physician, the chemist, the geologist, the physiologist, one which ought also to be passed over by the historian. We reject the supernatural for the same reason that we reject the existence of centaurs and hippogriffes; and this reason is, that nobody has ever seen them. It is not because it has been previously demonstrated to me that the evangelists do not merit absolute credence that I reject the miracles which they recount. It is because they do recount miracles that I say, "The Gospels are legends; they may contain history, but, certainly, all that they set forth is not historical."

It is hence impossible that the orthodox person and the rationalist who denies the supernatural can be of much assistance in such questions. In the eyes of theologians, the Gospels and the books of the Bible in general are books like no others, books more historic than the best histories, inasmuch as they contain no errors. To the rationalist, on the contrary, the Gospels are texts to which the ordinary rules of criticism ought to be applied; we are, in this respect, like the Arabs in presence of the Koran and the hadith, like the Hindoos in presence of the Vedas and the Buddhist books. Is it because the Arabs regard the Koran as infallible? Is it because we accuse them of falsifying history that they relate the origins of Islamism differently from the Mussulman theologians? Is it because the Hindoos hold the Lalitavistara to be a biography?

How are such opinions, in setting out from opposed principles, to be mutually reconciled? All rules of criticism assume that a document subjected to examination has but a relative value, that it may be in error, and that it may be improved by comparing it with a better document. The profane savant, persuaded that all books which have come down to us as legacies are the work of man, did not hesitate to do an injury to texts when the texts contradicted one another, when they set forth absurd or formal statements which had been refuted by witnesses of greater authority. Orthodoxy, on the contrary, positive in advancing that the sacred books do not contain an error or a contradiction, tolerates the most violent tactics, expedients the most desperate, in order to get out of difficulties. Orthodox exegesis is, in this way, a tissue of subtleties. An isolated subtlety may be true; but a thousand subtleties cannot at once be true. If there were in Tacitus or Polybius errors so pronounced as those committed by Luke apropos of Quirinius and of Theudas, we should say that Tacitus and Polybius have been deceived. Reasonings which we would not admit if the question were one of Greek or Latin literature, hypotheses which a Boissonade, or even a Rollin, would never think of, are held to be plausible when the question is one of exculpating a sacred author.

Hence it is orthodoxy which is guilty of a petitio principii, when it reproaches rationalism with changing history, because the latter does not accept word for word the documents which orthodoxy holds to be sacred. Because a fact is written down, it does not thence follow that it is true. The miracles of Mahomet have been put into writing as well as those of Jesus; and certainly the Arab biographies of Mahomet, that of Ibn-Haschim, for example, has a much more historical character than the Gospels. Do we on this account admit the miracles of Mahomet? We follow Ibn-Haschim with more or less confidence when we have no reasons for doubting him. But when he relates to us things that are perfectly incredible we make no difficulty about abandoning him. Certainly, if we had four lives of Buddha, which were partly fabulous, and as irreconcilable amongst themselves as the four Gospels are to one another, and if a savant essayed to purge the four Buddhist narratives of their contradictions, we should not accuse that savant of falsifying the texts. It might well be that he attempted to unite discordant passages, that he sought a compromise, a sort of middle course, a narrative which should embrace nothing that was impossible, in which opposing testimony was balanced and misrepresented as little as possible. If, after that, the Buddhists believed in a lie, in the falsification of history, we would have a right to say to them: "The question here is not one of history, and if we must at times discard your texts it is the fault of those texts which contain things impossible of belief, and, moreover, which are contradictory."

At the bottom of all discussion on such matters is the question of the supernatural. If the miracle and the inspiration of certain books are actual facts, our method is detestable. If the miracle and the inspiration of some books are beliefs without any reality, our method is the proper one. Now, the question of the supernatural is determined to us with absolute certainty, by this simple reason, that there is no room for belief in a thing of which the world can offer no experimental trace. We do not believe in a miracle, just as we do not believe in dreams, in the devil, in sorcery, or in astrology. Have we any need to refute step by step the long reasonings of astrology in order to deny that the stars influence human events? No. It is sufficient for this wholly negative, as well as demonstrable experience, that we give the best direct proof--such an influence has never been proved.

God forbid that we should be unmindful of the services that the theologians have rendered to science! The research and the constitution of the texts which serve as the basis of this history have been the work in many cases of orthodox theologians. The labour of criticism has been the work of liberal theologians. But there is one thing that a theologian can never be--I mean a historian. History is essentially disinterested. The historian has but one care, art and truth (two inseparable things; art guards the secret of the laws which are the most closely related to truth). The theologian has an interest -- his dogma. Minimise that dogma as much as you will, it is still to the artist and the critic an insupportable burden. The orthodox theologian may be compared to a caged bird; every movement natural to it is intercepted. The liberal theologian is a bird, some of the feathers of whose wings have been clipped. He believes he is master of himself, and he in fact is until the moment he seeks to take his flight. Then it is seen that he is not completely the creature of the air. We proclaim it boldly; critical inquiries relative to the origin of Christianity will not have said their last word until they shall have cultivated, in a purely secular and profane spirit, the method of the Hellenists, the Arabs, the Hindoos, people strangers to all theology, who think neither of edifying, nor of scandalising, nor of defending, nor of overthrowing dogmas.

Day and night, if I might so speak, I have reflected on these questions, questions which ought to be agitated without any other prejudices than those which constitute the essence of reason itself. The most serious of all unquestionably is that of the historic value of the fourth Gospel. Those who have not disagreed on such problems give room for the belief that they have not comprehended the whole difficulty. We may range the opinions on this Gospel into four classes, of which the following is the abridged expression. First opinion: "The fourth Gospel was written by the Apostle John, the son of Zebedee. The statements contained in that Gospel are all true; the discourses which the author puts into the mouth of Jesus were actually held by Jesus." This is the orthodox opinion. From the point of view of rational criticism, this is wholly untenable.

Second opinion: "The fourth Gospel is, in fact, by the Apostle John, although it may have been revised and retouched by his disciples. The facts recounted in that Gospel are direct traditions in regard to Jesus. The discourses are often from compositions expressing only the manner in which the author had conceived the mind of Jesus." This is the opinion of Ewald, and in some respects that of Lücke, Weisse, and Reuss. This is the opinion that I adopted in the first edition of this work.

Third opinion: "The fourth Gospel is not the work of the Apostle John. It was attributed to him by some of his disciples about the year 100. The discourses are almost entirely fictitious; but the narrative parts contain valuable traditions, ascending in part to the Apostle John." This is the opinion of Weizsaecker and of Michael Nicolas. It is the opinion which I now hold.

Fourth opinion: "The fourth Gospel is in no sense the work of the Apostle John. And whether, as regards the facts or the discourses which are reported in it, it is not a historic book; it is a work of the imagination and in part allegorical, concocted about the year 150, in which the author has proposed to himself, not to recount actually the life of Jesus, but to make believe in the idea that he himself had formed of Jesus." Such is, with some variations, the opinion of Baur, Schwegler, Strauss, Zeller, Volkmar, Helgenfeld, Schenkel, Scholten, and Rénille.

I cannot quite ally myself to this radical party. I am convinced that the fourth Gospel has an actual connection with the Apostle John, and that it was written about the end of the first century. I avow, however, that in certain passages of my first edition I inclined too much in the direction of authenticity. The probative force of some arguments upon which I insisted appear to me now of less importance. I no longer believe that Saint Justin may have put the fourth Gospel on the same footing as the synoptics amongst the "Memoires of the Apostles." The existence of Presbyteros Joannes, a personage distinct from the Apostle John, appears to me now as very problematical. The opinion according to which John, the son of Zebedee, could have written the work, an hypothesis which I have never altogether admitted, but for which, at moments, I might have shown a certain weakness, is here discarded as improbable. Finally, I acknowledge that I was wrong in repudiating the hypothesis of a false writing, attributed to an apostle who lived in the apostolic age. The second epistle of Peter, the authenticity of which no person can reasonably sustain, is an example of a work, much less important no doubt than the fourth Gospel, counterfeited under such conditions. Moreover, this is not for the moment the capital question. The essential question is to know what use it is proper to make of the fourth Gospel when one essays to write the life of Jesus. I persist in believing that that Gospel possesses a fund of valuable information, equal to that of the synoptics, and even sometimes superior. The development of this point possesses so much importance that I have made it the basis of an appendix at the end of this volume. The portion of the introduction relating to the criticism of the fourth Gospel has been revised and completed.

In the body of the narrative several passages have also been modified in consequence of what has been just stated. All passages in a sentence which implied more or less that the fourth Gospel was by the Apostle John. or by an ocular witness of the evangelical facts, have been cut out. In order to trace the personal character of John, the son of Zebedee, I have thought of the rude Boanerge of Mark, of the terrible visionary of the Apocalypse, and not of the mystic, so full of tenderness, who has written the Gospel of love. I insist, with less confidence, on certain little details which are furnished us by the fourth Gospel. The limited quotations I have made from the discourses of that Gospel have been still further restricted. I had allowed myself to follow too far the opinions of the alleged apostle in what concerned the promise of the Paraclete. In like manner I am not now so sure that the fourth Gospel is right in respect of its disagreement with the synoptics as to the day on which Jesus died. As to the time of the Lord's Supper, on the contrary, I persist in my opinion. The synoptic account which places the eucharistic institution on the last evening of Jesus appears to me to contain an improbability, equivalent to a quasi-miracle. It is hence, in my opinion, an adapted version, and founded upon a certain confusion of recollections.

The critical examination of the synoptics has not been modified throughout. It has been completed and determined on some points, notably in that which concerns Luke. As regards Lysanias, a study of the inscription of Zenodorus at Baalbeck, which I did for the Phoenician Mission, has led me to believe that the evangelist could not have made so grievous a mistake as the ingenious critics think. As regards Quirinius, on the contrary, the last memoir of M. Mommsen has settled the question against the third Gospel. Mark seems to me more and more the primitive type of the synoptic narrative and the most authoritative text.

The paragraph relative to the Apocrypha has been explained. The important texts published by M. Ceriani have been employed to advantage. I have great doubts in regard to the book of Enoch. I reject the opinion of Weisse, Volkmar, and Graetz, who believe that the whole book is posterior to Jesus. As to the most important portion of the book, which extends from chapter xxvii. to chapter lxxi., I dare not decide between the arguments of Helgenfeld and Colani, who regard this portion as posterior to Jesus; and the opinion of Hoffmann, Dillmann, Koestlin, Ewald, Lücke, and Weizsaecker, who hold it to be anterior. How much is it to be desired that the Greek text of that important writing could be found! I do not know why I persist in believing that this is not a vain hope. I have, in any case, stamped with doubt the inductions drawn from the aforenamed chapters. I have shown, on the contrary, the singular correspondences between the discourses of Jesus contained in the last chapters of the synoptic Gospels and the Apocalypses attributed to Enoch, relations in regard to which the discovery of the complete Greek text of the epistle attributed to Barnabas has cast much light, and which has been much enhanced by M. Weizsaecker. The certain results obtained by M. Volkmar in regard to the fourth book of Esdras, and which agree, in almost every particular, with those of M. Ewald, have been equally taken into consideration. Several new Talmudist citations have been introduced The portion accorded to Essenism has been enlarged.

The position I have taken in discarding the bibliography has frequently been wrongly interpreted. I believe I have loudly enough proclaimed that which I owe to the masters of German science in general, and to each of them in particular, so that such a silence might not be taxed with ingratitude. Bibliography is only useful when it is complete. Now the German genius has displayed such activity in the field of evangelical criticism that if I had cited all the works relative to the questions treated in this book I would have tripled the extent of the notes and changed the character of my narrative. One cannot accomplish everything at once. I have restricted myself, therefore, to the rule of only admitting citations at first hand. Their number has been greatly multiplied. Besides, for the convenience of French readers who are not conversant with these studies, I have continued the revision of the summary list of the writings, composed in our language, wherever I could find details which I may have omitted. Many of these works are far removed from my ideas; but all are of a nature to make the enlightened man reflect and to make him understand our discussions.

The thread of the narrative has been much changed. Certain expressions, too strong for communistic minds, which were of the essence of nascent Christianity, have been softened down. Among those holding personal relations with Jesus I have admitted some whose names do not figure in the Gospels, but who are known to us through evidence worthy of credence. That which relates to the name of Peter has been modified. I have also adopted another hypothesis in regard to Levi, son of Alpheus, and his relations with the Apostle Matthew. As to Lazarus, I unhesitatingly adopt now the ingenious hypothesis of Strauss, Baur, Zeller, and Scholten, according to which the pious pauper of the parable of Luke and the person restored to life by Jesus are one and the same individual. It will nevertheless be seen how I retain some reality in associating him with Simon the Leper. I adopt likewise the hypothesis of M. Strauss in respect of divers discourses attributed to Jesus during his last days, which appear to be quotations from writings spread over the first century. The discussion of the texts as to the duration of the life of Jesus has been reduced to greater precision. The topography of Bethphage and Dalmanutha has been altered. The account of Golgotha has been reproduced from the works of M. Vogüé. A person well-versed in the history of botany has taught me to distinguish, in the orchards of Galilee, between trees which have grown there for eighteen hundred years and those which have only been transplanted there since then. Some facts have also been communicated to me in regard to the potion administered to the crucified, to which I have given a place. In general, in the account of the last hours of Jesus, I have toned down some phraseology which might have too historical an appearance. It is in such cases where the favourite explanations of M. Strauss find their best application, where symbolic and dogmatic designs let themselves be seen at each step.

I have said, and I repeat it, that if in writing the life of Jesus one confines oneself to advancing only details which are certain, it would be necessary to limit oneself to a few lines. He existed. He was from Nazareth in Galilee. There was a charm in his preaching, and he implanted in the minds of his disciples aphorisms which left a deep impression there. His two principal disciples were Peter and John, sons of Zebedee. He excited the hatred of the orthodox Jews, who brought him before Pontius Pilate, then procurator of Judæa, to have him put to death. He was crucified without the gates of the city. It was believed that a short time after he was restored to life. This is what is known to us for certain, even though the Gospels had not existed or were falsehoods, through authentic texts and incontestable data, such as the evidently authentic epistles of St. Paul, the epistle to the Hebrews, the Apocalypse, and other texts believed in by all. Beyond that, it is permissible to doubt. What was his family? What in particular was his affinity to that James, "brother of the Lord," who after his death plays an important part? Was he actually related to John the Baptist? and did the most celebrated of his disciples belong to the school of baptism before they belonged to his? What were his Messianic ideas? Did he regard himself as the Messiah? What were his apocalyptic ideas? Did he believe that he would appear as the Son of Man in the clouds? Did he imagine he could work miracles? Were the latter attributed to him during his life? Did his legend grow up round himself, and had he cognisance of it? What was his moral character? What were his ideas in regard to the admission of Gentiles into the Kingdom of God? Was he a pure Jew like James, or did he break with Judaism, as did the most enthusiastic party of the Church subsequently? What was the order of his mental development? Those who seek only the indubitable in history must keep silent upon these points. The Gospels, in respect of these questions, are not much to be relied on, seeing that they frequently furnish arguments for two opposing theses, and seeing that the character of Jesus is therein modified to suit the views of the authors. For my part I think that on such occasions it is allowable to make conjectures, provided that they are presented as such. The texts, not being historic, give no certitude, but they give something. It is not necessary to follow them with a blind confidence, it is not necessary to reject their testimony with unjust disdain. We must strive to divine what they conceal, without being absolutely certain of having found it.

It is singular that, in regard to almost all these points, it is the liberal school of theology which proposes the most sceptical solutions. The more sensible defenders of Christianity have come to consider it as advantageous to leave a gap in the historical circumstances bearing upon the birth of Christianity. Miracles, Messianic prophecies, formerly the bases of the Christian apology, have become an embarrassment to it; people seek to discard them. If we would believe the partisans of this theology, amongst whom I could cite so many eminent critics and noble thinkers, Jesus never pretended to perform a miracle; he did not believe himself to be the Messiah; he had no idea of the apocalyptic discourses which have been imputed to him as touching the final catastrophe. That Papias, so excellent a traditionist, and so zealous a collector of the words of Jesus, was an enthusiastic millenarian; that Mark, the oldest and the most authoritative of the evangelical narrators, was almost exclusively preoccupied with miracles, matters little. The career of Jesus is in this way so belittled that we are many times at a loss to tell what he was. His being condemned to death has no more right to be embraced in such a hypothesis than the accident which has made of him the chief of an apocalyptic and a Messianic movement. Was it on account of his moral precepts or his discourses on the Mount that Jesus was crucified? Certainly not. These maxims had for a long time been the current coin of the synagogue. No one has ever been put to death for repeating them. When Jesus was put to death, it was for saying something more than that. A learned man, who has taken an active part in these discussions, wrote me lately: "As in former times it was necessary to prove at all hazards that Jesus was God, so in our own times the question that the Protestant theological school has to prove is that he was not only a mere man, but also that he always regarded himself as such. People persist in representing him as a man of good sense, as a practical man par excellence, and transform him into the image and according to the spirit of modem theology. I believe with you that this is not doing justice to historical truth, but is neglecting an essential side of it."

This tendency has already been more than once logically produced in the bosom of Christianity. What did Marcion aim at? What did the Gnostics of the second century try to do? Simply to discard the material circumstances of a biography, the human details of which shocked them. Baur and Strauss yielded to analogous philosophical necessities. The divine Æon which was developed by humanity has nothing to do with anecdotic incidents, with the particular life of an individual. Scholten and Schenkel held certainly to a historic and actual Jesus, but their historic Jesus is neither a Messiah, nor a prophet, nor a Jew. People do not know what he aimed at, nor comprehend either his life or his death. Their Jesus is an æon after his own manner, a being impalpable, intangible. Genuine history is not acquainted with any such beings. Genuine history must construct its edifice out of two kinds of materials, and, if I may so speak, out of two factors: the first, the general state of the human soul in a given age and in a given country; the second, the particular incidents which, uniting with general causes, determined the course of events. To explain history by accidental facts is as false as to explain it by principles which are purely philosophic. The two explanations ought mutually to sustain and complete each other. The history of Jesus and of the apostles must, above all histories, be constructed out of a vast mixture of

9

ideas and sentiments; nor would that even be sufficient. A thousand conjectures, a thousand whims, a thousand trifles, are mixed up with ideas and sentiments. To trace at this time of day the exact details of these conjectures, whims, and trifles is impossible; what legend has taught us in regard to this may be true, but it may also not be true. In my opinion, the best course to hold is to follow as closely as possible the original narratives, to discard impossibilities, to sow everywhere the seeds of doubt, and to put forth as conjectural the diverse manners in which the event might have taken place. I am not quite sure that the conversion of St. Paul came about as we have it related in the Acts; but it took place in a manner not widely different from that, for St. Paul himself has informed us that he had a vision of the resurrected Jesus, which gave an entirely new direction to his life. I am not sure whether the narrative of the Acts as to the descent of the Holy Spirit on the day of Pentecost is quite historic; but the ideas which were spread abroad as to the baptism of fire leads me to believe that a scene took place in the apostolic circle in which thunder played a part, as at Sinai. The visions of the resurrected Jesus were likewise occasionally the cause of the fortuitous circumstances interpreted by vivid and already preoccupied imaginations.

If liberal theologians repudiate explanations of this kind, it is because they do not wish to subject Christianity to the laws common to other religious movements; because also, perhaps, they are not sufficiently acquainted with the theory of spiritual life. There are no religious movements in which such deceptions do not play a great part. It may even be affirmed that they hold a permanent position in certain communities, such as the pietist Protestants, the Mormons, and the convent Catholics. In those little excited worlds it is not rare that conversions are the result of some accident, in which the anxious soul sees the finger of God. These accidents, which always contain something puerile, are concealed by the believers; it is a secret between heaven and them. A fortuitous event is nothing to a cold or indifferent soul; it is a divine symbol to a susceptible soul. To say that it was an accident which changed St. Paul and St. Ignatius Loyola through and through, or rather which gave a new turn to their activity, is certainly inexact. It was the interior movement of those strong natures which had prepared the clap of thunder; yet the thunderclap had been determined by an exterior cause. All these phenomena, moreover, had reference to a moral state which no longer belongs to us. In the majority of their actions they were governed by dreams which they had seen the preceding night, by inductions drawn from a fortuitous object which struck their first waking view, or by sounds which they believed they heard. It has happened that the wings of a bird, currents of air, or headaches, have determined the fate of the world. In order to be sincere and exhaustive it is necessary to say this; and when certain commonplace documents tell us of incidents of this kind we must take care to pass them over in silence. In history there are but few details which are certain; details, nevertheless, possess always some significance. The historian's talent consists in making a true narrative out of details which are of themselves but half true.

We can hence accord a place in history to particular incidents, without being on that account a rationalist of the old school or a disciple of Paulus. Paulus was a theologian who, wishing to have as little as possible to do with miracles, and not daring at the same time to treat the Bible narratives as legends, twisted them about so as to explain them in a wholly natural fashion. In this way Paulus desired to retain for the Bible all its authority and to enter into the real thoughts of the sacred authors. But I am a profane critic; I believe that no supernatural writing is true to the letter; I think that out of a hundred narratives of the supernatural there are eighty which have been pieced together by popular imagination. I admit, nevertheless, that in certain very rare cases legend has been derived from an actual fact and trans-formed in the imagination. As to the mass of supernatural data recounted by the Gospels and by the Acts, I shall attempt to show in five or six instances how the illusion may have been created. The theologian who is invariably methodical would have that a single explanation should hold good from one end of the Bible to the other. Criticism believes that every explanation should be attempted, or rather, that the possibility of each explanation should be successively demonstrated. That an explanation is repugnant to one's ideas is no reason for rejecting it. The world is at once an infernal and a divine comedy, a strange "round," led by a choragus of genius, now good, now evil, now stupid; the good defile into the ranks which have been assigned to them, in view of the accomplishment of a mysterious end. History is not history if in reading it one is not by turns charmed and disgusted, grieved and consoled.

The first task of the historian is to make a careful sketch of the manner in which the events he recounts took place. Now, the history of religious beginnings transports us into a world of women and children, of brains ardent or foolish. These facts, placed before minds of a positive order, are absurd and unintelligible, and this is why countries such as England, of ponderous intellects, find it impossible to comprehend anything about it. That which is a drawback to the arguments, formerly so celebrated, of Sherlock or of Gilbert West upon the resurrection, of Lyttelton upon the conversion of Saint Paul, is not the reasoning; that is a triumph of solidity; it is the just appreciation of the diversity of means. Every tentative religion with which we are acquainted exhibits unmistakably an enormous mixture of the sublime and the ridiculous. Read these narratives of primitive Saint Simonism, written with admirable candour by the surviving adepts. By the side of repulsive rôles, insipid declamations, what charm! what sincerity, when the man or the woman of the people enters upon the scene, hearing the artless confession of a soul which is open to the first gentle ray which has struck it! There is more than one example of beautiful durable things which have been founded upon singular puerilities. It were useless to seek for any proportion between the conflagration and the spark which lighted it. The devotion of Salette is one of the grandest religious events of our age. These basilicas, so respectable, of Chartres and of Laon, were reared upon illusions of the same sort. The Fête-Dieu originated in the visions of a female religionist of Liège who believed that in her prayers she always saw the full moon through a small hole. We could instance movements, absolutely sincere, which have been brought about by impostors. The discovery of the holy lance at Athens, in which the fraud was so patent, decided the fortune of the Crusades. Mormonism, the beginnings of which are so shameful, has inspired courage and devotion. The religion of the Druzes rests upon a tissue of absurdities which stagger the imagination, but it has its devotees. Islamism, which is the second great event in the history of the world, would not have existed if the son of Amina had not been an epileptic. The gentle and immaculate Francis d'Assisi would not have succeeded without Brother Elia. Humanity is so feeble of mind that the purest thing has need of the co-operation of some impure agent.

Let us guard against applying our conscientious distinctions, our reasonings of cool and clear heads, to the appreciation of these extraordinary events, which are at once so much beyond and beneath us. There are those who would make Jesus a sage, a philosopher, a patriot, a good man, a moralist, or a saint. He was neither or any of these. He was a charmer. Let us not make the past our idol. Let us not believe that Asia is Europe. With us, for example, the fool is a creature outside the rules of society; we torture him so as to make him re-enter it; the horrible treatment of fools by ancient houses was the result of scholastic and Cartesian logic. In the East, the fool is a privileged being; he enters the highest councils without any one daring to stop him; people listen to him, he is consulted. He is a being believed to be in close proximity to God, inasmuch as, his individual reason being extinguished, he is believed to be a partaker in the divine reason. The wit which, through delicate raillery, rises above all defects of reason, exists only in Asia. A person educated in Islamism told me that, repairs having become necessary at the tomb of Mahomet, people at Medina for several years made an appeal to the masons, and announced that he who should descend into that dreadful place should have his head cut off on reascending. "It was necessary," said my interlocutor to me, "to picture those places to oneself in a certain manner, and it was not for any person to say that they were otherwise."

Troubled consciences cannot have the clearness of good sense. Now, it is only troubled consciences which can lay powerful foundations. I have tried to draw a picture in which the colours should be disposed as they are in nature, that is to say, at once grand and puerile, in which one sees the divine instinct threading its way with safety through a thousand peculiarities. If the picture had been without shade, this would have been the proof that it was false. The condition of the written proofs does not permit of us telling in what instances the illusion was consistent with itself. All that we can say is, that sometimes it has happened thus. One cannot lead for years the life of a thaumaturgist without being often cornered--without having one's hand forced by the public. The man who has a legend attaching to his life is led tyrannically by his legend. One begins by artlessness, credulity, absolute innocence; one ends in all sorts of embarrassments, and, in order to sustain the divine power which is at fault, one gets out of these embarrassments through the most desperate expedients. When one is put to the wall must one leave the work of God to perish, because God is slow of coming to the relief? Did not Joan of Arc more than once make her voice heard in response to the necessities of the moment? If the account of the secret revelation which she made to King Charles VII. has any reality, a supposition which it is difficult to deny, it must have been that that innocent girl had represented that she had received through supernatural intuition that which she had heard in confidence. An exposé of religious history which does not some day disclose indirectly suppositions of this sort is for the same reason argued to be incomplete.

Every true, or probable, or possible circumstance most then have its proper place in my narration, together with its shade of probability. In such a history it will be necessary to speak not only of that which has taken place, but also of that which had a likelihood of taking place. The impartiality with which I have treated my subject has interdicted me from not accepting a conjecture, even one that shocks; for undoubtedly there were many shocking ones in the fashion of the things which are past and gone. I have applied from beginning to end the same process in an inflexible manner. I have given the good impressions which the texts have suggested to me; I could not, therefore, be silent as to the bad. I intend that my book shall retain its value even in the day when people shall have reached the point of regarding a certain amount of fraud as an element inseparable from religious history. It will be necessary to make my hero beautiful and charming (for undoubtedly he was so), and that, too, in spite of actions which, in our days, might be characterised in an unfavourable manner. People have praised me for having tried to construct a narrative lovely, human, and possible. Would my work have received these eulogiums if it had represented the origin of Christianity as absolutely immaculate? That would have been to admit the greatest of miracles. The result thence would have been a picture lifeless to the last degree. I do not say that this is for want of faults I may have made in the composition. Nevertheless,

I must leave each text to produce its melodious or discordant note. If Goethe had been alive he would, with this reserve, have commended me. That great man would not have forgiven me for producing a portrait wholly celestial: he would have desired to find repellent details; for, assuredly, in actual life things happen which would wound us, if only it were given to us to see them.

The same difficulty presents itself, moreover, in the history of the apostles. This history is admirable in its way. But what can be more shocking than the glossolaly, which is attested by the unexceptionable texts of St. Paul? Liberal theologians admit that the disappearance of the body of Jesus was one of the grounds for the belief in the resurrection. What does that signify, unless the Christian conscience at that moment was two-sided, that a moiety of that conscience gave birth to the illusion of the other moiety? If the disciples themselves had taken away the body and spread themselves over the city crying, "He is risen!" the imposture would have been discovered. But there can be no doubt that it was not they themselves who did the two things. For belief in a miracle to be accepted it is indeed necessary that someone be responsible for the first rumour which is spread abroad; but, ordinarily, this is not the principal author. The rôle of the latter is limited to not exclaiming against the reputation which people have given him. Moreover, even if he did exclaim, it would be useless; popular opinion would prove stronger than he. In the miracle of Salette, people possessed a clear idea of the artifice; but the conviction that it would do good to religion carried all before it. The fraud was divided between several unconscionable persons, or rather it had ceased to be a fraud and became a misapprehension. Nobody, in that case, deceives deliberately; everybody deceives innocently. Formerly it was taken for granted that every legend implied deceivers and deceived; in our opinion, all the collaborators of a legend are at once deceived and deceivers. A miracle, in other words, presupposes three conditions: first, general credulity; second, a little complaisance on the part of some; third, tacit acquiescence in the principal author. Through a reaction against the brutal explanations of the eighteenth century, we did not fall into the trap of hypotheses which implied effects without causes. Legend does not wholly create itself: people assist in giving it birth. These points d'appui in a legend are often of a rare elasticity. It is the popular imagination which makes the ball of snow; there, nevertheless, must have been an original nucleus. The two persons who composed the two genealogies of Jesus knew quite well that the lists were not of any great authenticity. The apocryphal books, the alleged apocalypses of Daniel, Enoch, and Esdras, proceeded from persons of strong convictions; but the authors of these works knew well they were neither Daniel, Enoch, nor Esdras. The priest of Asia who composed the romance of Thekla declared that he had done it out of love for Paul. It is incumbent that we should say a great deal about the author of the fourth Gospel, who was assuredly a personage of the first order. If you chase the illusion of religious history out of one door, it will re-enter by another. In fine, it would be difficult to cite a great event of the past, whatever it might be, in an entirely defensible manner. Shall we cease to be Frenchmen because France has been founded by centuries of perfidy? Shall we refuse to profit by the benefits of the Revolution because the Revolution committed crimes without number? If the house of Capet had succeeded in creating for us a good constitutional assize, similar to that of England, would we have wrangled over the cure of the king's evil?

Science alone is pure; for science possesses nothing practical; it does not touch men; the Propaganda takes no notice of it; its duty is to prove, not to persuade or to convert. He who has discovered a theorem publishes its demonstration for those who are capable of comprehending it. He does not mount a chariot; he does not gesticulate; he does not have recourse to oratorical artifices in order to induce people to adopt it who do not perceive its truth. Enthusiasm, certainly, has its good faith, but it is an ingenuous good faith; it is not the deep reflective good faith of the savant. Only the ignorant yield to bad reasonings. If Laplace had been able to gain the multitude over to his system of the world, he would not have limited himself to mathematical demonstrations. M. Littré, in writing the life of a man whom he regarded as his master, pressed sincerity to the point of leaving nothing unsaid that would render that man more amiable. That is without example in religious history. Science alone seeks after pure truth. She alone offers good reasons for truth, and brings a severe criticism into the employment of the methods of conviction. This is no doubt the reason why, up till now, she has had no influence on the people. It may be that in the future, when people are better instructed, even as we have been led to hope, they will yield only to good and carefully deduced proofs. But it would not be equitable to judge the great men of the past according to these principles. There are natures who resign themselves to impotence, who accept humanity, with all its weaknesses, such as it is. Many great things have not been accomplished without lies and without violence. If to-morrow the incarnate ideal were to come and offer itself to men in order to govern them, it would find itself confronted by the foolish, who wish to be deceived; by the wicked, who wish to be subdued. The sole irreproachable person is the contemplative man, who only aims at finding the truth, without either caring about making it a triumph or of applying it.

Morality is not history. To paint and to record is not to approve. The naturalist who describes the transformations of the chrysalis neither blames nor praises it. He does not tax it with ingratitude because it abandons its shroud; he does not describe it as bold because it has found its wings: he does not accuse it of folly because it aspires to plunge into space. One may be the passionate friend of the true and the beautiful, and show oneself indulgent at the same time to the simple ignorance of the people. Our happiness has cost our fathers torrents of tears and deluges of blood. In order that pious souls may taste at the foot of the altar the inward consolation which gives them life, it has taken centuries of severe constraint, the mysteries of a sacerdotal polity, a rod of iron, funereal piles. The success which one owes to a wholly great institution does not demand the sacrifice of the sincerity of history. Formerly, to be a good Frenchman, it was necessary to believe in the dove of Clovis, in the national antiquities of the Treasure of Saint Denis, in the virtues of the oriflamme, in the supernatural vision of Joan of Arc; it was necessary to believe that France was the first of nations, that French royalty was superior to all other royalties, that God had for that crown a predilection altogether peculiar and was constantly engaged in protecting it. To-day we know that God protects equally all kingdoms, all empires, all republics; we own that many of the kings of France have been contemptible men; we recognise that the French character has its faults; we greatly admire a multitude of things which come from abroad. Are we on that account worse Frenchmen? We can say, on the contrary, that we are better patriots, since, in place of being blind to our faults, we seek to correct them; that, in place of depreciating the foreigner, we seek to imitate that which he has in him of good. In like manner we are Christians. He who speaks with irreverence of the royalty of the Middle Ages, of Louis XIV., of the Revolution, of the Empire, commits an act of bad taste. He who does not speak kindly of Christianity and of the Church of which he forms a part renders himself guilty of ingratitude. But filial recognition ought not to be carried to the length of closing our eyes to the truth. One is not wanting in respect to the government in making the remark that it is not able to satisfy the conflicting needs that are in man, nor to a religion in saying that she is not free from the formidable objections which science has raised against all supernatural belief. Responding to certain social exigencies and not to some others, governments fall by reason of the same causes which have founded them and which have been their strength. Responding to the aspirations of the heart at the expense of the protestations of reason, religions crumble away in turn, because no force here below can succeed in stifling reason.

That day will be unfortunate for reason when she would stifle religion. Our planet, believe me, labours at some profound work. Do not pronounce rashly upon the inutility of such and such of its parts; do not say that it is necessary to suppress this wheel-work, which to appearance makes but the contrary play of the others. Nature, which has endowed the animal with an infallible instinct, has not put into humanity anything deceptive. From his organs you may boldly conclude his destiny. Est Deus in nobis. Religions are false when they attempt to prove the infinite, to determine it, to incarnate it, if I may so speak, but they are true when they affirm it. The greatest errors that they import into that affirmation are nothing compared to the price of the truth which they proclaim. The greatest simpleton, provided he practises the worship of the heart, is more enlightened as to the reality of things than the materialist who thinks he explains everything by accident, and leaves it there.

INTRODUCTION

WHICH TREATS PRINCIPALLY OF THE ORIGINAL DOCUMENTS OF THIS HISTORY.

A HISTORY of the "Origins of Christianity" ought to embrace the whole obscure and, so to speak, subterranean period which extends from the first beginnings of this religion to the time when its existence became a public fact, notorious and apparent to everybody. Such a history ought to consist of four parts. The first, which is now presented to the public, treats of the particular fact which was the starting point of the new religion, and is wholly concerned with the sublime personality of the Founder. The second should treat of the Apostles and their immediate disciples, or rather, of the revolutions which took place in religious thought in the first two generations of Christianity. This should end about the year 100, when the last friends of Jesus were just dead, and when the whole of the books of the New Testament had almost assumed the form in which they are now read. The third book should set forth the state of Christianity under the Antonines. We should then observe its slow development and its waging of an almost permanent war against the empire, which latter, having at that moment attained to the highest degree of administrative perfection and being governed by philosophers, combated in the nascent sect a secret and theocratic society, which the latter obstinately disowned, but which was a continual source of weakness. This book would embrace the whole of the second century. The fourth and last part should show the decided progress which Christianity had made from the time of Syrian emperors. In it we should see the learned constitution of the Antonines crumble away, the decadence of ancient civilisation set in irrevocably and Christianity profit by its ruin, Syria conquer the entire West, and Jesus, in combination with the gods and the deified sages of Asia, take possession of a society which philosophy and a purely civil government were unable longer to cope with. It was then that the religious ideas of the races established upon the coasts of the Mediterranean underwent a great change; that the Eastern religions everywhere took the lead; that Christianity, having become a large Church, totally forgot its millennium dreams, broke its last connections with Judaism, and passed entirely into the Greek and Roman world. The strifes and the literary labours of the third century, which had already taken place openly, have to be described only in their general features. Again, the persecutions of the commencement of the fourth century, the last effort of the empire to return to its old principles, which denied to religious associations a place in the State, should be recounted more briefly. Finally, the change of policy which, under Constantine, inverted the position, and made of the most free and most spontaneous religious movement an official worship subject to State control, and in its turn persecutor, would need only to be foreshadowed.

I do not know whether I shall have life and strength to execute no vast a plan. I should be satisfied if, after writing the life of Jesus, it is given to me to relate, as I understand it, the history of the Apostles; the condition of the Christian conscience during the weeks which immediately succeeded the death of Jesus; the formation of the cycle of legends touching the resurrection; the first acts of the Church of Jerusalem, the life of St. Paul, the crisis at the time of Nero, the appearance of the Apocalypse, the ruin of Jerusalem, the foundation of the Hebrew-Christian sects of Batanea, the compilation of the Gospels, and the rise of the great schools of Asia Minor. Everything pales by the side of that marvellous first century. By a peculiarity rare in history, we can judge better of what passed in the Christian world from the year 50 to 75 than from the year 80 to 150.

The plan upon which this history proceeds prevents the introduction into the text of long critical dissertations upon controversial points. A continuous succession of notes places likewise the reader in a position to verify the sources of all the propositions in the text. These notes are strictly limited to quotations at first hand--I mean, to the indication of the original passages upon which each assertion or hypothesis rests. I am aware that, to persons who have had little experience in these studies, many other explanations might be necessary; but it is not my habit to do over again what has once been done and done well. To cite only books written in French, the following can be recommended: [1]

The above works are for the most part excellent, and in them will be found explained a multitude of details upon which I have had to be very succinct. In particular, the criticism of the details of evangelical texts has been done by M. Strauss in a manner which leaves little to be desired. Although M. Strauss may at first have been deceived in his theory in regard to the authorship of the Gospels, and although his book, in my opinion, has the fault of occupying too much theological and too little historical ground, it is indispensable, so as to understand the motives which have guided me in a multitude of details, to follow the argument (always judicious, though sometimes a little subtle) of the book which has been so well translated by my learned co-worker M. Littré.

I am not aware that, in respect of ancient testimony, I have overlooked any source of information. Not to mention a multitude of scattered data respecting Jesus and the times in which he lived, we still have five great collections of writings. These are: first, the Gospels and the New Testament writings in general; second, the compositions called the "Apocrypha of the Old Testament;" third, the works of Philo; fourth, those of Josephus; fifth, the Talmud. The writings of Philo have the inestimable advantage of showing us the thoughts which, in the time of Jesus, stirred souls occupied with great religious questions. Philo lived, it is true, in quite a different sphere of Judaism from Jesus; yet, like him, he was quite free from the pharisaic spirit which reigned at Jerusalem; Philo is in truth the elder brother of Jesus. He was sixty-two years of age when the prophet of Nazareth had reached the highest point of his activity, and he survived him at least ten years. What a pity it is that the accidents of life did not direct his steps into Galilee! What would he not have taught us!

Josephus, who wrote chiefly for the Pagans, did not exhibit the some sincerity. His meagre accounts of Jesus, John the Baptist, and of Judas the Gaulonite are colourless and lifeless. We feel that he sought to represent these movements, so profoundly Jewish in character and spirit, in a form which would be intelligible to the Greeks and Romans. Taken as a whole I believe the passage in regard to Jesus to be authentic. It is perfectly in the style of Josephus, and, if that historian mentioned Jesus at all, it is indeed in this manner that he would have spoken of him. We feel, however, that the hand of a Christian has retouched the fragment, and has added to it passages without which it would have been well nigh blasphemous, as well as abridged and modified some expressions. It is necessary to remember that Josephus owed his literary fortune to the Christians, who adopted his writings as essential documents of their sacred history. It is probable that in the second century they circulated an edition of them, corrected according to Christian ideas. At all events that which constitutes the immense interest of the books of Josephus in respect of our present subject is the vivid picture he gives of the times. Thanks to this Jewish historian, Herod, Herodias, Antipas, Philip, Annas, Kaïaphas, and Pilate are personages whom, so to speak, we can touch, and whom we can actually see living before us.

The Apocrypha of the Old Testament, especially the Jewish part of the Sibylline verses, the book of Enoch, the Assumption of Moses, the fourth book of Esdras, the Apocalypse of Baruch, together with the book of Daniel, which is also itself a real Apocrypha, possess a primary importance in the history of the development of the Messianic theories, and in the understanding of the conceptions of Jesus in regard to the kingdom of God. The book of Enoch, in particular, and the Assumption of Moses, were much read in the circle of Jesus. Some expressions imputed to Jesus by the synoptics are presented in the epistle attributed to Saint Barnabas as belonging to Enoch: Ος Ενὸχ λεγει. It is very difficult to determine the date of the different sections of which the book attributed to that patriarch in composed. None of them are certainly anterior to the year 150 B.C.: some of them may even have been written by a Christian pen. The section containing the discourses entitled "Similitudes," and extending from chapter xxvii. to chapter lxxi., is suspected of being a Christian work. But this has not been proved. Perhaps this part is only a proof of alterations. Other additions or Christian revisions are recognisable here and there.

The collection of the Sibylline verses needs to be regarded in the same light; but the latter is more easily established. The oldest part in the poem contained in Book III., v. 97-817; it appeared about the year 140 B.C. Respecting the date of the fourth book of Esdras everybody now is nearly agreed in assigning this Apocalypse to the year 97 A.D. It has been altered by the Christians. The Apocalypse of Baruch has a great resemblance to that of Esdras; we find there, as in the book of Enoch, several utterances imputed to Jesus. As to the book of Daniel, the character of the two languages in which it is written, the use of Greek words, the clear, precise, dated announcements of events which go back as far as the times of Antiochus Epiphanes; the false descriptions which are there drawn of ancient Babylon; the general tone of the book, which has nothing suggestive of the writings of the captivity, but, on the contrary, corresponds, by numerous analogies, to the beliefs, the manners, the turn of imagination of the epoch of Seleucidæ; the Apocalyptic form of the visions; the position of the book in the Hebrew canon which is outside the series of the prophets; the omission of Daniel in the panegyrics of chapter xlix. of Ecclesiasticus, in which his position is all but indicated; and a thousand other proofs, which have been deduced a hundred times, do not permit of a doubt that this book was but the product of the general exaltation produced among the Jews by the persecution of Antiochus. It is not in the old prophetic literature that it most be classed; its place is at the head of Apocalyptic literature, the first model of a kind of composition, after which were to come the various Sibylline poems, the book of Enoch, the Assumption of Moses, the Apocalypse of John, the Ascension of Isaiah, the fourth book of Esdras.

Hitherto, in the history of the origins of Christianity, the Talmud has been too much neglected. I think with M. Geiger that the true notion of the circumstances which produced Jesus must be sought in this peculiar compilation, in which so much knowledge is mixed with the most insignificant scholasticism. The Christian theology and the Jewish theology having followed uniformly two parallel paths, the history of the one cannot be understood without the history of the other. Innumerable material details in the Gospels find, moreover, their commentary in the Talmud. The vast Latin collections of Lightfoot, Schoettgen, Buxtorf, and Otho contained already on this point a mass of information. I have taken upon myself to verify in the original all the quotations which I have made use of, without an exception. The assistance which has been given in this part of my task by a learned Israelite, M. Newbauer, well-versed in Talmudic literature, has enabled me to go further and to elucidate certain parts of my subject by some new researches. The distinction here between epochs is very important, the compilation of the Talmud extending from the year 200 to the year 500, or thereabout. In the actual condition of these studies, we have brought to it as much discernment as it was possible in the actual state of these studies. Dates no recent will excite fears among persons accustomed to attach value to a document only for the epoch in which it was written. But such scruples would here be out of place. Jewish teaching from the Asmonean epoch up to the end of the second century was chiefly oral. These sorts of intellectual states must not be judged by the customs of an age in which much writing takes place. The Vedas, the Homeric poems, the ancient Arabic poems, were for centuries preserved only in memory, and yet these compositions present a very distinct and delicate form. In the Talmud, on the other hand, the form possesses no value. Let us add that before the Mischnah of Juda the saint, which obliterated the recollection of all others, there had been several essays at compilation, the commencement of which goes further back perhaps than is commonly supposed. The style of the Talmud is that of careless notes; the editors probably did no more than range under certain titles the enormous medley of writings which, for generations, had accumulated in the different schools.

It remains for us to speak of the documents which, pretending to be biographies of the Founder of Christianity, must naturally take the place of honour in a life of Jesus. A complete treatise upon the compilation of the Gospels would be a work of itself. Thanks to the excellent work which, for the last thirty years, has been devoted to this question, a problem which was formerly held to be insoluble has been resolved, and, though there is room still left for much uncertainty, it is quite sufficient for the requirements of history. We shall have occasion later on to revert to this in our second book, seeing that the composition of the Gospels was one of the most important facts in the future of Christianity in the second half of the first century. We shall only touch in this place a single aspect of the subject, but one which is indispensable to the solidarity of our narrative. Putting to one side all that belongs to a picture of the apostolic times, we will inquire only to what extent the data furnished by the Gospels can be employed in a history arranged according to rational principles.

That the Gospels are in part legendary is quite evident, inasmuch as they are full of miracles and of the supernatural; but there are legends and legends. Nobody disputes the principal traits in the life of Francis d'Assisi, although at every step the supernatural is encountered in it. Contrariwise, no one gives credence to the "Life of Apollonius of Tyana," for the reason that it was written long after the hero, and avowedly as a pure romance. When, by whom, and under what conditions were the Gospels compiled? This is the chief question upon which the opinion, it is necessary to form of their credibility, depends.

We know that each of the four Gospels bears at its head the name of a personage known either in Apostolic history or in evangelical history itself. If these titles are correct it is clear that the Gospels, without ceasing to be in part legendary, possess a high value, since they take us back to the half century which followed the death of Jesus, and even in two cases to eyewitnesses of his acts.

As for Luke, doubt is hardly possible. The Gospel of Luke is a studied composition, founded upon anterior documents. It is the work of a man who selects, adapts, and combines. The author of this Gospel is undoubtedly the same as that of the Acts of the Apostles. Now, the author of the Acts appears to be a companion of Paul, an appellation which exactly fits Luke. I am aware that more than one objection can be raised against this opinion; but one thing is beyond question, to wit, the author of the third Gospel and of the Acts is a man belonging to the second Apostolic generation, and that is sufficient for our purpose. The date of that Gospel may, however, be determined with quite enough precision by considerations drawn from the book itself. The 21st chapter of Luke, which is an inseparable part of the work, was certainly written subsequently to the siege of Jerusalem, but not very long afterwards. We are here, then, upon solid ground; for the work in question has been written by the same person, and its unity is perfect.

The Gospels of Matthew and Mark do not nearly possess the same stamp of individuality. They are impersonal compositions, in which the author wholly disappears. A proper name inscribed at the head of such works does not count for much.

We cannot, moreover, reason here as in the case of Luke. The date which belongs to a particular chapter (to Matthew xiv. and Mark xiii. for example) cannot he rigorously applied to the works as a whole, for the latter are made up of fragments of epochs and of productions which are quite distinct. In general, the third Gospel appears to be posterior to the two first, and exhibits the character of a much more advanced composition. We cannot, nevertheless, conclude hence that the two Gospels of Mark and Matthew were in the some condition as we have them when Luke wrote his. These two works, entitled Mark and Matthew, in fact, remained for a long time in a loose state, if I may so speak, and were susceptible of additions. On this point we have an excellent witness, who lived in the first half of the second century. This was Papias, bishop of Hierapolis, a grave man, a traditionist, who was busy all his life in collecting what was known by any one of Jesus. After declaring that in such cases he preferred oral tradition to books, Papias mentions two accounts of the acts and words of Christ. First a writing of Mark, the interpreter of the Apostle Peter, a short incomplete composition, without chronological order, including narratives and discourses (λεχθέντα ἤ πραχθέντα), composed from the information and recollections of the Apostle Peter; second, a collection of sayings (λόγια) written in Hebrew by Matthew, which everybody has translated as he listed. Certain it is that these two descriptions accord pretty well with the general tenor of the two books now called the Gospel according to Matthew and the Gospel according to Mark--the former characterised by its long discourses; the second, above all, by anecdote, and being much more exact than the other on minor details--brief even to dryness, the discourses few in number and indifferently composed. Nevertheless, that these two works as read by us are absolutely identical with those which were read by Papias is not sustainable, because, first, the writings of Matthew which were perused by Papias were composed solely of discourses in Hebrew, different translations of which were in circulation, and, secondly, because the writings of Mark and those of Matthew were to him perfectly distinct, written without any collusion, and it would seem m different languages. Now in the actual state of the texts, the Gospel according to Matthew and the Gospel according to Mark present parallelisms so long, and so perfectly identical, that it must be supposed that the final compiler of the first had the second before him, or vice versâ, or that both copied from the same source. That which appears the most probable is that we have not the original compilation of either Matthew or Mark, that the two first Gospels as we have them are adaptations in which each sought to fill up the lacunes of one text from the other. In fact, each was desirous of possessing a complete copy. He whose copy contained discourses only filled it out with narratives, and contrariwise. It is in this way that "The Gospel according to Matthew" is found to have appropriated all the anecdotes of Mark, and that "The Gospel according to Mark" contains to-day many of the details which have come from the Λόγια of Matthew. Each, moreover, imbibed largely of the oral tradition which floated around him. This tradition is so far from having been exhausted by the Gospels that the Acts of the Apostles, and of the most ancient Fathers, cite many sayings of Jesus which appear authentic and are not found in the Gospels that we possess.

It matters little for our present purpose that we should press this analysis further, or attempt, on the one hand, to reconstruct in a kind of way the original Λόγια of Matthew, or, on the other, to restore the primitive narrative to what it was when it left the pen of Mark. The Λόγια are doubtless presented to us in the great discourses of Jesus, which make up a considerable portion of the first Gospel. These discourses, in fact, form, when detached from the rest, a complete enough narrative. As for the original narratives of Mark, the text of them seems to make its appearance now in the first, now in the second Gospel, but most often in the second. In other words, the plan of the life of Jesus in the synoptics is founded upon two original documents: first, the discourses of Jesus collected by the Apostle Matthew; second, the collection of anecdotes and of personal information which Mark committed to writing from the recollections of Peter. It may be said that we still possess these two documents, mixed up with the facts of another production, in the two first Gospels, which bear, not without reason, the titles of "The Gospel according to Matthew" and "The Gospel according to Mark" respectively.

In any case, that which is indubitable is that very early the discourses of Jesus were reduced to writing in the Aramean tongue; also, that very early his remarkable actions were taken down. These were not texts to be settled and fixed dogmatically. Besides the Gospels which have come down to us, there might be others which professed equally to set forth the tradition of eyewitnesses. We attach little importance to these writings, while their preservers, such as Papias, who lived in the first half of the second century, preferred always to them oral tradition. Seeing that the world was believed to be near an end, people had not much inclination to write books for the future; they were solely concerned about preserving in their heart the living image of him whom they hoped to see soon again in the clouds. Hence, the small authority which, for nearly a hundred years, evangelical texts enjoyed. People made no scruple about inserting paragraphs in them, of combining various narratives, and in perfecting the one by the other. The poor man who had only one book was anxious that it should contain all that was dear to his heart. These little books were lent by one to another; each transcribed into the margin of his copy the phrases and parables he found in others which affected him. The most beautiful thing in the world has thus proceeded from an obscure and wholly popular elaboration. No edition possessed an absolute value. The two editions attributed to Clement Romanus quote the sayings of Jesus with two notable variances. Justin, who often appeals to that which he calls "The Memoirs of the Apostles," had before him a set of evangelical documents a little different from that which we have; at all events, he does not take the trouble to give them textually. The evangelical quotations in the pseudo-Clementine homilies of Ebionite origin present the some character. The spirit was everything; the letter nothing. It was when tradition, in the latter half of the second century, lost its power, that the text bearing the names of apostles or of apostolic men assumed a decisive authority and obtained the force of law. Even then free compositions were not absolutely interdicted; following the example of Luke people continued to write special Gospels by changing the ensemble of older texts.

Who does not recognise the value of documents constructed thus out of the tender recollections and simple narratives of the first two Christian generations, still full of the strong impressions produced by the illustrious Founder, and which seems to have survived him for a long time? Let us add that those Gospels seemed to proceed from those branches of the Christian family which were most closely related to Jesus. The final labour of compilation of the text which bears the name of Matthew appears to have been done in one of the countries situated to the north-east of Palestine, such as Gaulonitis, Auranitis, and Batanea, where many Christians took refuge at the time of the Roman war, where were still to be found at the end of the second century relatives of Jesus, and where the first Galilean tendency was longer felt than elsewhere.

So far we have only spoken of the three Gospels called the synoptic. It now remains to speak of the fourth, the one which bears the name of John. Here the question is much more difficult. Polycarp, the most intimate disciple of John, who often quotes the synoptics in his epistle to the Philippians, makes no allusion to the fourth Gospel. Papias, who was equally attached to the school of John, and who, if he had not been his disciple, as Irenæus believes he was, had associated a great deal with his immediate disciples--Papias, who had eagerly collected all the oral accounts relative to Jesus, does not say a word of a "Life of Jesus" written by the Apostle John. If such a mention could have been found in his work, Eusebius, who notices everything in it which bears on the literary history of the apostolic age, would undoubtedly have mentioned it. Justin, perhaps, knew the fourth Gospel; but he certainly did not regard it as the work of the Apostle John, since he expressly designates that apostle as the author of the Apocalypse, and takes not the least account of the fourth Gospel in the numerous facts which he extracts from the "Memoirs of the Apostles." More than this, upon all the points where the synoptics and the fourth Gospel differ he adopts opinions at complete variance with the latter. This is all the more surprising, seeing that the dogmatic tendencies of the fourth Gospel are marvellously adapted to Justin.

The same remarks apply to the pseudo-Clementine homilies. The words of Jesus quoted by that book are of the synoptic type. In two or three places there are, it would seem, facts borrowed from the fourth Gospel. But the author of the Homilies certainly does not accord to that Gospel an apostolic authority, since on many points be puts himself in direct contradiction with him. It appears that Marcion (about 140) could not have known the said Gospel, or attributed to it no importance as an inspired book. This Gospel accorded so well with his ideas that, if he had known it, he would have adopted it eagerly, and would not have been obliged, so as to have an ideal Gospel, to make a corrected edition of the Gospel of Luke. Finally, the apocryphal Gospels which may be referred to the second century, like the Protevangel of James, the Gospel of Thomas the Israelite, embellished the synoptic canvas, but they took no account of the Gospel of John.

The intrinsic difficulties which result from the reading of the fourth Gospel itself are not less forcible. How is it that, by the side of information so precise, and in places felt to be that of eyewitnesses, we find discourses totally different from those of Matthew? How is it that the Gospel in question does not contain a parable or an exorcism? How is it to be explained that side by side with a general plan of the life of Jesus, which plan in some respects seems more satisfactory and more exact than that of the synoptics, appear those singular passages in which one perceives a dogmatic interest peculiar to the author, ideas most foreign to Jesus, and sometimes indications which put us on our guard to the good faith of the narrator? How is it, finally, that by the side of views the most pure, the most just, the most truly evangelical, we find those blemishes which we would rather look upon as the interpolation of an ardent sectary? Is this indeed John, son of Zebedee, the brother of James (who is not mentioned once in the fourth Gospel), who has written in Greek those abstract lessons on metaphysics, to which the synoptics offer no analogy? Is this the essentially Judaising author of the Apocalypse, who, in so few years, should have been stripped to this extent of his style and of his ideas? Is it an "Apostle of Circumcision," who is likely to have composed a narrative more hostile to Judaism than the whole of St. Paul's, a narrative in which the word "Jew" is almost equivalent to That of "enemy of Jesus"? Is it indeed he whose example was invoked by the partisans of the celebration of the Jewish passover in favour of their opinion, who could speak with a sort of disdain of the "Feasts of the Jews" and of the "Passover of the Jews"? All of this is important. For my part, I reject the idea that the fourth Gospel could have been written by the pen of a quondam Galilean fisherman. But that, taken all in all, this Gospel may have proceeded, about the end of the first century or the beginning of the second, from one of the schools of Asia Minor which was attached to John, that it presents to us a version of the life of the Master worthy of high consideration and often of being preferred, is indeed rendered probable, both by external evidence and by examining the document under consideration.

And, in the first place, no one doubts that about the year 170 the fourth Gospel did exist. At that date there broke out at Laodicea on the Lycus a controversy relative to the Passover, in which our Gospel played an important part. Apollinaris, Athenagoras, Polycrates, the author of the epistle to the Churches of Vienne and of Lyons, professed already in regard to the alleged narrative of John the opinion that it would soon become orthodox. Theophilus of Antioch (about 180) said positively that the Apostle John was the author of it. Irenæus and the Canon of Muratori attest the complete triumph of our Gospel, a triumph in respect of which there could no longer be any doubt.

But, if about the year 170 the fourth Gospel appeared as a writing of the Apostle John and invested with full authority, is it not evident that at this date it was not of ancient creation? Tatian, the author of the epistle to Diogenatus, seems indeed to have made use of it. The part played by our Gospel in Gnosticism, and especially in the system of Valentinus, in Montanism and in the controversy of the Aloges, is not less remarkable, and shows that from the last half of the second century this Gospel was included in every controversy, and served as a corner stone for the development of the dogma. The school of John is the one whose progress is the most apparent during the second century; Irenæus proceeded from the school of John, and between him and the Apostle there was only Polycarp. Now, Irenæus has not a doubt as to the authenticity of the fourth Gospel. Let as add that the first epistle attributed to Saint John is, according to all appearances, by the same author as the fourth Gospel; now the epistle seems to have been known to Polycarp; it was, it is said, cited by Papias; Irenæus recognised it as John's.

But, as some light is now required to be cast upon the reading of the work itself, we shall remark, first, that the author therein always speaks as an eyewitness. He wishes to pass for the Apostle John, and it is clearly seen that he writes in the interest of that apostle. In each he betrays the design of fortifying the authority of the son of Zebedee, of showing that he was the favourite of Jesus, and the most far-seeing of his disciples; that on all the most solemn occasions (at the Supper, at Calvary, at the Tomb), he occupied the chief place. The relations of John with Peter, which were on the whole fraternal, although not excluding a certain rivalry; the hatred, on the other hand, of Judas, a hatred probably anterior to the betrayal, seem to break through here and there. At times one is constrained to believe that John, in his old age, having perused the evangelical narratives which were in circulation, on the one hand, remarked various inaccuracies; on the other, was chagrined at seeing that in the history of Christ he was not accorded an important enough place; that then he commenced to recount a multitude of things which were better known to him than to the others, with the intention of showing that, in many instances where Peter only was mentioned, he had figured with and before him. Even during the life of Jesus these petty sentiments of jealousy had been betrayed between the sons of Zebedee and the other disciples. Since the death of James, his brother, John remained the sole inheritor of the intimate remembrances of which the two apostles, by common consent, were the depositaries. Those clear remembrances were preserved in the circle of John, and as the ideas of the times in the matter of literary good faith differed much from ours, a disciple, or rather one of those numerous sectaries, already semi-Gnostics, who from the end of the first century, in Asia Minor, commenced to modify greatly the idea of Christ, might have been tempted to take the pen for the apostle and to make on his own account a free revision of his Gospel. It would cost him no more to speak in the name of John than it cost the pious author of the second Epistle of Peter to write a letter in the name of the latter. To identify himself with the beloved Apostle of Jesus, he espoused all his sentiments, even his littlenesses. Hence this perpetual design of the alleged author to recall that he is the last surviving eyewitness, and the pleasure he takes in relating circumstances which could only be known to him. Hence, so many petty minute details which he would like passed off as the commentaries of an annotator: "It was the sixth hour;" "it was night;" "that man was called Malchus;" "they had lighted a fire, for it was cold;" "the coat was without seam." Hence, finally, the bad arrangement of the compilation, the irregularity of the narrative, the disjointedness of the first chapters--so many inexplicable features, if we go on the supposition that our Gospel is a mere theological thesis without any historic value, yet perfectly comprehensible if we regard it as the recollections of an old man arranged without the assistance of those from whom they proceeded--recollections, sometimes possessing uncommon freshness, at others having been subjected to singular modifications.

An important distinction, in fact, is to he remarked in the Gospel of John. This Gospel, on the one hand, presents a sketch of the life of Jesus which differs considerably from that of the synoptics. On the other, it puts into the mouth of Jesus discourses whose tone, style, character and doctrines have nothing in common with the Λόγια contained in the synoptics. In respect of the latter, the difference is such that one must make an unqualified choice. If Jesus spoke as Matthew would have us believe, he could not have spoken in the manner represented by John. Between these two authorities no one has hesitated, or will ever hesitate. Removed by a thousand leagues from the simple, disinterested and impersonal tone of the synoptics, the Gospel of John shows at every step the prepossession of the apologist, the arrière pensée of the sectary, the desire to establish a thesis and to overcome his adversaries. It was not by pretentious tirades, clumsy, badly written, and appealing little to the moral sense, that Jesus founded his divine work. Even though Papias had not informed us that Matthew wrote the sayings of Jesus in their original tongue, the natural, the ineffable truth, the incomparable charm contained in the synoptic Gospels, the profoundly Hebraic turn of these discourses, the analogies which they present to the sayings of the Jewish doctors of the period, their perfect harmony with the Galilean nature--all these characteristics, compared with the obscure Gnosticism and the distorted metaphysics which fill the discourses of John, speak loudly enough. We do not mean to say that there are not to be found in the discourses of John some brilliant flashes, some traits which really proceeded from Jesus. But the mystical tone of these discourses corresponds in nothing to the character of the eloquence of Jesus, such as it is pictured to us in the synoptics. A new spirit breathes through them; Gnoticism has previously found a footing; the Galilean era of the kingdom of God is at an end, the hope of the near advent of Jesus is further off; we enter the arid realm of metaphysics, into the darkness of abstract dogmatism. The spirit of Jesus is not there, and if the son of Zebedee has indeed traced those pages, it is to be supposed that in writing them he had forgotten the Lake of Gennesareth and the charming conversations he had heard upon its banks.

One circumstance, moreover, which proves indeed that the discourses reported by the fourth Gospel are historical fragments, but that they ought to be regarded as compositions, intended to cover, with the authority of Jesus, certain doctrines dear to the author, is their complete harmony with the intellectual condition of Asia Minor at the time they were written. Asia Minor was then the theatre of a strange movement of syncretic philosophy; all the germs of Gnosticism existed there already. Cerinthus, a contemporary of John, said that æon named Christos was united by baptism to the man named Jesus, and had separated from him on the cross. Some of the disciples of John would appear to have drunk deeply from these strange springs. Can we affirm that the Apostle himself had not been subject to the same influences, that he did not experience something anologous to the change which was wrought in St. Paul, and of which the epistle to the Colossians is the principal witness? No, certainly not. It may be that after the crisis of 68 (the date of the Apocalypse), and of the year 70 (the ruin of Jerusalem), the old Apostle, with an ardent and plastic soul, disabused of the belief of the near appearance of the Son of Man in the clouds, inclined towards the ideas that he found around him, many of which amalgamated quite well with certain Christian doctrines. In imputing these new ideas to Jesus, he only followed a very natural leaning. Our recollections are, like everything else, transformable; the ideal of a person we have known changes as we change. Regarding Jesus as the incarnation of truth, John has succeeded in attributing to him that which he had come to accept as the truth.

It is nevertheless much more probable that John himself had no part in them, that the change was made around him rather than by him, and doubtless after his death. The long age of the apostle may have terminated in such a state of feebleness that he was in a measure at the mercy of those around him. A secretary might take advantage of this state to speak in his name that which the world called par excellence, "the old man," Ὁ Πρεσβύτερος. Certain parts of the fourth Gospel have been added subsequently; such is the whole xxi. chapter, in which the author seems to have resolved to render homage to the apostle Peter after his death, and to answer the objections which might be drawn or were already drawn from the death of John himself (v. 21-23). Several other places bear the traces of erasures and of corrections. Not being accounted as wholly the work of John, the book could well remain fifty years in obscurity. Little by little people got accustomed to it, and finished by accepting it. Even before it had become canonical many simply made use of it as a book of mediocre authority, yet very edifying. On the other hand, the contradictions that it offered to the synoptic Gospels, which were much more widely circulated, prevented its being taken into account when setting forth the contexture of the life of Jesus, such as it was imagined to be.

In this mode some explain away the whimsical contradictions presented in the writings of Justin and in the pseudo-Clementine Homilies, in which are to be found traces of our Gospel, but which certainly are not to be placed upon the same footing as the synoptics. Hence also those species of allusions, which are not faithful quotations, but were made from it about the year 180. Hence, finally, this singularity, that the fourth Gospel appeared to emerge slowly from the Church of Asia in the second century, was first adopted by the Gnostics, but only obtained in the orthodox Church very limited credence, as can be seen from the controversy on the Passover, then it was universally recognised. I am sometimes led to believe that it was the fourth Gospel of which Papias was thinking when he opposed to the exact information in regard to the life of Jesus the long discourses and the singular precepts which others have attributed to him. Papias and the old Jadæo-Christian party came to esteem such novelties as very reprehensible. This could not have been the only instance that a book which was at first heretical would have forced the gates of the orthodox Church and become one of its rules of faith.

There is one thing, at least, which I regard as very probable, and that is, that the book was written before the year 100; that is to say, at a time when the synoptics had not yet a complete canonicity. After this date it is impossible any longer to conceive that the author could force himself to go beyond the limits of the "Apostolic Memoirs." To Justin, and apparently to Papias, the synoptic cadre constitutes the true and only plan of the life of Jesus. An impostor who wrote about the year 120 to 130 a fantastic gospel contented himself with treating in his own way the received version, as had been done in the apocryphal Gospels, and did not reverse from top to bottom what was regarded as the essential lines of the life of Jesus. This is so true that, from the second half of the second century, these contradictions became a serious difficulty in the hands of the aloges, and obliged the defenders of the fourth Gospel to invent the most embarrassing solutions. There is nothing to prove that the author of the fourth Gospel had, when writing, any of the synoptic Gospels under his eyes. The striking similarities of his narrative to the other three Gospels as touching the Passion leads one to suppose that there was then for the Passion as well as for the Last Supper an almost fixed account, which people knew by heart.

It is impossible at this distance of time to comprehend all these singular problems, and we should undoubtedly encounter many surprises if it were given to us to penetrate the secrets of that mysterious school of Ephesus, which appeared frequently to take pleasure in pursuing obscure paths. But the latter is a capital test. Every person who sets himself to write the life of Jesus without having a decided opinion upon the relative value of the Gospels, who allows himself to be guided solely by the sentiment of the subject, would, in many instances, be induced to prefer the narrative of the fourth Gospel to that of the synoptics. The last months of the life of Jesus especially are explained only by John; several details of the Passion, which are unintelligible in the synoptics, assume both probability and possibility in the narrative of the fourth Gospel. On the other hand, I can defy anybody to compose a life of Jesus that is understandable, which takes into account the discourses that the alleged John imputes to Jesus. This fashion of his of incessantly preaching himself up and of exhibiting himself, this perpetual argumentation, this studied stage-effect, these long reasonings attached to each miracle, these lifeless and incoherent discourses, the tone of which is so often false and unequal, could not be endured by a man of taste alongside of the delightful phraseology which, according to the synoptics, constituted the soul of the teaching of Jesus. There are here evidently fictitious fragments, which represent to us the sermons of Jesus in the same way as the dialogues of Plato set forth the conversations of Socrates. They resemble the variations of a musician improvising on his own account upon a given theme. The theme in question may have existed previously; but in the execution the artist gives his fancy free scope. We perceive the factitious progressions, the rhetoric, the verisimilitude. Let us add that the vocabulary of Jesus is nowhere to be found in the fragments of which we speak. The expression of "Kingdom of God," which was so common with the master, does not appear even once. But, contrariwise, the style of the discourses attributed to Jesus by the fourth Gospel offers the most complete analogy to that of parts of the narrative of the same Gospel and to that of the author of the epistles called John. We see that the author of the fourth Gospel, in writing these discourses, did not give his recollections, but the somewhat monotonous workings of his own thought. Quite a new mystical language is displayed in them, language characterised by the frequent employment of the words "world," "truth," "life," "light," "darkness," and which resembles much less that of the synoptics than that of the book of the sages-- Philo and the Valentinians. If Jesus had ever spoken in that style, which is neither Hebraic nor Jewish, how does it come that, amongst the auditors, only a single one of the latter has kept the secret?

For the rest, literary history offers one example which presents a certain analogy to the historic phenomenon we have just been describing, and which serves to explain it. Socrates, who, like Jesus, did not write, is known to us through two of his disciples, Xenophon and Plato; the former corresponding with the synoptics by reason of his compilation, at once consecutive, transparent and impersonal; the latter, by reason of his robust individuality, recalling the author of the fourth Gospel. In order to describe the Socratic teaching must we follow the "Dialogues" of Plato, or the "Discourses" of Xenophon? In such a case doubt is not possible; everyone sticks to the "Discourses" and not to the "Dialogues." Does Plato nevertheless teach us nothing concerning Socrates? In writing the biography of the latter, would it be good criticism to neglect the dialogues? Who would dare to maintain this?

Without pronouncing upon the question, it is material to know as to what hand indited the fourth Gospel; even if we were persuaded it was not that of the son of Zebedee, we can at least admit that this work possesses some title to be called "the Gospel according to John." The historical sketch of the fourth Gospel is, in my opinion, the life of Jesus, such as it was known to the immediate circle of John. It is also my belief that this school was better acquainted with the different exterior circumstances of the life of the Founder than the group whose recollections go to make up the synoptic Gospels. Notably, in regard to the sojourns of Jesus at Jerusalem, it was in possession of facts that the other Gospels had not. Presbyteros Joannes, who is probably not a different person from the Apostle John, regarded, it is said, the narrative of Mark as incomplete and confused; he even had a theory which explained the omissions of the latter. Certain passages in Luke, which are a kind of echo of the Johannine traditions, prove, moreover, that the traditions preserved by the fourth Gospel were not to the rest of the Christian family something which was entirely unknown.

These explanations will suffice, I think, to show the motives which in the course of my narrative have determined me to give the preference to this or that one of the four guides which we have for the life of Jesus. On the whole, I admit the four canonical Gospels to be important documents. All four ascend to the century which succeeded the death of Jesus; but their historic value is very diverse. Matthew evidently merits unlimited confidence in respect of the discourses; the latter are the Λόγια, the very notes which have been extracted from a clear and lively memory of the teaching of Jesus. A species of éclat at once mild and terrible, a divine force, if I may so speak, underlines these words, detaches them from the context, and to the critic renders them easily distinguishable. The person who undertakes the task of carving out of evangelical history a consecutive narrative possesses, in this regard, an excellent touchstone. The actual words of Jesus, so to speak, reveal themselves; as soon as we touch them in this chaos of traditions of unequal authority, we feel them vibrate; they translate themselves spontaneously and fit into the narrative naturally, where they constitute an unsurpassable relief.

The narrative parts which are grouped in the first Gospel around this primitive nucleus do not possess the same authority. In them are to be found many silly enough legends, which proceeded from the piety of the second Christian generation. The accounts which Matthew gives in common with Mark present faults of transcription which prove a mediocre acquaintance with Palestine. Many of the episodes are repeated twice, several persons are duplicated, which shows that different sources have been utilised and largely amalgamated. The Gospel of Mark is much more firm, more precise, and less weighted with circumstances which have been added. Of the three synoptics it is the one which has remained the most primitive, the most original, the Gospel to which has been annexed the fewest posterior elements. Material details are given in Mark with a clearness which we should seek in vain for in the other evangelists. He delights to report certain sayings of Jesus in Syro-Chaldean. His observations are most minute, and come, no doubt, from an eyewitness. There is nothing to disprove that this eyewitness, who evidently had followed Jesus, who had loved him and observed him very closely, and who had preserved a lively image of him, was the Apostle Peter himself, as is maintained by Papias.

As for the work of Luke, its historic value is sensibly more feeble. It is a document at second hand. Its manner of narration is more matured. The sayings of Jesus are there more reflective, more sententious. Some sentences are carried to excess and are false. Writing outside Palestine, and certainly after the siege of Jerusalem, the author indicates the places with less exactness than the two other synoptics; he is too fond of representing the temple as an oratory, where people go to do their devotions; he does not speak of the Herodians; he modifies details in order to bring the different narratives into closer agreement; he softens down passages which had become embarrassing because of the more exalted idea which people around him had attained to in regard to the divinity of Jesus; he exaggerates the marvellous; he commits errors of geography and of topography; he omits the Hebraic glosses; he appears to know little of Hebrew; he does not quote a word of Jesus in that language; he calls all the localities by their Greek names; he corrects at times in a clumsy manner the sayings of Jesus. We perceive in the author a compiler, a man who has not seen directly the witnesses, who labours at the texts, and permits himself to do them great violence in order to make them agree. Luke had probably under his eyes the original narrative of Mark and the Λόγια of Matthew. But he treats them with great freedom; at times he runs two anecdotes or two parables together to make one; sometimes he divides one in order to make two. He interprets the documents according to his own mind; he has not the absolute impassibility of Matthew and Mark. We might affirm this of his tastes and of his personal tendencies: he is a very exact devotee; he holds that Jesus has accomplished all the Jewish rites; he is a passionate democrat and Ebionite; that is to say, much opposed to property, and is persuaded that the poor will soon have their revenge; he is specially partial to the anecdotes which put into relief the conversion of sinners and the exaltation of the humble; he frequently modifies the ancient traditions so as to give them this acceptation. In his first pages he includes the legends touching the infancy of Jesus, related with the long amplifications, the canticles and the conventional proceedings which constitute the essential feature of the apocryphal Gospels. Finally, in the account of the last hours of Jesus, he introduces some circumstances which are full of a tender sentiment, as well as certain sayings of Jesus of rare beauty, which are not to be found in the more authentic narratives, and in which can be detected the hand of the legendary. Luke has probably borrowed them from a more recent collection, in which it is seen his chief aim was to excite sentiments of piety.

A great reserve was naturally bespoken in regard to a document of this nature. It would have been as little scientific to neglect it as to employ it without discernment. Luke had under his eyes originals which we no longer have. He is less an evangelist than a biographer of Jesus, a "harmonist," a reviser, after the manner of Marcion and Tatian. But he is a biographer of the first century, a divine artist who, independently of the information he has extracted from more ancient sources, shows us the character of the Founder with a happiness of treatment, a uniformity of inspiration, and a clearness that the other two synoptic do not possess. His Gospel is the one the reading of which possesses most charm: for, not to mention the incomparable beauty of its common basis, he combines a degree of art and of skill in composition which singularly enhances the effect of the picture, without seriously marring its truthfulness.

To sum up, we are warranted in saying that the synoptic compilation has passed through three stages: first, the original documentary stage (λόγια of Matthew, λεχθέντα ἢ πραχθέντα of Mark), primary compilations no longer in existence; second, the simple amalgamation stage, in which the original documents were thrown together without any regard to literary form, and without any personal traits on the part of the authors becoming manifest (the present Gospels of Matthew and Mark); third, the combination stage, that of careful composition and reflection, in which we are conscious of an effort made to reconcile the different versions (the Gospel of Luke, the Gospels of Marcion, Tatian, &c.). The Gospel of John, as we have above said, is a composition of another order and altogether distinct.

It will be observed that I have not made any use of apocryphal Gospels. In no sense ought these compositions to be placed on the same footing as the canonical Gospels. They are tiresome and puerile amplifications, having almost entirely the canonicals for a basis, and adding almost nothing to them of any particular value. Contrariwise, I have been most careful in collecting the shreds which have been preserved by the Fathers of the Church, by the ancient Gospels which formerly existed simultaneously with the canonicals, but which are now lost, such as the Gospel according to the Hebrews, the Gospel according to the Egyptians, the Gospels attributed to Justin, Marcion, and Tatian. The first two possess a peculiar importance, inasmuch as they were indited in Aramean like the Λόγια of Matthew; as they appear to have formed a version of the Gospel attributed to that apostle, and as they were the Gospel of Ebionim, that is to say, of those small Christian sects of Batanea who preserved the use of the Syro-Chaldean tongue, and appear to have continued, to some extent, in the footsteps of Jesus. But it most be owned that, in the condition they have come down to us, these Gospels are inferior, for the purposes of criticism, to the edition of the Gospel of Matthew which we possess.

It will now, I presume, be understood what sort of historic value I put upon the Gospels. They are neither biographies after the manner of Suetonius, nor fictitious legends, after the manner of Philostratus; they are legendary biographies. I place them at once alongside of the legends of the saints, the lives of Plotinus, Proclus, Isidore, and other compositions of the same sort, in which historical truth and the desire to present models of virtue are combined in divers degrees. Inexactitude, a trait common to all popular compositions, makes itself particularly felt in them. Let us suppose that fifteen or twenty years ago three or four old soldiers of the Empire had individually set themselves to write a life of Napoleon from recollections of him. It is clear that their narratives would present numerous errors, great discordances. One of them would place Wagram before Marengo; another would boldly state that Napoleon ousted the government of Robespierre from the Tuileries; a third would omit expeditions of the highest importance. But one thing, possessing a great degree of truthfulness, would certainly result from these simple narratives--that is, the character of the hero, the impression he made around him. In this sense such popular narratives would be worth more than a solemn and official history. The same can also be said of the Gospels. Bent solely on bringing out strongly the excellency of the master, his miracles, his teaching, the evangelists manifest entire indifference to everything that is not of the very spirit of Jesus. The contradictions in respect of time, place, and persons were regarded as insignificant; for just as the greater the degree of inspiration that is attributed to the words of Jesus, so the less was granted to the compilers themselves. The latter looked upon themselves as simple scribes, and cared only for one thing--to omit nothing they knew. [2]

Without doubt some certain preconceived ideas must have been associated with such recollections. Several narratives, especially in Luke, are invented in order to bring out more vividly certain traits of the personality of Jesus. This personality itself underwent alteration each day. Jesus would be a unique phenomenon in history if, with the part which he played, he had not soon become imbued with it. The legend respecting Alexander was concocted before the generation of his companions in arms was extinct; that respecting St. Francis d'Assisi began in his lifetime. A rapid work of transformation went on in the same manner in the twenty or thirty years which followed the death of Jesus, and imposed upon his biography the absolute traits of an ideal legend. Death makes perfect the most perfect man; it renders him faultless to those who have loved him. At the same time, the wish to paint the Master created likewise the desire to explain him. Many anecdotes were concocted in order to prove that the prophecies regarded as Messianic had been fulfilled in him. But this procedure, the importance of which is undeniable, would not suffice to explain everything. No Jewish work of the time gives a series of prophecies declaring formally what the Messiah was to accomplish. Many of the Messianic allusions referred to by the evangelists are so subtle, so indirect, that it is impossible to believe they all had relation to a generally admitted doctrine. Sometimes they reasoned thus: "The Messiah was to do such a thing; now Jesus is the Messiah; therefore Jesus has done such a thing." Sometimes they reasoned inversely: "Such a thing has happened to Jesus; now Jesus is the Messiah; therefore such a thing was to happen to the Messiah." [3] Explanations which are too simple are always false when it is a question of analysing the tissues of those profound creations of popular sentiment which baffle all science by their fulness and infinite variety.

It is scarcely necessary to say that with such documents, in order to present only what is incontestable, we must confine ourselves to general lines. In almost all ancient histories, even in those which are much less legendary than these, details give rise to infinite doubts. When we have two accounts of the some fact, it is extremely rare that the two accounts are in accord. Is not this a reason, when we are confronted with but one perplexity, for falling into many? We may say that amongst the anecdotes, the discourses, the celebrated sayings reported by the historians, there is not one strictly accurate. Were there stenographers to take down these fleeting words? Was there an annalist always present to note the gestures, the conduct, the sentiments, of the actors? Let any one essay to attain to the truth as to the manner in which such or such a contemporary fact took place; he will not succeed. Two accounts of the same event given by two eyewitnesses differ essentially. Must we, hence, reject all the colouring of the narratives, and confine ourselves to recording the bare facts only? That would be to suppress history. Certainly I think, however, that if we except certain short and almost mnemonic axioms, none of the discourses reported by Matthew are textual; there is hardly one of our stenographic reports which is so. I willingly admit that that admirable account of the Passion embraces a multitude of trifling inaccuracies. Would it, however, be writing the history of Jesus to omit those sermons which exhibit to us in such a vivid manner the nature of his discourses, and to limit ourselves to saying, with Josephus and Tacitus, "that he was put to death by the order of Pilate" at the instigation of the priests"? That would be, in my opinion, a kind of inexactitude worse than that to which one exposes himself when admitting the details supplied by the texts. These details are not true to the letter, but they are rendered true by a superior truth; they are more true than the naked truth, in the sense that they are truths rendered expressive and articulate and raised to the height of an idea.

I beg those who think that I have placed an exaggerated confidence in narratives which are in great part legendary to take note of the observation I have just made. To what would the life of Alexander be reduced if it were limited to that which is materially certain? Even partly erroneous traditions contain a portion of truth which history may not pass over. No one has reproached M. Sprenger for having, in writing the life of Mahomet, set much store by the hadith or oral traditions concerning the prophet, and for often having imputed to his hero words which are only known through this source. The traditions respecting Mahomet, nevertheless, do not have a superior historical character to the discourses and narratives which compose the Gospels. They were written between the year 50 and the year 140 of the Hegira. When the history of the Jewish schools in the ages which immediately preceded and followed the birth of Christianity shall be written, no one will make any scruple of attributing to Hillel, Shammai, Gamaliel, the maxims imputed to them by the Mishna and the Gemara, although these great compilations were written many centuries after the time of the doctors just mentioned.

Contrariwise, those who believe that history ought to consist of a reproduction without comments of the documents which have come down to us, I beg them to take notice that such a course is not allowable. The four principal documents are in flagrant contradiction with one another; Josephus, moreover, sometimes rectifies them. It is necessary to make a choice. To allege that an event cannot take place in two ways at once, or in an absurd manner, is not to impose à priori philosophy upon history. Because he possesses several different versions of the same fact, or because credulity has mixed with all these versions fabulous circumstances, the historian most not conclude that the fact is not a fact; but he ought, in such a case, to be very cautious,--to examine the texts, and to proceed by induction. There is one class of narratives especially, apropos of which this principle must necessarily be applied--narratives of the supernatural. To seek to explain these narratives, or to transform them into legends, is not to mutilate facts in the name of theory; it is to begin with the observation of the very facts themselves. None of the miracles with which the old histories are filled took place under scientific conditions. Observation, which has not once been falsified, teaches us that miracles never take place save in times and countries in which they are believed, and in presence of persons disposed to believe them. No miracle ever took place in presence of an assembly of men capable of testing the miraculous character of the event. Neither common people nor men of the world are equal to the latter. It requires great precautions and long habit of scientific research. In our own days, have we not seen the great majority of people become dupes of the grossest frauds or of puerile illusions! Marvellous facts, attested by the populations of small towns, have, thanks to closer investigation, been condemned. [4] Since it is proved that no contemporary miracle will bear discussion, is it not probable that the miracles of the past, which have all been performed in popular gatherings, would equally present their share of illusion, if It were possible to criticise them in detail?

It is not, then, in the name of this or that philosophy, but in the name of unbroken experience, that we banish the miracle from history. We do not say, "The miracle is impossible." We say, "So far, a miracle has never been proved." If to-morrow a thaumaturgist were to come forward with credentials sufficiently important to be discussed; if he were to announce that he was able, say, to raise the dead; what would be done? A commission, composed of physiologists, physicists, chemists, persons accustomed to historical criticism, would be named. That commission would choose a corpse, would assure itself that the death was indeed real, would designate the room in which the experiment should be made, would arrange a whole series of precautions, so as to leave no chance of doubt. If, under such conditions, resuscitation were effected, a probability, almost equal to certainty, would be established. As, however, it ought always to be possible to repeat an experiment--to do over again that which has been done once--and as, in the case of miracle, there can be no question of facility or difficulty, the thaumaturgist would be invited to reproduce his marvellous feat under different circumstances, upon other corpses, in another place. If the miracle was repeated each time, two things would be proved: first, that supernatural facts take place in the world; second, that the power of producing them belongs, or is delegated to, certain individuals. But who does not perceive that a miracle never took place under these conditions? that hitherto the thaumaturgist has always chosen the subject of the experiment, chosen the spot, chosen the public; that, moreover, it is the people themselves who most often, in consequence of the invincible desire to see something divine in great events and great men, create afterwards the marvellous legends? Until the order of things changes, we maintain it, then, as a principle of historical criticism, that a supernatural account cannot be admitted as such, that it always implies credulity or imposture, that it is the duty of the historian to explain it, and search out what share of truth, or of error, it may conceal.

Such are the rules which have been adhered to in the composition of this narrative. In the reading of the texts, I have been able to combine with it an important source of information--the viewing of the places where the events occurred. The scientific mission, having for its object the exploration of ancient Phoenicia, which I directed in 1860 and 1861, [5] led me to reside on the frontiers of Galilee, and to travel thither frequently. I have traversed, in every sense of the term, the country of the Gospels; I have visited Jerusalem, Hebron, and Samaria; scarcely any important locality in the history of Jesus has escaped me. All this history, which seems at a distance to float in the clouds of an unreal world, took thus a form, a solidity, which astonished me. The striking agreement of the texts and the places, the marvellous harmony of the evangelical idea, and of the country which served it as a framework, were to me a revelation. Before my eyes I had a fifth Gospel, disfigured though still legible, and from that time, in the narratives of Matthew and Mark, I saw instead of an abstract being, who could be said never to have existed, an admirable human figure living and moving. During the summer, having to go up to Ghazir, in Lebanon, to take a little repose, I fixed, in rapid sketches, the picture as it had appeared to me, and from them resulted this history. When a cruel affliction came to hasten my departure, I had only a few pages to write. In this manner the book was almost entirely composed near the very places where Jesus was born and lived. Since my return, I have laboured unceasingly to complete and arrange in detail the rough sketch which I had hastily written in a Maronite cabin, with five or six volumes around me.

Many will perhaps regret the biographical form which my work has thus taken. When, for the first time, I conceived the idea of writing a history of the origins of Christianity, my intention was, in fact, to produce a history of doctrines, in which men and their actions would have hardly had a place. Jesus was scarcely to be named; I was especially bent on showing how the ideas which, under cover of his name, were produced, took root and covered the world. But I have since learned that history is not a simple game of abstractions; that men are more important than doctrines. It was not a certain theory in regard to justification and redemption which caused the Reformation; it was Luther and Calvin. Parseeism, Hellenism, Judaism, might have been able to combine under all forms; the doctrines of the Resurrection and of the Word might have gone on developing for ages without producing that grand, unique, and fruitful fact, which is called Christianity. That fact is the work of Jesus, of St. Paul, and of the apostles. To write the history of Jesus, of St. Paul, and of the apostles, is to write the history of the origins of Christianity. The anterior movements do not belong to our subject except as serving to explain the characters If these extraordinary men, who, naturally, could not be severed from that which preceded them.

In such an effort, to make the great souls of the past live again, some degree of divination and of conjecture must be permitted. A great life is an organic whole which cannot be exhibited by the mere agglomeration of small facts. It requires a profound sentiment to embrace the whole, and to make it a perfect unity. The artist method in such a subject is a good guide; the exquisite tact of a Goethe would discover how to apply it. The essential condition of the creations of art is to form a living system of which all the parts are mutually dependent and connected. In histories of this kind, the great indication that we hold to the truth is to have succeeded in combining the texts in such a fashion that they shall constitute a logical and probable narrative, in which nothing shall be out of tune. The secret laws of life, of the progression of organic products, of the action of minute particles, ought to be consulted at each moment; for what is required to be reproduced is not the material circumstance, which it is impossible to verify; it is the soul itself of history; what most be sought after is not the petty certainty of minutiæ, it is the correctness of the general sentiment, the truthfulness of the colouring. Each detail which departs from the rules of classic narration ought to warn us to be on our guard; for the fact which requires to be related has been confined to the necessities of things, natural and harmonious. If we do not succeed in rendering it such by our narrative, it is only because we have not attained to seeing it aright. Suppose that, in restoring the Minerva of Phidias according to the texts, we produced an ensemble at once dry, jarring artificial; what must we conclude? Only one thing: the texts lack an appreciative interpretation; we must inquire into them calmly until they can be made to approximate and furnish a whole in which all the parts are happily blended. Should we then be sure of having feature for feature of the Greek statue? No; but we should not, at least, have the caricature of it; we should have the general spirit of the work--one of the forms in which it might have existed.

This sentiment of a living organism we have not hesitated to take as our guide in the general arrangement of the narrative. The reading of the Gospels would be sufficient to prove that the authors, although conceiving a very true idea of the Life of Jesus, have not been guided by very rigorous chronological data; Papias, moreover, expressly teaches this, and bases his opinion upon evidence which seems to emanate from the Apostle John himself. The expressions, "At this time . . . after that . . . then . . . and it came to pass . . ." &c., are the simple transitions designed to connect different narratives with each other. To leave all the information furnished by the Gospels in the disorder in which tradition gives it, would no more be writing the history of Jesus than it would be writing the history of a celebrated man to give pell-mell the letters and anecdotes of his youth, his old age, and of his maturity. The Koran, which presents to us, in the loosest manner possible, fragments of the different epochs in the life of Mahomet, has discovered its secret to ingenious criticism; the chronological order in which the fragments were composed has been hit upon in such a way as to leave little room for doubt Such a re-arrangement is much more difficult in the Gospel, owing to the public life of Jesus having been shorter and less eventful than the life of the founder of Islamism. Nevertheless, the attempt to find a thread which shall serve as a guide through this labyrinth, ought not to be taxed with gratuitous subtlety. There is no great abuse of hypothesis in premising that a religious founder commences by attaching himself to the moral aphorisms which are already in circulation, and to the practices which are in vogue; nor, as he advances and gets full possession of his idea, that he delights in a kind of calm and poetical eloquence, remote from all controversy, sweet and free as pure feeling; nor, as he gradually warms, that he is animated by opposition, and finishes by polemics and strong invectives. Such are the periods which are plainly distinguishable in the Koran. The order which, with extremely fine tact, is adopted by the synoptic, supposes an analogous progress. If we read Matthew attentively, we shall find, in the arrangement of the discourses, a gradation greatly analogous to that just indicated. We may observe also the studied turns of expression which are made use of when it is desired to show the progress of the ideas of Jesus. The reader may, if he prefers, see in the divisions adopted in this respect, only the breaks indispensable for the methodical exposition of a profound and complicated thought.

If love for a subject can assist in the understanding of it, it will also, I hope, be recognised that I have not been wanting in this condition. To construct the history of a religion, it is necessary first to have believed it (without this, we should not be able to understand why it has charmed and satisfied the human conscience); in the second place, to believe it no longer in an absolute manner, for absolute faith is incompatible with sincere history. But love exists apart from faith. In order not to attach one's self to any of the forms which captivate the adoration of men, one need not renounce the appreciation of that which they contain of good and of beautiful. No transitory apparition exhausts the Divinity; God was revealed before Jesus--God will reveal Himself after him. Profoundly unequal, and so much the more Divine, because they are grander and more spontaneous, the manifestations of God which are hidden in the depths of the human conscience are all of the same order. Jesus cannot then belong solely to those who call themselves his disciples. He is the common honour of him who carries a human heart. His glory does not consist in being banished from history; we render him a truer worship in showing that all history is incomprehensible without him.

Footnotes:

1. See Volume VIII. of this series, which contains the author's notes of the whole seven volumes of the series, together with a complete index.--Ed.

2. See the passage from Papias, before cited.

3. See, for example, John xix. 23, 24.

4. See the Gazette des Tribunaux, 10th Sept, and 11th Nov., 1851; 28th May, 1857.

5. The work which will contain the results of this mission is in the press.

CHAPTER I

PLACE OF JESUS IN THE HISTORY OF THE WORLD

The chief event in the world's history is the revolution by which the noblest portions of humanity passed from the ancient religions comprised under the name of Paganism to a religion based on the divine unity, the trinity, and the incarnation of the Son of God. It took nearly a thousand years to make this conversion. The new religion itself was three hundred years in forming. But the revolution in question had its origin in the reigns of Augustus and Tiberius. There lived then a superior person, who, through his daring originality and the love he could inspire, created the object and fixed the point of departure of the future faith of humanity.

Man, since he distinguished himself from the animal, has been religious: we mean, he sees something in nature beyond appearances, and in himself something beyond death. This sentiment, for thousands of years, was debased in the most singular manner. With many races it went no further than a belief in sorcerers, under the gross form in which it is still to be found in certain parts of Oceania. With other peoples the religious sentiment degenerated into the hideous scenes of butchery which characterised the ancient religion of Mexico. In other countries, Africa in particular, it did not get beyond Fetichism: we mean the adoration of a material object to which were attributed supernatural powers. Like the instinct of love, which at moments elevates the most vulgar man above himself, it sometimes takes the form of perversion and ferocity; similarly, this divine faculty of religion had for a long time the appearance of a cancer, which it was necessary to extirpate from the human species, the source of errors and of crimes which it was the duty of wise men to seek to suppress.

The brilliant civilisations developed at a remote period in China, in Babylonia, and in Egypt, were the cause of a certain progress in religion. China attained early to a sort of good common sense, which prevented her from going wildly astray. She was cognisant neither of the advantages nor the abuses of the religious spirit. At all events, she had in this instance no influence in directing the great current of human thought. The religions of Babylonia and Syria never disengaged themselves from a substratum of strange sensuality; those religions continued to be, until their extinction in the fourth and fifth centuries of our era, schools of immorality from which, at times, thanks to a kind of poetical instinct, glimpses of the divine world emanated. Egypt, in spite of an apparent kind of Fetichism, was able very early to embrace metaphysical dogmas and a lofty symbolism. But these interpretations of a refined theology were unquestionably not intuitive. Man, when possessed of a clear idea, has never amused himself by clothing it in symbols; most often it is the result of long reflection, and the impossibility felt by the human mind of giving itself up to the absurd, that we seek for ideas whose meaning is lost to us behind ancient mystic images. It is not from Egypt, moreover, whence has come the faith of humanity. The elements in the Christian religion which, after undergoing a thousand transformations, came from Egypt and Syria, are exterior forms of little consequence, or of dross such as is always retained in the purest worships. The grand defect of the religions in question was their superstitious character; they only threw into the world millions of amulets and charms. No great moral thought could emanate from races debased by a secular despotism and accustomed to institutions which prevented almost any exercise of individual liberty.

The poetry of the soul, faith, liberty, sincerity, devotion, appeared simultaneously in the world with the two great races which, in a sense, have made humanity; we refer to the Indo-European and the Semitic races. The first religious intuitions of the Indo-European race were essentially naturalistic. But it was a profound and moral naturalism, an amorous embrace of nature by man, a delicious poetry, full of the sentiment of the infinite; the principle, in a word, of all that which the Germanic and Celtic genius, of that which, in later times, a Shakespeare and a Goethe, should express. This was neither religion nor moral reflection; it was melancholy, tenderness, and imagination; above all, it was extreme earnestness--that is to say, the essential condition of morals and religion. The faith of mankind, nevertheless, could not issue thence, for the reason that these old religions had much difficulty in detaching themselves from polytheism, and could not attain to a very distinct symbolism. Brahmanism has survived to our day only by virtue of the astonishing conservatism which India seems to possess. Buddhism has been stranded in all its attempts to reach the West. Druidism was an exclusively national form, and without universal application. The Greek attempts at reform, Orpheism, the Mysteries, were not able to give solid nourishment to the soul. Persia alone attained to the making of a dogmatic religion, which was almost monotheistic, besides being skilfully organised; but it is very possible that this organisation itself was only an imitation or borrowed. In any case, Persia has not converted the world; on the contrary, she was converted when she saw the flag of the divine unity proclaimed by Islam appear on her frontiers.

It is the Semitic race whose glory it is to have founded the religion of humanity. Away beyond the confines of history, the Bedouin patriarch, resting under his tent and free from the disorders of an already corrupted world, prepared the faith of humanity. His superiority consisted in his strong antipathy against the voluptuous religions of Syria, a marked simplicity of ritual, a complete absence of temples, and the idol reduced to insignificant theraphim. Amongst all the tribes of the nomadic Semites that of the Beni-Israel was already marked out for a great future. From its ancient relations with Egypt there resulted impressions whose extent it would be difficult to determine, but this only served to enhance its hatred for idolatry. A "Law," or Thora, written in very ancient times on tables of stone, which they attributed to Moses, their great liberator, was already the code of monotheism, and contained, when compared with the institutions of Egypt and Chaldea, powerful germs of social equality and of morality. A portable ark, surmounted by a sphinx, with staples on the two sides through which to pass poles, constituted all their religious matériel; all the sacred books of the nation were collected, its relics, its souvenirs, and, finally, the "book," the journal of the tribe, which was always open, but in which entries were made with great discretion. The family charged with holding the poles and keeping watch over these portable archives, being near and having control of the book, acquired very soon some importance. The institution, however, which was to determine the future did not proceed thence. The Hebrew priest differed little from other priests of ancient times. The character which essentially distinguishes Israel among theocratic peoples is, that sacerdotalism has always been subordinated to individual inspiration. Besides its priests, each nomadic tribe had its nabi, or prophet, a sort of living oracle, who was consulted upon obscure questions, the solution of which presupposed the gift of clairvoyance in a high degree. The nabis of Israel, who were formed into groups or schools, possessed great superiority. Defenders of the ancient democratic spirit, enemies of the rich, opposed to all political organisation and to whatever might attract Israel into the paths of other nations, they were the true agents of the religious pre-eminence of the Jewish people. Very early they held forth boundless hopes, and when the people, victims to some extent of their impolitic counsels, were crushed by the might of Assyria, they proclaimed that an endless reign was in store for Judah, that Jerusalem would one day be the capital of the whole world, and that the human race would be made Jews. Jerusalem, with its temple, appeared to them as a city placed upon the summit of a mountain, towards which all peoples should turn, as an oracle whence universal law should issue, as the centre of an ideal kingdom, where the human race, pacified by Israel, should find once more the delights of Eden.

Obscure utterances began already to be heard, which extolled the martyrdom and celebrated the power, of "the Man of Sorrows." Apropos of one of these sublime sufferers, who, like Jeremiah, were to dye the streets of Jerusalem with their blood, one of the inspired composed a song upon the sufferings and the triumph of the "servant of God," in which all the prophetic force of the genius of Israel seemed concentrated.

" For he shall grow up before him as a tender plant and as a root out of a dry ground; he hath no form nor comeliness. He is despised and rejected of men; and we hid as it were our faces from him; he was despised, and we esteemed him not. Surely he hath borne our grief, and carried our sorrows; yet we did esteem him stricken, smitten of God, and afflicted. But he was wounded for our transgressions, he was bruised for our iniquities; the chastisement of our peace was upon him; and with his stripes we are healed. All we like sheep have gone astray; we have turned every one to his own way; and the Lord hath laid on him the iniquity of us all. He was oppressed and he was afflicted, yet he opened not his mouth; he is brought as a lamb to the slaughter, and as a sheep before her shearers is dumb, so he openeth not his mouth. And he made his grave with the wicked. When thou shalt make his soul an offering for sin, he shall see his seed, he shall prolong his days, and the pleasure of the Lord shall prosper in his hand." [Isaiah lii. 13 et seq., and liii. entirely.]

Great alterations were made at the same time in the Thora. New texts, such as Deuteronomy, assuming to represent the true law of Moses, were produced, which inaugurated in reality a spirit very different from that of the old nomads. An ardent fanaticism was the dominant characteristic of this spirit. Infatuated believers provoked incessant persecutions against all who strayed from the worship of Jehovah; a code of blood, prescribing the penalty of death for religious derelictions, was successfully established. Piety almost always brings in its train the singular contradictions--vehemence and gentleness. This zeal, unknown to the coarser simplicity of the age of the Judges, inspired tones of eager prophecy and of tender unction of which the world until now had never heard. A strong tendency towards social questions already made itself felt. Utopias, dreams of a perfect society, were admitted to the code. The Pentateuch, a mélange of patriarchal morality and of ardent devotion, primitive intuitions and pious subtleties, like those with which the souls of Hezekiah, Josiah, and Jeremiah were charged, was thus determined in its present form, and was for ages the absolute rule of the national mind.

This great book once created, the history of the Jewish people developed with an irresistible force The great empires which succeeded each other in Western Asia, in destroying the hope of a terrestrial kingdom, threw them into religious dreams, which they cherished with a kind of sombre passion. Caring little for the national dynasty or for political independence, they accepted all governments which permitted them to practise freely their worship and to follow their usages. Israel will no longer have other guidance than that of its religious enthusiasts, other enemies than those of the Divine unity, other country than its Law.

And this Law, it must be remarked, was entirely social and moral. It was the work of men penetrated with a high ideal of the present life, who believed they had found the best means of realising it. The general conviction was that the Thora, closely followed, could not fail to give perfect felicity. This Thora has nothing in common with the Greek or Roman "Laws," which are cognisant of little else than abstract right, and entered little into the questions of private happiness and morality. We feel beforehand that the results which will proceed from the Jewish Law will be of a social, and not of a political order, that the work at which this people labours is a kingdom of God, not a civil republic; a universal institution, not a nationality or a country.

Despite numerous failures, Israel admirably sustained this vocation. A series of pious men, Ezra, Nehemiah, Onias, the Maccabees, eaten up with zeal for the Law, succeeded each other in the defence of the ancient institutions. The idea that Israel was a holy people, a tribe chosen by God and bound to Him by a covenant, took more and more a firm root. A great expectation filled their souls. The whole of the Indo-European antiquity had placed paradise in the beginning; its poets, who had wept a golden age, had passed away. Israel placed the age of gold in the future. The perennial poesy of religious souls, the Psalms, with their divine and melancholy harmony, blossomed from this exalted piety. Israel became actually and par excellence the people of God, while around it the Pagan religions were more and more reduced; in Persia and Babylonia to an official charlatanism, in Egypt and Syria to a gross idolatry, and in the Greek and Roman world to parade. That which the Christian martyrs did in the first centuries of our era; that which the victims of persecuting orthodoxy have done, even in the bosom of Christianity, up to our time, the Jews did during the two centuries which preceded the Christian era. They were a living protest against superstition and religious materialism. An extraordinary activity of ideas, terminating in the most opposite results, made of them, at this epoch, a people the most striking and original in the world. Their dispersion along the whole Mediterranean littoral, and the use of the Greek language, which they adopted when out of Palestine, prepared the way for a propagandism of which ancient societies, broken up into small nationalities, had not yet presented an example.

Up to the time of the Maccabees, Judaism, in spite of its persistence in announcing that it would one day be the religion of the human race, had had the characteristic of all the other worships of antiquity--it was a worship of the family and the tribe. The Israelite thought, indeed, that his worship was the best, and spoke with contempt of strange gods. Nevertheless, he believed also that the religion of the true God had only been made for himself. One embraced the religion of Jehovah when one entered the Jewish family; not otherwise. No Israelite dreamed of converting the stranger to a worship which was the patrimony of the sons of Abraham. The development of the pietistic spirit, beginning with Ezra and Nehemiah, led to a much firmer and more logical conception. Judaism became, in a more absolute manner, the true religion; the right of entering it was given to him who wished it; soon it became a work of piety to bring into it the greatest number possible. True, the generous sentiment which elevated John the Baptist, Jesus, and St. Paul above the petty ideas of race did not yet exist; for, by a strange contradiction, these converts (proselytes) were little respected, and were even treated with disdain. But the idea of an exclusive religion, the idea that there was something in the world superior to country, to blood, to laws, the idea which was to make apostles and martyrs, was founded. A profound pity for the Pagans, however brilliant might be their worldly fortune, was henceforward the sentiment of every Jew. By a series of legends, destined to furnish established models (Daniel and his companions, the mother of the Maccabees and her seven sons, the romance of the racecourse of Alexandria), the guides of the people sought above all to inculcate this idea--that virtue consists in a fanatical attachment to fixed religious institutions.

The persecutions of Antiochus Epiphanes made of this idea a passion, almost a frenzy. It was something very analogous to what happened under Nero two hundred and thirty years later. Rage and despair threw believers into the world of visions and of dreams. The first apocalypse, "The Book of Daniel," appeared. It was like a revival of prophecy, though under a very different form from the ancient one, and with a much larger conception of the destinies of the world. The Book of Daniel gave, in a manner, to the Messianic hopes their last expression. The Messiah was no longer a king, after the manner of David and Solomon, a theocratic and Mosaic Cyrus; he was a "Son of man" appearing in the clouds, a supernatural being, invested with human form, charged to rule the world, and to preside over the golden age. Perhaps the Sosiosch of Persia, the great prophet who was to come, charged with preparing the reign of Ormuzd, furnished some features for this new ideal. The unknown author of the Book of Daniel had, in any case, a decisive influence on the religious event which was going to transform the world. He devised the mise-en-scène, and the technical terms of the new Messianism; and it might be applied to him what Jesus said of John the Baptist,--"Before him, the prophets; after him, the kingdom of God." A few years later the same ideas were reproduced under the name of the patriarch Enoch. Essenism, which seems to have been in direct relationship with the apocalyptic school, was created about the same time, and offered a first rough sketch of the grand discipline which was soon to constitute the education of humanity.

It must not, however, be supposed that this movement, so profoundly religious and soul-stirring, had particular dogmas to give it impulse, as was the case in all the conflicts which have broken out in the bosom of Christianity. The Jew of this time had as little of the theologian about him as may be. He did not speculate upon the essence of the Divinity; the beliefs about angels, about the end of man, about the Divine hypostasis, of which the first germs might already be perceived, were quite optional--they were meditations, which each one cherished according to the turn of his mind, but of which a great number of men had never heard. Those who did not share in these particular imaginings were even the most orthodox, and who adhered to the simplicity of the Mosaic law. No dogmatic power, analogous to that which orthodox Christianity has given to the Church, then existed. It was not until the beginning of the third century, when Christianity had fallen into the hands of reasoning races, crazy about dialectics and metaphysics, that that fever for definitions commenced which made the history of the Church the history of a great controversy. There were disputes also among the Jews; some ardent schools brought opposite solutions to almost all the questions which were agitated; but in these contests, the principal details of which are preserved in the Talmud, there is not a single word of speculative theology. Observe and maintain the Law, because the Law was just, and because, in being well observed, it gave happiness; this was the whole of Judaism. No credo, no theoretical symbol. A disciple of the boldest Arabic philosophy, Moses Maimonides, succeeded in becoming the oracle of the synagogue, because he was a well-informed canonist.

The reigns of the last Asmoneans, and that of Herod, saw the excitement grow still stronger. They were filled with an uninterrupted series of religious movements. In proportion as that power became secularised, and passed into the hands of unbelievers, the Jewish people lived less and less for the earth, and allowed themselves to become more and more absorbed by the strange force which was operating in their midst. The world, distracted by other spectacles, knew nothing of what was passing in this forgotten corner of the East. The minds in touch with their age were, however, better informed. The tender and prescient Virgil seems to respond, as by a secret echo, to the second Isaiah; the birth of a child throws him into dreams of a universal palingenesis. These dreams were general, and formed a species of literature which was indicated by the name Sibylline. The quite recent formation of the empire exalted the imagination; the great era of peace on which it entered, and that impression of melancholy sensibility which souls experience after long periods of revolution, gave rise everywhere to boundless hopes.

In Judæa expectation was at its zenith. Holy persons, such as old Simeon, who, legend tells us, held Jesus in his arms; Anna, daughter of Phanuel, regarded as a prophetess, passed their life about the temple, fasting and praying, that it might please God not to withdraw them from the world until they should see the fulfilment of the hopes of Israel. They felt a powerful presentiment of the approach of something unknown.

This confused mixture of clear views and of dreams, this alternation of deceptions and of hopes, these ceaseless aspirations, which were driven back by an odious reality, found at last their expression in the incomparable man, to whom the universal conscience has most justly decreed the title of Son of God, because he has given to religion a direction which no other can or probably ever will be able to emulate.

CHAPTER II

INFANCY AND YOUTH OF JESUS--HIS FIRST IMPRESSIONS

Jesus was born at Nazareth, a small town of Galilee, which until his time had no celebrity. During the whole of his life he was designated by the name of "the Nazarene," and it is only by a puzzling enough evasion that, in the legends concerning him, it can be shown that he was born at Bethlehem. We shall see later on the motive for this supposition, and how it was the necessary consequence of the Messianic character attributed to Jesus. The precise date of his birth is not known. It took place during the reign of Augustus, about 750 of the Roman year, that is to say, some years before the first of that era which all civilised nations date from--the day on which it is believed he was born.

The name of Jesus, which was given him, is an alteration from Joshua. It was a very common name; but people naturally sought later on to discover some mystery in it, as well as an allusion to his character of Saviour. Perhaps Jesus himself, like all mystics, exalted himself in this respect. It is thus that more than one great vocation in history has been caused by a name given to a child without premeditation. Ardent natures never can bring themselves to admit chance in anything that concerns them. God has ordained everything for them, and they see a sign of the supreme will in the most insignificant circumstances.

The population of Galilee, as the name indicates, was very mixed. This province reckoned amongst its inhabitants, in the time of Jesus, many who were not Jews (Phoenicians, Syrians, Arabs, and even Greeks). The conversions to Judaism were not rare in mixed countries like this. It is therefore impossible to raise any question of race here, or to try to discover what blood flowed in the veins of him who has most of any contributed to efface the distinctions of blood in humanity.

He sprang from the ranks of the people. His father Joseph and his mother Mary were of humble position, artisans living by their work, in that condition which is so common in the East, and which is neither ease nor poverty. The extreme simplicity of life in such countries, by dispensing with the need of modern comforts, renders the privileges of the wealthy almost useless, and makes every one voluntarily poor. On the other hand, the total absence of taste for art and for that which tends to the elegance of material life, gives a naked aspect to the house of the man who otherwise wants for nothing. If we take into account the sordid and repulsive features which Islamism has carried into the Holy Land, the town of Nazareth, in the time of Jesus, did not perhaps much differ from what it is to-day. The streets where he played as a child we can see in the stony paths or in the little cross-ways which separate the dwellings. The house of Joseph no doubt closely resembled those poor shops, lighted by the door, which serve at once as workshop, kitchen, and bedroom, the furniture consisting of a mat, some cushions on the ground, one or two earthenware pots, and a painted chest.

The family, whether it proceeded from one or several marriages, was rather numerous. Jesus had brothers and sisters, of whom he seems to have been the eldest. All have remained obscure, for it appears that the four personages who are given as his brothers--one of whom at least, James, had acquired great importance in the earliest years. of the development of Christianity--were his cousins-german. Mary, in fact, had a sister also named Mary, who married a certain Alpheus or Cleophas (these two names appear to designate the same person), and was the mother of several sons, who played a considerable part among the first disciples of Jesus. These cousins-german, who adhered to the young Master, while his own brothers opposed him, took the title of "brothers of the Lord." The real brothers of Jesus, as well as their mother, had no notoriety until after his death. Even then they do not appear to have equalled in importance their cousins, whose conversion had been more spontaneous, and whose characters seem to have had more originality. Their names were unknown to the extent that, when the evangelist put in the mouth of the men of Nazareth the enumeration of the brothers according to natural relationship, the names of the sons of Cleophas first presented themselves to him.

His sisters were married at Nazareth, and he spent there the first years of his youth. Nazareth was a small town situated in a hollow, opening broadly at the summit of the group of mountains which close the plain of Esdraelon on the north. The population is now from three to four thousand, and it can never have varied much. The cold is keen there in winter, and the climate very healthy. Nazareth, like all the small Jewish towns at this period, was a heap of huts built without plan, and would exhibit that withered and poor aspect which characterise villages in Semitic countries. The houses, as it would seem, did not differ much from those cubes of stone, without exterior or interior elegance, which cover to-day the richest parts of the Lebanon, and which, surrounded with vines and fig-trees, are far from being disagreeable. The environs, moreover, are charming; and no place in the world was so well adapted for dreams of absolute happiness. Even to-day Nazareth is a delightful abode, the only place, perhaps, in Palestine in which the soul feels itself relieved from the burden which oppresses it in the midst of this unequalled desolation. The people are amiable and cheerful; the gardens fresh and green. Anthony the Martyr, at the end of the sixth century, gives an enchanting picture of the fertility of the environs, which he compares with paradise. Some valleys on the western side fully bear out his description. The fountain, where formerly the life and gaiety of the little town were concentrated, is destroyed; its broken channels contain now only a muddy stream. But the beauty of the women who meet there in the evening,--that beauty which was already remarked in the sixth century, and which was looked upon as a gift of the Virgin Mary,--is still most strikingly preserved. It is the Syrian type in all its grace, so full of languor. There is no doubt that Mary was there almost every day, and took her place with her jar on her shoulder in the file of her obscure companions. Anthony the Martyr remarks that the Jewish women, usually disdainful to Christians, were here very affable. At the present day religious animosity is less pronounced at Nazareth than elsewhere.

The prospect from the town is limited; but if we ascend a little and reach the plateau, swept by a perpetual breeze, which overlooks the highest houses, the view is splendid. On the west are displayed the fine outlines of Carmel, terminated by an abrupt spur which seems to plunge into the sea. Next are spread out the double summit which dominates Megiddo; the mountains of the country of Shechem, with their holy places of patriarchal age; the hills of Gilboa, the small picturesque group to which are attached the graceful or terrible recollections of Shunem and of Endor; and Tabor, with its rounded form, which antiquity compared to a bosom. Through a crevice between the mountains of Shunem and Tabor are seen the valley of the Jordan and the high plains of Peræa, which on the east side form a continuous line. On the north, the mountains of Safed, in inclining towards the sea, conceal St.-Jean-d'Acre, but reveal the outline of the Gulf of Khaifa. Such was the country of Jesus. This enchanted circle, this cradle of the kingdom of God, was the world of Jesus for years. Even in his later life he did not depart much from the familiar scenes of his childhood. For, yonder northwards, a glimpse is caught, almost on the flank of Hermon, of Cæsarea-Philippi, the furthest point he had reached in the Gentile world; and southwards, the more sombre aspect of these Samaritan hills foreshadows the dreariness of Judea beyond, parched as by a scorching wind of desolation and death.

If the world, should it remain Christian, though it should attain to a better idea of the esteem in which the origins of its religion should be held, ever wishes to replace by authentic holy places the mean and apocryphal sanctuaries to which the piety of dark ages attached itself, it is upon this ground of Nazareth that it will rebuild its temple. There, at the spot where Christianity was born, and at the centre of the activity of its Founder, the great church ought to be raised in which all Christians might worship. There, also, on the spot where sleep Joseph the carpenter and thousands of forgotten Nazarenes, who never passed beyond the outskirts of their valley, would be a better station than any in the world for the philosopher to contemplate the course of human events, to console himself for the disappointments which those inflict upon our most cherished instincts, and to reassure himself as to the divine end which the world pursues through endless falterings, and in spite of the universal vanity.

CHAPTER III

EDUCATION OF JESUS

Nature here, at once smiling and grand, was the whole education of Jesus. He learnt to read and to write, no doubt, according to the Eastern method, which consisted in putting into the hands of the child a book, which he repeated rhythmically with his little comrades, until he knew it by heart. It is doubtful, however, whether he understood the Hebrew writings in their original tongue. His biographers make him quote them according to the translations in the Aramean language; and his methods of exegesis, as far as we can make them out from his disciples, much resembled those which were then common, and which form the spirit of the Targummim and the Midraschim.

The schoolmaster in the small Jewish towns was the hazzan, or reader in the synagogues. Jesus frequented little the higher schools of the scribes or sopherim (Nazareth had perhaps none of them), and he had not any of those titles which confer, in the eyes of the vulgar, the privileges of knowledge. It would, nevertheless, be a great error to imagine that Jesus was what we call an ignoramus. Scholastic education among us draws a great distinction, in respect of personal worth, between those who have received and those who have been deprived of it. It was different in the East, and in the good old days. The rude state in which among us the person remains who has not passed through the schools--in consequence of our isolated and entirely individual life--was unknown in those societies where moral culture, and, above all, the general spirit of the age, was transmitted by the constant intercourse between men of all kinds. The Arab, who has never had a teacher, is, notwithstanding that, a decidedly superior man; for the tent is a sort of academy, always open, where, from meeting with well-educated people, very considerable intellectual and even literary activity is produced. Refinement of manners and acuteness of intellect have, in the East, nothing in common with what we call education. The men of the schools, on the contrary, are those who pass for pedantic and badly-trained people. In this social state, ignorance, which among us at once relegates a man to an inferior grade, is the condition of great things and of great originality.

It is not at all likely that Jesus knew Greek. This language had spread only to a small extent in Judæa beyond the classes who participated in the government, and the towns which were inhabited by Pagans, like Cæsarea. The mother tongue of Jesus was the Syrian dialect mixed with Hebrew, which was spoken in Palestine at that time. There is even greater reason to conclude that he knew nothing of Greek culture. This culture was indeed proscribed by the doctors of Palestine, who included in the same malediction "the man who breeds swine, and the person who teaches his son Greek science." At all events, it had not penetrated to little towns such as Nazareth. Notwithstanding the anathema of the doctors, some Jews, it is true, had already embraced the Hellenic culture. Without speaking of the Jewish school of Egypt, in which the attempts to amalgamate Hellenism and Judaism had been in operation nearly two hundred years, a Jew, Nicholas of Damascus, had become, even at this time, one of the most distinguished men, one of the best informed, and one of the most respected of his age. Josephus was destined soon to furnish another example of a Jew completely Grecianised. But Nicholas was only a Jew in blood. Josephus declares that he himself was an exception among his contemporaries; and the whole schismatic school of Egypt was detached to such a degree from Jerusalem that we do not find the least allusion to it either in the Talmud or in Jewish tradition. At Jerusalem itself Greek was very little studied: indeed, Greek studies were considered to be dangerous, and even servile; at the best they were held to be only an effeminate accomplishment. The study of the Law stood alone as "liberal," and worthy of a thoughtful man. When he was asked as to the time when it would be right to teach children "Greek wisdom," a learned Rabbi replied: "At the time which is neither day nor night; for it is written of the Law, Thou shalt study it day and night."

It seems clear, therefore, that neither directly nor indirectly did any element of "profane" culture reach Jesus. He knew nothing beyond Judaism; his mind preserved that free innocence which is invariably weakened by an extended and varied culture. In the very bosom of this Judaism he remained a stranger to many efforts somewhat parallel to his own. On the one hand, the asceticism of the Essenes or Therapeutæ did not seem to have had any direct influence upon him; on the other, the fine efforts of religious philosophy made by the Jewish school of Alexandria, of which Philo, his contemporary, was the ingenious interpreter, were unknown to him. The frequent resemblances which may be discovered between himself and Philo, those excellent maxims concerning the love of God, of charity, and rest in God, which sound like an echo between the Gospel and the writings of the illustrious Alexandrian thinker, arise from the common tendencies which the demands of the age inspired in all lofty minds.

Happily for him, he was also ignorant of the strange scholasticism which was taught at Jerusalem, and which soon was to form the Talmud. If some Pharisees had already brought it into Galilee, Jesus did not associate with them, and when later he met this silly casuistry face to face, it only inspired him with disgust. We may believe, however, that the principles of Hillel were not unknown to him. This Rabbi, fifty years before him, had uttered certain aphorisms which were almost analogous to his own. By his poverty so meekly borne, by the sweetness of his character, by his antagonism to priests and hypocrites, Hillel was the true master of Jesus, if it may be allowed that one should speak of a master in connection with such a lofty genius as his.

The perusal of the books of the Old Testament made a deep impression on Jesus. The canon of the holy books was composed of two principal parts--the Law, that is to say, the Pentateuch, and the Prophets, such as we possess them now. An extensive and allegorical method of interpretation was applied to all these books; and the attempt was made to draw from them what was a response to the aspirations of the age. The Law, which did not represent the ancient laws of the country, but Utopias-- the factitious laws, and the pious frauds of the pietistic kings--had become, since the nation had ceased to govern itself, an inexhaustible theme of subtle interpretations. As to the Prophets and the Psalms, the popular persuasion was that almost all the somewhat mysterious details that were in these books had reference to the Messiah, and it was sought to find there the type of him who should realise the hopes of the nation. Jesus participated in the liking which every one had for these allegorical interpretations. But the true poetry of the Bible which escaped the doctors of Jerusalem disclosed itself most fully to the fine genius of Jesus. The Law does not seem to have had much charm for him; he believed he could accomplish better things. But the religious poetry of the Psalms discovered a wonderful agreement with his own lyrical soul; and they remained, during his whole life, his nourishment and support. The prophets, especially Isaiah and the writer who continued his record of the times of the captivity, with their brilliant dreams of the future, their impetuous eloquence, and their invectives mingled with enchanting pictures, were his true masters. He, doubtless, also read many apocryphal works--somewhat modern writings, whose authors, in order to give their productions an authority which would not be granted except to very ancient scriptures, had invested themselves with the names of prophets and patriarchs. One of these books above all others moved him; that was the book of Daniel. This work, composed by an enthusiastic Jew of the time of Antiochus Epiphanes, and headed by the name of an ancient sage, was the resumé of the spirit of these later days. Its author, a true creator of the philosophy of history, was the first who had been bold enough to see in the onward march of the world and the succession of empires only a series of facts subordinated to the destinies of the Jewish people. Jesus was at an early age penetrated by these high hopes. Perhaps, moreover, he had read the books of Enoch, then regarded with equal reverence as the holy books, and the other writings of the same class, which kept up so much excitement in the popular imagination. The advent of the Messiah, with its glories and terrors, the nations falling to pieces one after another, the cataclysm of heaven and earth, were the familiar food of his imagination; and, as these revolutions were believed to be so close at hand that numbers of people sought to calculate their exact dates, the supernatural state into which men are led by such visions appeared to Jesus from the first quite simple and perfectly natural.

That he had no acquaintance with the general condition of the world is a fact which is seen in each feature of his best authenticated discourses. The earth to him appeared as still divided into kingdoms making war upon each other; he seemed to ignore the "Roman peace," and the new state of society which its age inaugurated. He had no exact idea of the Roman power; the name of "Cæsar" was all that had reached him. He saw being built, in Galilee or its neighbourhood, Tiberias, Julias, Diocæsarea, Cæsarea--splendid works of the Herods, who sought by these magnificent structures to prove their admiration for Roman civilisation, and their devotion to the members of the family of Augustus; and the names of these places, although strangely altered, now serve to designate, as by a caprice of fate, miserable hamlets of Bedouins. Jesus probably also saw Sebaste, a work of Herod the Great, a showy city, whose ruins would make one believe that it had been transported there ready made, like some machine which had only to be set up in its place. This ostentatious piece of architecture was shipped to Judæa in portions; the hundreds of columns, all of the same diameter, the ornament of some insipid "Rue de Rivoli"--these were what he called "the kingdoms of the world and all the glory of them." But this luxury of power, this administrative and official art, displeased him. What he really loved were his Galilean villages, a confused mixture of huts, of nests and holes cut in the rocks, of wells, of tombs, of fig-trees and olives. He always clung closely to nature. The courts of kings constantly presented to him the idea of places where men wear fine clothes. The charming impossibilities with which his parables abound, when he brings kings and mighty ones on the stage, prove that he never had any conception of aristocratic society except as a young villager who sees the world through the prism of his own simplicity.

Jesus was still less acquainted with the new idea, created by Grecian science, which is the basis of all philosophy and which modern science has largely confirmed, viz., the exclusion of the supernatural forces to which the simple faith of the ancient times attributed the government of the universe. Almost a century before him, Lucretius had expressed, in an admirable manner, the unchangeableness of the general system of nature. The negation of miracle -- the idea that everything in the world happens by laws in which the personal intervention of superior beings has no share--was universally admitted in the great schools of all the countries which had accepted Grecian science. Perhaps even Babylon and Persia were not strangers to it. Jesus knew nothing of this progress. Although born at a time when the principle of positive science was already proclaimed, he lived entirely in the supernatural. Never, perhaps, had the Jews been more possessed with the thirst for the marvellous. Philo, who lived in a great intellectual centre, and who had received a very complete education, possessed only a chimerical and inferior knowledge of science.

Jesus on this point differed in no respect from his companions. He believed in the devil, whom he regarded as a kind of evil genius, and he imagined, like all the world, that nervous maladies were produced by demons who possessed the patient and agitated him. The marvellous was not the exceptional to him; it was his normal state. The idea of the supernatural, with its impossibilities, does not arise except with the birth of the experimental science of nature. The man who is a stranger to all idea of physical law, and who believes that by prayer he can alter the path of the clouds, can arrest disease and even death, finds nothing extraordinary in miracle, inasmuch as the whole course of things is for him the result of the freewill of the Divinity. This intellectual condition was always that of Jesus. But in his great soul such a belief produced effects altogether opposed to those wrought on the vulgar. Among the latter, faith in the special action of God led to a foolish credulity, and deceptions on the part of charlatans. With him it led to a profound idea of the familiar relations of man with God, and to an exaggerated belief in the power of man--beautiful errors which were the secret of his influence; for, if they became one day the means of putting him in a position of error in the eyes of the natural philosopher and the chemist, they gave him, over his own age, a power which no individual has ever possessed before or since.

At an early age his extraordinary character revealed itself. Legend delights to show him even in his infancy in revolt against parental authority, and deviating from the common lines to follow his vocation. It is at least certain that for the relations of kinship he cared little. His family do not seem to have loved him, and more than once he appears to have been severe towards them. Jesus, like all men exclusively preoccupied by an idea, came to think little of the ties of blood. It is the bond of thought alone which natures like his recognise. "Behold my mother and my brethren," said he, extending his hand towards his disciples; "he that doeth the will of my Father, the same is my brother and sister." The simple people did not understand this view of things, and one day a woman who was passing near him cried out, "Blessed is the womb that bare thee, and the paps that thou hast sucked!" But he replied, "Yea, rather, blessed are they that hear the word of God and keep it!" Soon, in his daring revolt against nature, he went still further; we shall soon see him trample under foot everything that is human--blood, love, country--preserving soul and mind simply for the idea which presented itself to him in the guise of absolute goodness and truth.

CHAPTER IV

THE ORDER OF THOUGHT FROM WHOSE CENTRE JESUS WAS DEVELOPED

As the cooled earth no longer permits us to comprehend the phenomena of primitive creation, because the fire which once penetrated it is extinct, so deliberate explanations contain always something insufficient, when the question is one of applying our timid methods of analysis to the revolutions of the creative epochs which have decided the fate of humanity. Jesus lived at one of those epochs when the game of public life is freely played, when the stake of human activity is increased a hundredfold. Every great part, then, entails death; for such movements suppose liberty and an absence of preventive measures, which could not exist without a terrible alternative. In the present day, man risks little and gains little. In the heroic periods of human activity, man risked all and gained all. The good and the wicked, or at least those who believe themselves and are believed to be such, form opposing armies. The apotheosis is attained by the scaffold; characters have distinctive features, which engrave them as eternal types in the memory of men. Except in the French Revolution, no historical centre was as appropriate as that in which Jesus was formed, for developing those hidden forces which humanity holds as in reserve, and which are not seen except in days of excitement and peril.

If the government of the world were a speculative problem, and the greatest philosopher was the man best fitted to tell his fellow-men what they ought to believe, it would be from calmness and reflection that those great moral and dogmatic truths which we call religions would proceed. But it is nothing of the kind. If we except Sakya-Mouni, the great religious founders have not been metaphysicians. Buddhism itself, which is based on pure thought, has conquered one-half of Asia by motives wholly political and moral. As for the Semitic religions, they are as little philosophical as it is possible to be. Moses and Mahomet were not speculators: they were men of action. It was by proposing action to their fellow-countrymen, and to their contemporaries, that they governed humanity. Jesus, in like manner, was not a theologian or a philosopher, having a more or less well-constructed system. To be a disciple of Jesus, it was not necessary to sign any formulary, or to repeat any confession of faith; one thing only was necessary--to attach oneself to him, to love him. He never disputed about God, for he felt Him directly in himself. The rock of metaphysical subtleties, against which Christianity has dashed since the third century, was in no wise erected by the founder. Jesus had neither dogma nor system; he had a fixed personal resolution, which, exceeding in intensity every other created will, directs to this hour the destinies of humanity.

The Jewish people have had the advantage, from the Babylonian captivity up to the Middle Ages, of being always in a state of extreme tension. This is why the interpreters of the spirit of the nation, during this long period, seem to have written under the action of a violent fever, which placed them constantly either above or under reason, rarely in its middle pathway. Never did man seize the problem of the future and of his own destiny with a more desperate courage, or was more determined to go to extremes. Not separating the fate of humanity from that of their little race, the Jewish thinkers were the first who sought to discover a general theory of the progress of our species. Greece, always confined within itself, and only concerned with its petty provincial quarrels, has had admirable historians. Stoicism had enounced the highest maxims upon the duties of man considered as a citizen of the world and as a member of a great brotherhood; but previous to the Roman period it would be a vain attempt to discover in classic literature a general system of the philosophy of history, embracing all humanity. The Jew, on the contrary, thanks to a sort of prophetic sense, has made history enter into religion. Possibly he owes a little of this spirit to Persia, which, from an ancient date, conceived the history of the world as a series of evolutions, over which a prophet presided.

Each prophet had his reign of a thousand years, and out of those successive ages, analogous to the millions of ages devolved to each Buddha of India, was composed the train of events which prepared the reign of Ormuzd. At the end of the time when the circle of the revolutions shall be completed, the perfect Paradise will appear. Men will then live happily: the earth will be like a great plain; there will be only one language, one law, and one government for all men. But this advent is to be preceded by terrible calamities. Dahak (the Satan of Persia) will break his chains and fall upon the world. Two prophets will then come to comfort mankind, and to prepare for the great advent.

These ideas ran through the world, and penetrated even to Rome, where they inspired a cycle of prophetic poems, whose fundamental ideas were the division of the history of humanity into periods, the succession of the gods representing these epochs, a complete renewal of the world, and the final coming of a golden age. The book of Daniel, certain parts of the book of Enoch, and the Sibylline books are the Jewish expression of the same theory. It was certainly not the case that these thoughts were universal. They were, on the contrary, embraced at first only by some people of vivid imaginations and readily impressed by strange doctrines. The dry and narrow author of the book of Esther never thought of the rest of the world except to despise it and to wish it evil. The sated and undeceived Epicurean who writes Ecclesiastes thinks so little of the future that he considers it even useless to work for his children. In the eyes of this egotistical celibate, the highest advice of wisdom is to find one's chief good in mis-spent money. But great achievements made by any people are generally the work of the minority. In spite of all their defects, hard, egotistical, scoffing, cruel, narrow, subtle, sophistical, the Jews are nevertheless the authors of the finest movement of disinterested enthusiasm of which history speaks. Opposition always makes the glory of a country. In one sense, the greatest men of a nation are often those whom it puts to death. Socrates honoured the Athenians, who would not suffer him to live. Spinoza was the greatest modern Jew, and the synagogue expelled him with ignominy. Jesus was the glory of the people of Israel, and they crucified him.

A gigantic dream haunted for centuries the Jewish people, constantly renewing its youth in its decrepitude. A stranger to the theory of individual recompenses which Greece had spread under the name of immortality of the soul, Judæa concentrated on her national future all her power of love and longing. She believed herself to possess divine promises of a boundless future; and as the bitter reality which, from the ninth century before our era, gave the domination of the world more and more to physical force brutally crushed these aspirations, she took refuge in the union of the most impossible ideas, and attempted the strangest gyrations. Before the captivity, when all the earthly future of the nation disappeared in consequence of the separation of the northern tribes, they had dreamt of the restoration of the house of David, the reconciliation of the two divisions of the people, and the triumph of theocracy and the worship of Jehovah over idolatrous systems. At the time of the captivity, a poet full of harmony foresaw the splendour of a future Jerusalem, to which the nations and distant isles should be tributaries, under colours so charming that it teemed a glance from the eyes of Jesus had leached him from a distance of six centuries.

The victories of Cyrus at one time appeared to realise all that had been hoped for. The grave disciples of the Avesta and the adorers of Jehovah believed themselves brothers. Persia had begun by banishing the multiple dévas and by transforming them into demons (divs), to draw from the old Arian imagination, which was essentially naturalistic, a species of monotheism. The prophetic tone of many of the teachings of Iran resemble greatly certain compositions of Hosea and Isaiah. Israel reposed under the Achemenidæ, and under Xerxes (Ahasuerus) made itself feared by the Iranians themselves. But the triumphant and often cruel entrance of Greek and Roman civilisation into Asia, threw it back upon its dreams. More than ever it invoked the Messiah as the judge and avenger of the nations. In fact, there was a complete renovation--a revolution which should take hold of the world by its roots, and shake it from top to bottom--in order to satisfy the fearful longing for vengeance excited in Israel by the consciousness of its superiority and the sight of its humiliations.

If Israel had possessed the doctrine called spiritualism, which divides man into two parts--the body and the soul--and finds it quite natural that while the body decays the soul survives, this paroxysm of rage and of energetic protestation would have had no raison d'être. But such a doctrine, proceeding from the Grecian philosophy, was not in the traditions of the Jewish mind. The ancient Hebrew writings contain no trace of future rewards or punishments. Whilst the idea of the solidarity of the tribe existed, it was natural that a strict retribution according to individual merits should not be thought of. So much the worse for the pious man who happened to live in a time of impiety; he suffered like the rest the public misfortunes consequent on the general irreligion. This doctrine, bequeathed by the sages of the patriarchal era, produced day by day unsustainable contradictions. Already at the time of Job it was much shaken; the old men of Teman who professed it were considered behind the age, and the young Elihu, who intervened in order to combat them, dared to utter as his first thesis this essentially revolutionary sentiment, "Great men are not always wise; neither do the aged understand judgment." With the complications which had taken place in the world since the time of Alexander, the old Temanite and Mosaic principle became still more intolerable. Never had Israel been more faithful to the Law, and yet it was subjected to the atrocious persecution of Antiochus. Only a declaimer, accustomed to repeat old phrases denuded of sense, would dare to assert that these evils proceeded from the unfaithfulness of the people. What! these victims who died for their faith, these heroic Maccabees, this mother with her seven sons, will Jehovah forget them eternally? Will he abandon them to the corruption of the grave? Worldly and incredulous Sadduceeism might possibly not recoil before such a consequence, and a consummate sage, like Antigonus of Soco, might indeed maintain that we must not practise virtue like a slave in expectation of a recompense--that we must be virtuous without hope. But the mass of the nation could not be contented with that. Some, attaching themselves to the principle of philosophical immortality, imagined the righteous living in the memory of God, glorious for ever in the remembrance of men, and judging the wicked who had persecuted them. "They live in the sight of God; . . . they are known of God." That was their reward. Others, especially the Pharisees, had recourse to the doctrine of the resurrection. The righteous will live again in order to participate in the Messianic reign. They will live again in the flesh, and for a world of which they will be the kings and the judges; they will be present at the triumph of their ideas and at the humiliation of their enemies.

We find among the ancient people of Israel only very indecisive traces of this fundamental dogma. The Sadducee, who did not believe it, was in reality faithful to the old Jewish doctrine; it was the Pharisee, the believer in the resurrection, who was the innovator. But in religion it is always the zealous sect which innovates, which progresses, and which has influence. Besides this, the resurrection, an idea totally different from that of the immortality of the soul, proceeded very naturally from the anterior doctrines and from the position of the people. Perhaps Persia also furnished some of its elements. In any case, combining with the belief in the Messiah, and with the doctrine of a speedy renewal of all things, the dogma of the resurrection formed those apocalyptic theories which, without being articles of faith (the orthodox Sanhedrim of Jerusalem does not seem to have adopted them), pervaded all imaginations, and produced an extreme fermentation from one end of the Jewish world to the other. The total absence of dogmatic rigour caused very contradictory notions to be admitted at one time, even upon so primary a point. Sometimes the righteous were to await the resurrection; sometimes they were to be received at the moment of death into Abraham's bosom; sometimes the resurrection was to be general; sometimes it was to be reserved only for the faithful; sometimes it presupposed a new earth and a new Jerusalem; sometimes it implied a previous annihilation of the universe.

Jesus, from the moment he began to think, entered into the burning atmosphere which had been created in Palestine by the ideas we have just referred to. These ideas were taught in no school; but they were "in the air" around him, and his soul was early penetrated by them. Our hesitations and doubts never reached him. On this summit of the hill of Nazareth, where no man of the present day can sit without an uneasy, although frivolous, feeling as to his own destiny, Jesus sat habitually without a doubt. Free from selfishness, the source of our troubles, he thought of nothing but his work, his race, and humanity at large. Those mountains, that sea, that azure sky, those high plains in the horizon, were for him not the melancholy vision of a soul which interrogates nature upon her fate, but the certain symbol, the transparent shadow of an invisible world and a new heaven.

He never attached much importance to the political events of his time, and he was probably badly informed regarding them. The dynasty of the Herods lived in a world so different from his own that he doubtless only knew it by name. Herod the Great died about the year in which Jesus was born, leaving imperishable memories--monuments which must compel the most malevolent posterity to associate his name with that of Solomon; his woks, nevertheless, was incomplete, and could not be continued. Profanely ambitious, lost in a maze of religious controversies, this astute Idumean had the advantage which coolness and judgment, stripped of morality, give one in the midst of passionate fanatics. But his conception of a secular kingdom of Israel, even if it had not been an anachronism in the state of the world in which it was conceived, would have miscarried, like the similar project which Solomon formed, in consequence of the difficulties arising from the peculiar character of the nation. His three sons were nothing but lieutenants of the Romans, analogous to the rajahs of India under the English Government. Antipater, or Antipas, Tetrarch of Galilee and Peræa, whose subject Jesus was all his life, was an idle and empty prince, a favourite and flatterer of Tiberius, and too often misled by the evil influence of his second wife Herodias. Philip, Tetrarch of Gaulonitis and Batanea, into whose territories Jesus made frequent journeys, was a much better sovereign. As to Archelaus, Ethnarch of Jerusalem, he could not have known him. Jesus was about ten years of age when this man, weak and characterless, although sometimes violent, was deposed by Augustus. The last trace of self-government was, in this way, lost to Jerusalem. United to Samaria and Idumea, Judæa formed a kind of dependency of the province of Syria, in which the senator Publius Sulpicius Quirinius, a well-known consular personage, was the imperial legate. A series of Roman procurators, subordinate in affairs of importance to the imperial legate of Syria--Coponius, Marcus Ambivius, Annius Rufus, Valerius Gratus, and lastly (in the 26th year of our era) Pontius Pilate--followed each other, and were incessantly occupied in extinguishing the volcano which was rumbling beneath their feet.

Continual seditions, excited by the zealots of Mosaism, were constantly during this period agitating Jerusalem. The death of the seditious was certain; but death, when the matter concerned the integrity of the Law, was sought for with avidity. To overturn the Roman eagles, to destroy the works of art raised by the Herods, in which the Mosaic regulations were not always respected, to rebel against the votive escutcheons raised by the procurators, and whose inscriptions seemed to them tainted by idolatry, were perpetual temptations to fanatics who had reached that degree of exaltation which removes all regard for life. Thus it was that Judas, son of Sariphea, and Matthias, son of Margaloth, two greatly celebrated doctors of the Law, formed against the established order a party of bold aggression, which continued after their execution. The Samaritans were agitated by movements of the same kind. The Law seems never to have counted more impassioned votaries than at this period, when there already lived that man who, by the full authority of his genius and of his great soul, was about to abrogate it. The "zelotes" (kanaïm) or "sicarii," pious assassins, who imposed on themselves the task of killing whoever in their estimation broke the Law, began to appear. Representatives of a totally different spirit, the Thaumaturges, considered as in some measure divine, found credence in consequence of the imperious necessity which the age expressed for the supernatural and the divine.

A movement which had much more influence on Jesus was that of Judas, the Gaulonite or Galilean. Of all the constraints to which countries newly conquered by Rome were subjected, the census was the most unpopular. This measure, which always irritates nations little accustomed to the responsibilities of great central administrations, was specially odious to the Jews. Already, under David, we see how a numbering of the people provoked violent recriminations, and the threatenings of the prophets. The census, in fact, was the basis of taxation. Now, taxation, in the estimation of a pure theocracy, was almost an impiety. God being the sole Master whom man ought to recognise, to pay tithe to a secular sovereign was, in a manner, to put him in the place of God. Completely ignorant of the idea of the State, the Jewish theocracy only acted up to its logical induction -- the negation of civil society and of all government. The money in the public treasury was regarded as stolen. The census ordered by Quirinius (in the sixth year of the Christian era) powerfully awakened these ideas, and caused a tremendous ferment. A disturbance broke out in the northern provinces. One Judas, of the town of Gamala, on the eastern shore of the lake of Tiberias, and a Pharisee named Sadoc, by denying the lawfulness of the impost, created a numerous party, which soon broke out into open revolt. The fundamental maxims of this school were that liberty was better than life, and that no man ought to be called "master," this title belonging to God alone. Judas had, doubtless, many other principles, which Josephus, always careful not to compromise his co-religionists, designedly suppresses; for it is impossible to understand how, for so simple an idea, the Jewish historian should give him a place among the philosophers of his nation, and should regard him as the founder of a fourth school, equal to those of the Pharisees, the Sadducees, and the Essenes. Judas was evidently the chief of a Galilean sect, which was imbued with Messianic ideas, and became a political movement. The procurator, Coponius, crushed the sedition of the Gaulonite; but the party survived and preserved its chiefs. Under the leadership of Menahem, son of its founder, and of one Eleazar, his kinsman, we find it again very active in the last struggles of the Jews with the Romans. Jesus, it may be, saw this Judas, who had conceived a Jewish revolution of a kind so different from his own ideal; at all events, he knew the opinions of his school, and it was probably by a reaction against his mistake that he pronounced the axiom upon the "penny" of Cæsar. Wisely standing aloof from all sedition, Jesus profited by the fault of his predecessor, and dreamed of another kingdom and of another deliverance.

Galilee was thus a vast furnace, in which the most diverse elements were heaving to a boiling point. An extraordinary contempt for life, or, to speak more correctly, a kind of longing for death, was the result of these agitations. Experience counts for nothing in great fanatical movements. Algeria, in the first days of the French occupation, saw arise, each springtime, inspired men who declared that they were invulnerable and were sent by God to expel the infidels; the following year their death was forgotten, and their successors found an undiminished credence. Very stern on the one hand, the Roman power was not at all meddlesome, and permitted much liberty. These great brute-force despotisms, terrible in repression, were not so suspicious as powers which have some dogma to uphold. They allowed everything to be done up to the point at which they thought they ought to use vigorous measures. In his wandering career, Jesus does not appear to have been once annoyed by the civil authorities. Such a liberty, and above all the happiness which Galilee enjoyed in being much less restrained by the bonds of Pharisaic pedantry, gave to this province a real advantage over Jerusalem. The revolution, or, in other words, the Messianic expectations, caused a general mental fermentation here. Men believed that they were on the eve of beholding the great renovation; the Scriptures, tortured into a variety of meanings, became food for the most colossal hopes. In each line of the simple writings of the Old Testament they saw the assurance, and, in a certain sense, the programme of the future reign, which should bring peace to the righteous, and seal for ever the work of God.

From all time this division into two parties, opposed to each other in interest and spirit, had been for the Hebrew people a principle which had been fertile in moral growth. Every nation called to high destinies ought to form a complete little world, including within it the opposite poles. Greece presented, a few leagues apart, Sparta and Athens, the two antipodes to a superficial observer, but in reality rival sisters, each necessary to the other. It was the same with Judæa. Less brilliant in one sense than the development of Jerusalem, that of the north was on the whole much more fruitful; the noblest works of the Jewish people have always proceeded thence. A complete absence of the love of nature, almost amounting to something dry, narrow, and even ferocious, has stamped upon all purely Jerusalemitish works a character grand indeed, but sad, arid, and repulsive. With its solemn doctors, its insipid canonists, its hypocritical and atrabilious devotees, Jerusalem could not conquer humanity. The north has given to the world the simple Shulamite, the humble Canaanite, the passionate Magdalene, the good foster-father Joseph, and the Virgin Mary. It is the north alone which has made Christianity; Jerusalem, on the contrary, is the true home of that obstinate Judaism which, founded by the Pharisees and fixed by the Talmud, has traversed the Middle Ages and come down to us.

A beautiful aspect of nature contributed to the formation of this less austere, though less sharply monotheistic spirit, if I may venture so to call it, which impressed all the dreams of Galilee with a charming and idyllic character. The region round about Jerusalem is, perhaps, the gloomiest country in the world. Galilee, on the contrary, was exceedingly verdant, shady, smiling, the true home of the Song of Songs and the Canticles of the well-beloved. During the two months of March and April the country is a carpet of flowers, with an incomparable variety of colouring. The animals are small and extremely gentle,--delicate and lively turtle-doves, blue-birds so light that they rest on a blade of grass without bending it; crested larks which advance nearly under the very feet of the traveller; little river-tortoises with sweet and lively eyes, and also storks with grave and modest mien, which, dismissing all timidity, allow themselves to be approached quite closely, and seem almost to invite the companionship of men. In no country in the world do the mountains spread themselves out with more harmony, or inspire loftier thought. Jesus seems to have specially loved them. The most important acts of his career took place on mountains. It was there he was the most inspired; it was there he held secret communings with the ancient prophets; it was there he showed himself transfigured before the eyes of his disciples.

This lovely country, which at the present day has become (through the woful impoverishing influence which Islamism has wrought on human life) so sad and wretched, but where everything that man cannot destroy breathes still an air of freedom, sweetness, and tenderness, overflowed with happiness and joy at the time of Jesus. The Galileans were reckoned brave, energetic and laborious. If we except Tiberias, built by Antipas in the Roman style, in honour of Tiberius (about the year 15), Galilee had no large towns. The country was nevertheless covered with small towns and large villages well peopled, and cultivated with skill in every direction. From the ruins of its ancient splendour which survive we can trace an agricultural people in no way gifted in art, caring little for luxury, indifferent to the beauties of form, and exclusively idealistic. The country abounded in fresh streams and fruits; the large farms were shaded with vines and fig-trees; the gardens were a mass of apple and walnut trees, and pomegranates. The wine was excellent, if it may be judged from what the Jews still obtain at Safed, and they drank freely of it. This contented and easily satisfied life did not at all resemble the gross materialism of our peasantry, or the coarse happiness of agricultural Normandy, or the heavy mirth of the Flemings. It spiritualised itself in mysterious dreams, in a kind of poetical mysticism, blending heaven and earth. Leave the austere John Baptist in his desert of Judæa, to preach penitence, to inveigh unceasingly, and to live on locusts in the company of jackals! Why should the companions of the bridegroom fast while the bridegroom is with them? Joy will be a part of the kingdom of God. Is she not the daughter of the humble in heart, of the men of goodwill?

The entire history of infant Christianity is in this sense a delightful pastoral. A Messiah at the marriage supper, the courtesan and the good Zaccheus called to his feasts, the founders of the kingdom of heaven like a bridal procession;--this is what Galilee has dared to offer, and what the world has really accepted. Greece has drawn admirable pictures of human life in sculpture and poetry, but always without backgrounds or receding perspectives. Here were wanting the marble, the practised workmen, the exquisite and refined language. But Galilee has created for the popular imagination the most sublime ideal; for behind its idyll the fate of humanity moves, and the light which illumines its picture is the sun of the kingdom of God.

Jesus lived and grew up amidst those elevating surroundings. From his infancy, he went almost every year to the feast at Jerusalem. The pilgrimage was for the provincial Jews a solemnity of sweet associations. Several entire series of psalms were consecrated to celebrate the happiness of thus journeying in family society during several days in springtime across the hills and valleys, all having in prospect the splendours of Jerusalem, the solemnities of the sacred courts, and the joy of brethren dwelling together. The route which Jesus usually followed in these journeys was that which is taken in the present day, through Ginæa and Shechem. From Shechem to Jerusalem travelling is very toilsome. But the neighbourhood of the old sanctuaries of Shiloh and Bethel, near which the pilgrim passes, keeps the mind awake with interest. Ain-el-Haramié, the last halting-place, is a melancholy and yet charming spot; and few impressions equal that which one feels when encamping there for the night. The valley is narrow and sombre, while a dark stream issues from the rocks full of tombs, which form its banks. It is, I believe, "the valley of tears," or of dropping waters, which is sung of as one of the stations on the way in the delightful eighty-fourth Psalm; and it became, to the sweet and sad mysticism of the Middle Ages, the emblem of life. The next day, at an early hour, the travellers would be at Jerusalem; this expectation, even at the present day, sustains the caravan, rendering the night short and slumber light.

These journeys, during which the assembled nation exchanged its ideas, and which created annually in the capital centres of great excitement, placed Jesus in contact with the mind of his countrymen, and doubtless inspired him from his youth with a lively antipathy to the defects of the official representatives of Judaism. It is observable that very early the desert had been for him like a school, and to this he had made prolonged visits. But the God he found there was not his God. It was emphatically rather the God of Job, severe and terrible, and who is accountable to none. Sometimes Satan came to tempt him. He then returned from these sojourns into his beloved Galilee, and found again his heavenly Father, in the midst of the green hills and the clear fountains--among the crowds of women and children who, with joyous soul and the song of the angels in their hearts, waited for the salvation of Israel.

CHAPTER V

THE FIRST SAYINGS OF JESUS--HIS IDEAS OF A "FATHER-GOD" AND OF A PURE RELIGION--FIRST DISCIPLES

Joseph died before his son had assumed any public position. Mary remained, in a manner, the head of the family; and this explains why Jesus, when it was desired to distinguish him from others of the same name, was most frequently called "the son of Mary." It would seem that having, through her husband's death, become friendless in Nazareth, she retired to Cana, which was probably her native place. Cana was a little town about two or two and a half hours' journey from Nazareth, at the base of the hills which bound the plain of Asochis on the north. The prospect, less grand than that at Nazareth, extends over the whole plain, and is bounded in the most picturesque manner by the mountains of Nazareth and the hills of Sepphoris. Jesus appears to have resided in this place for some time. There he probably passed a part of his youth, and his first manifestations were made at Cana.

He followed the same occupation as his father--that of a carpenter. This was no humiliating or vexatious circumstance. The Jewish custom demanded that a man devoted to intellectual work should assume a handicraft. The most celebrated doctors had their trades; it was thus that St. Paul, whose education was so elaborate, was a tent-maker, or upholsterer. Jesus never married. All his power of loving expended itself on what he considered his heavenly vocation. The extremely delicate sentiment which one observes in his manner towards women did not interfere with the exclusive devotion he cherished for his idea. Like Francis d'Assisi and Francis de Sales, he treated as sisters the women who threw themselves into the same work as he did; he had his Saint Clare, and his Françoise de Chantals. However, it is probable that they loved himself better than his work; he was certainly more beloved than loving. As happens frequently in the case of very lofty natures, his tenderness of heart transformed itself into an infinite sweetness, a vague poetry, a universal charm. His relations, free and intimate, but of an entirely moral kind, with women of doubtful character, are also explained by the passion which attached him to the glory of his Father, and which made him jealously anxious for all beautiful creatures who could contribute to it.

What was the progress of thought in Jesus during this obscure period of his life? Through what meditations did he enter upon his prophetic career? We cannot tell, his history having come to us in the shape of scattered narratives and without exact chronology. But the development of living character is everywhere the same, and it cannot be doubted that the growth of a personality so powerful as that of Jesus obeyed very rigorous laws. An exalted conception of the Divinity--which he did not owe to Judaism, and which appears to have been in all its parts the creation of his great intellect--was in a manner the source of all his power. It is essential here that we put aside the ideas familiar to us, and the discussions in which little minds exhaust themselves. In order properly to understand the precise character of the piety of Jesus, we must forget all that is placed between the gospel and ourselves. Deism and Pantheism have become the two poles of theology. The paltry discussions of scholasticism, the dryness of spirit of Descartes, the deep-rooted irreligion of the eighteenth century, by lessening God, and by limiting Him, in a manner, by the exclusion of everything which is not His very self, have stifled in the breast of modern rationalism all fertile ideas of the Divinity. If God, in fact, is a fixed entity outside of us, he who believes himself to have peculiar relations with God is a "visionary," and, as the physical and physiological sciences have shown us that all supernatural visions are illusions, the logical Deist finds it impossible to understand the great beliefs of the past. Pantheism, on the other hand, in suppressing the Divine personality, is as far as it can be from the living God of the ancient religions. Were the men who have best comprehended God--Sakya-Mouni, Plato, St. Paul, St. Francis d'Assisi, and St. Augustine (at some periods of his fluctuating life)--Deists or Pantheists? Such a question has no meaning. The physical and metaphysical proofs of the existence of God were quite indifferent to them. They felt the Divine within themselves.

We must place Jesus in the first rank of this great family of the true sons of God. Jesus had no visions; God did not speak to him as to one outside of himself; God was in him; he felt himself with God, and he drew from his own heart all he said of his Father. He lived in the bosom of God by an unceasing communication; he did not see Him, but he understood Him, without need of the thunder or the burning bush of Moses, of the revealing tempest of Job, of the oracle of the old Greek sages, of the familiar genius of Socrates, or of the angel Gabriel of Mahomet. The imagination and the hallucination of a Saint Theresa, for example, are valueless here. The intoxication of the Soufi proclaiming himself identical with God is also a totally different thing. Jesus never once announced the sacrilegious theory that he was God. He believed himself to be in direct communication with God--he believed himself to be the Son of God. The highest consciousness of God which has existed in the bosom of humanity is that of Jesus.

We understand, on the other hand, that Jesus, commencing his work with such a disposition of mind, could never be a speculative philosopher like Sakya-Mouni. Nothing is further from scholastic theology than the Gospel. The speculations of the Greek doctors on the Divine essence proceed from an entirely different spirit. God, conceived simply as Father, was all the theology of Jesus. And this was not with him a theoretical principle, a doctrine more or less proved, which he sought to inculcate in others. He did not argue with his disciples; he demanded from them no effort of attention. He did not preach his opinions; he preached himself. Very great and very disinterested minds often present, associated with much elevation, that character of perpetual attention to themselves, and extreme personal susceptibility, which, in general, is peculiar to women. Their conviction that God is in them, and occupies Himself perpetually with them, is so strong that they have no fear of obtruding themselves upon others; our reserve, and our respect for the opinion of others, which is a part of our weakness, could not belong to them. This exaltation of self is not egotism; for such men, possessed by their idea, give their lives freely, in order to seal their work; it is the identification of self with the object it has embraced, carried to its utmost limit. It is regarded as vain glory by those who see in the new teaching only the personal phantasy of the founder; but it is the finger of God to those who see the result. The fool stands side by side here with the inspired man, only the fool never succeeds. It has not yet been given to mental aberration to influence seriously the progress of humanity.

Jesus, no doubt, did not reach at one step this high assertion of himself. But it is probable that, from the first, he looked on himself as standing with God in the relation of a son to his father. This was his grand act of originality; there was nothing here in common with his race. Neither the Jew nor the Mussulman has understood this delightful theology of love. The God of Jesus is not the tyrannical master who kills, damns, or saves us, just as it pleases Him. The God of Jesus is our Father. We hear Him while listening to the gentle inspiration which cries within us--"Father." The God of Jesus is not the partial despot who has chosen Israel for His people, and protects them against all the world. He is the God of humanity. Jesus would not be a patriot like the Maccabees, or a theocrat like Judas the Gaulonite. Boldly elevating himself above the prejudices of his nation, he would establish the universal Fatherhood of God. The Gaulonite maintained that it was better for one to die than to give the title of "Master" to any other than God; Jesus would allow any man to take this name, but reserves for God a title dearer still. Yielding to the powerful of the earth, who were to him the representatives of force, a respect full of irony, he establishes the supreme consolation--the recourse to the Father whom each one has in heaven, and the true kingdom of God which every man carries in his heart.

This expression--"the kingdom of God" or "the kingdom of heaven"--was the favourite term of Jesus to describe the revolution he was bringing into the world. Like nearly all the terms relating to the Messiah, it came from the book of Daniel. According to the author of that extraordinary book, the four profane empires destined to extinction would be succeeded by a fifth empire-- that of the saints, which should endure for ever. This reign of God upon earth naturally led to the most diverse interpretations. In the later days of his life Jesus believed that this reign would be realised in a material form by a sudden renovation of the world. But this was, doubtless, not his first idea. The admirable moral which he drew from the notion of the Father-God is not that of enthusiasts who believe the world to be nearly at an end, and who prepare themselves by asceticism for a chimerical catastrophe; it is that of a world which has lived and would live still. "The kingdom of God is within you," he said to those who cunningly sought for external signs. The realistic conception of the Divine Advent was only a cloud, a transient error, which his death has made us forget. The Jesus who founded the true kingdom of God, the kingdom of the meek and the humble, was the Jesus of early life, of those pure and cloudless days when the voice of his father re-echoed within his bosom in clearer tones. It was then for some months--a year perhaps-- that God truly dwelt on earth. The voice of the young carpenter acquired all at once an extraordinary sweetness. An infinite charm was exhaled from his person, and those who had hitherto seen him recognised him as the same no longer. He had not as yet any disciples, and the group of people which gathered round him was neither a sect nor a school; but there was already felt among them a common spirit, and an influence both sweet and penetrating. His amiable character, and doubtless one of those exquisite faces which sometimes appear in the Jewish race, threw around him a fascination from which no one, in the midst of these kindly and fresh-minded peoples, could escape.

Paradise would, in fact, have been brought to earth if the ideas of the young Master had not far transcended that level of ordinary goodness which the human race has found it hitherto impossible to pass. The brotherhood of men, as sons of God, and the moral consequences which have resulted from it, were deduced with exquisite feeling. Like all the rabbis of the period, Jesus little affected consecutive reasonings, but clothed his teaching in concise aphorisms, and in an expressive form, oft-times enigmatical and singular. Some of these maxims came from the books of the Old Testament. Others were the thoughts of more modern sages, especially of Antigonus of Soco, Jesus, son of Sirach, and Hillel, which had reached him, not through a course of learned study, but as oft-repeated proverbs. The synagogue was rich in very happily-expressed maxims, which formed a sort of current proverbial literature. Jesus adopted almost all this oral teaching, but imbued it with a superior spirit. Generally exceeding the duties laid down by the Law and the elders, he demanded perfection. All the virtues of humility, pardon, charity, abnegation, and self-denial--virtues which have been called with good reason Christian--if it is meant by this that they have been truly preached by Christ--were found in germ in this first declaration. As to justice, he contented himself with repeating the well-known axiom--"Whatsoever ye would that men should do unto you, do ye even so to them." But this old wisdom, selfish enough as it was, did not satisfy him. He went to excess, declaring--"Whosoever shall smite thee on thy right cheek, turn to him the other also. And if any man will sue thee at the law, and take away thy coat, let him have thy cloak also." "If thy right eye offend thee, pluck it out, and cast it from thee." "Love your enemies, do good to them that hate you; pray for them that persecute you." "Judge not, that ye be not judged." "Forgive, and ye shall be forgiven." "Be therefore merciful, as your Father also is merciful." "It is more blessed to give than to receive." "Whosoever shalt exalt himself shall be abased; and he that shall humble himself shall be exalted."

In regard to alms, pity, good works, kindness, the desire for peace, and complete disinterestedness of heart, he had little to add to the teaching of the synagogue. But he stamped them with an emphasis full of unction, and thus gave novelty to those aphorisms which had long been current. Morality is not composed of principles more or less well-expressed. The poetry of the precept, which makes one love it, is more than the precept itself, viewed as an abstract truth. Now, it cannot be denied that these maxims, borrowed by Jesus from his predecessors, produce quite a different effect in the Gospel to that in the ancient Law, in the Pirké Aboth, or in the Talmud. It is neither the ancient Law nor the Talmud which has conquered and changed the world. Little original in itself--if it is meant by that that one might recompose it almost entirely by means of more ancient maxims--the morality of the Gospel remains no less the loftiest creation of the human conscience, the most beautiful code of perfect life which any moralist has traced.

Jesus did not speak against the Mosaic law; but it is clear that he saw its insufficiency, and he let this be distinctly understood. He repeated constantly that more must be done than the ancient sages commanded. He forbade the least harsh word; he prohibited divorce, and all swearing; he censured revenge; he condemned usury; he held voluptuous desire to be as criminal as adultery. He demanded a universal forgiveness of injuries. The motive on which he grounded these maxims of exalted charity was always the same. . . . . "That ye may be the children of your Father which is in heaven; for He maketh His sun to rise on the evil and the good." "For if," he added, "ye love them that love you, what reward have ye? do not even the publicans the same? And if ye salute your brethren only, what do ye more than others? do not even the publicans so? Be ye therefore perfect, even as your Father which is in heaven is perfect."

A pure worship, a religion without priests or external observances, resting entirely on the feelings of the heart, on the imitation of God, on the direct communication between the conscience and the heavenly Father, was the result of these principles. Jesus never shrank from this daring consequence, which made him, in the very centre of Judaism, a revolutionist of the first rank. Why should there be any intermediaries between man and his Father? As God only looks on the heart, of what use are these purifications--these observances which only relate to the body? Even tradition, a thing so sacred to the Jew, is nothing compared to a pure feeling. The hypocrisy of the Pharisees, who, in praying, turned their heads to see if they were observed, who gave alms with ostentation, and put on their garments marks by which they might be recognised as pious persons--all these grimaces of false devotion disgusted him. "They have their reward," said he; "but thou, when thou doest thine alms, let not thy left hand know what thy right hand doeth, that thy alms may be in secret; and thy Father, which seeth in secret, Himself shall reward thee openly." "And thou, when thou prayest, enter into thy closet, and when thou hast shut thy door, pray to thy Father which is in secret; and thy Father, which seeth in secret, shall reward thee openly. But when ye pray, use not vain repetitions, as the heathen do; for they think that they shall be heard for their much speaking. Your Father knoweth what things ye have need of before ye ask him."

He did not affect any outward sign of asceticism, contenting himself with praying, or rather meditating, upon the mountains and in those solitary places where man has always sought God. This lofty idea of the relations of man with God, of which so few minds, even after him, have been capable, is summed up in a prayer which he compiled from some pious phrases already current amongst the Jews, and which he taught his disciples: --

"Our Father, which art in heaven, hallowed be thy name; thy kingdom come, thy will be done on earth as it is in heaven. Give us this day our daily bread. Forgive us our trespasses, as we forgive them that trespass against us. Lead us not into temptation; deliver us from the evil one." Jesus insisted particularly upon the idea that the heavenly Father knows better than we do what we need, and that we almost sin against Him in asking Him for this or that particular thing.

Jesus did nothing more in this matter than to carry out the consequences of the great principles which Judaism had established, but which the official classes of the nation inclined more and more to despise. The Greek and Roman prayers were almost always full of egotism. Never had Pagan priest said to the faithful, "If thou bring thy offering to the altar, and there rememberest that thy brother hath aught against thee, leave there thy gift before the altar and go thy way; first be reconciled with thy brother, and then come and offer thy gift." Alone in antiquity, the Jewish prophets, especially Isaiah, in their antipathy to the priesthood, had discovered a little of the true nature of the worship which man owes to God. "To what purpose is the multitude of your sacrifices unto me? I am full of the burnt-offerings of rams, and the fat of fed beasts; and I delight not in the blood of bullocks, or of lambs, or of he-goats. Incense is an abomination unto me: for your hands are full of blood; cease to do evil, learn to do well, seek judgment, and then come." In later times such doctors as Simeon the Just, Jesus son of Sirach, and Hillel, almost reached this point, and declared that the sum of the Law was righteousness. Philo, in the Judæo-Egyptian world, attained at the same time as Jesus ideas of a high moral sanctity; and the consequence of this was a decreasing regard for the customs of the Law. Shemaïa and Abtalion also more than once showed themselves very liberal casuists. Rabbi Johanan ere long went so far as to place works of mercy above even the study of the Law! Jesus alone, however, proclaimed this principle in an effective manner. Never has any man been less a priest than Jesus, and never has there been a greater enemy of forms which stifle religion under the pretext of protecting it. In this way we are all his disciples and his successors; in this way he has laid the eternal foundation-stone of true religion; and if religion is the essential thing for humanity, by this he has merited the divine rank which men have awarded him. An absolutely new idea--the idea of a worship founded upon purity of heart and on human brotherhood--made, through him, its entrance into the world--an idea so elevated that the Christian Church ought by this fact to disclose exhaustively its design, but an idea which, in our days, only some minds are able to grasp.

An exquisite sympathy with nature furnished Jesus with expressive images at every turn. Sometimes a wonderful ingenuity, which we call wit, adorned his aphorisms; at other times their vivacity consisted in the happy use of popular proverbs. "How wilt thou say to thy brother, Let me pull the mote out of thine eye; and behold, a beam is in thine own eye? Thou hypocrite; first cast out the beam out of thine own eye, and then thou shalt see clearly to cast the mote out of thy brother's eye."

These lessons, long concealed in the heart of the young Master, soon gathered round him a few disciples. The spirit of the age was in favour of small churches; it was the time of the Essenes or Therapeutæ. Certain Rabbis, each having his own distinctive teaching, Shemaïa, Abtalion, Hillel, Shammaï, Judas the Gaulonite, Gamaliel, and many others whose maxims form the Talmud, appeared on all sides. They wrote very little; the Jewish doctors of that age did not make books; everything was done by conversation and public lessons, to which it was sought to give a form easily remembered. The day when the youthful carpenter of Nazareth began openly to proclaim those maxims, for the most part already propagated, but which, thanks to him, have been able to regenerate the world, marked therefore no very startling event. It was only one Rabbi more (true, the most fascinating of them all), and around him a few young people, greedy to hear him and to search for the unknown. It requires time to awaken men from inattention. There was not as yet any Christian, though true Christianity was founded already, and doubtless it has never been more perfect than at this first period. Jesus added nothing more enduring to it afterwards. What do I say? In one sense he compromised it; for every idea, in order to prevail, must make sacrifices; we never come out of the battle of life unscathed.

To conceive the good, in fact, is not enough; it is necessary to make it succeed amongst men. To this end, less pure paths must be followed. No doubt, if the Gospel were confined to some chapters of Matthew and Luke, it would be more perfect, and would certainly not be open now to so many objections; but without miracles would it have converted the world? If Jesus had died at the period of his career which we have now reached, there would not have been in, his life a single page that could wound us; but, although greater thus in the eyes of God, he would have remained unknown to men; he would have been lost in the crowd of great unknown spirits--himself the noblest of them all; the truth would not have been promulgated, and the world would not have profited by the immense moral superiority with which the Father had endowed him. Jesus, the son of Sirach, and Hillel had uttered aphorisms nearly as elevated as his own. Hillel, however, will never be reckoned as the true founder of Christianity. In morals, as in art, precept is nothing; practice is everything. The idea which lies hidden in a picture of Raphael is of small moment; it is the picture itself which is prized. In the same manner, in morals, truth is very little thought of when it only reaches the condition of being a mere feeling; it only attains its full value when it is realised in the world as a certain fact. Some men of mediocre morality have written a number of good maxims. Some very virtuous men, on the other hand, have done nothing to continue in the world the tradition of virtue. The palm is his who has been powerful both in words and deeds, who has discerned the good, and at the price of his blood, has made it triumph. Jesus, from this double point of view, is without equal; his glory remains entire, and will ever be renewed.

CHAPTER VI

JOHN THE BAPTIST--VISIT OF JESUS TO JOHN, AND HIS ABODE IN THE DESERT OF JUDÆA--HE ADOPTS THE BAPTISM OF JOHN

An extraordinary man, whose position, in the absence of documents to describe it, remains to us in some measure enigmatical, appeared about this time, and was unquestionably connected to some extent with Jesus. This connection rather tended to make the young prophet of Nazareth deviate from his path; but it also suggested many important accessories to his religious institution, and, at all events, it furnished his disciples with a very strong authority to recommend their master in the eyes of a certain class of Jews.

About the year 28 of our era (the fifteenth year of the reign of Tiberius), there spread through all Palestine the fame of a certain Johanan or John, a young ascetic full of zeal and enthusiasm. John was of the priestly race, and was born, it would seem, at Juttah, near Hebron, or at Hebron itself. This city, which may be called patriarchal beyond all others, situated a short distance from the desert of Judæa, and within a few hours' journey of the great desert of Arabia, was at that time what it is still to-day, one of the bulwarks of monotheism in its most austere form.

From his infancy John was a Nazir--that is to say, subjected by vow to certain abstinences. The desert by which he was, so to speak, surrounded, attracted him from early life. He led there a life like that of a Yogui of India, clothed with skins or cloth of camel's hair, having for food only locusts and wild honey. A certain number of disciples were grouped around him, sharing his life or studying his severe doctrine. We might imagine ourselves transported to the banks of the Ganges, if special features had not revealed in this recluse the last descendant of the grand prophets of Israel.

Since the Jewish nation had begun to reflect upon its destiny with a kind of despair, the imagination of the people had reverted with much complacency to the ancient prophets. Now, of all the personages of the past, the remembrance of whom came like the dreams of a troubled night to awaken and agitate the people, the greatest was Elias. This giant of the prophets and his rough solitude of Carmel, where he shared the life of wild beasts, dwelling in the hollows of the rocks, whence he issued like a thunderbolt to make and unmake kings, had become, by successive transformations, a sort of superhuman being, sometimes visible, sometimes invisible, and one who had not tasted of death. It was generally believed that Elias would return and restore Israel. The austere life which he had led, the terrible remembrances he had left behind him--the impression of which is still vivid in the East--that sombre portraiture which, even in our own days, causes trembling and death; all this mythology, full of vengeance and terrors, powerfully struck the public imagination and stamped, as with a birth-mark, all the creations of the popular mind. Whoever aspired to any great influence over the people must imitate Elias; and, as a solitary life had been the essential characteristic of that prophet, they were accustomed to think of "the man of God" as a hermit. They imagined that all holy personages would have their days of penitence, of solitary life, and of austerity. The retreat to the desert thus became the condition and the prelude of high destinies.

There can be no doubt that this idea of imitation had occupied John's mind to a considerable degree. The anchorite life, so opposed to the spirit of the ancient Jewish people, and with which the vows, such as those of the Nazirs and the Rechabites, had no relation, pervaded all parts of Judæa. The Essenes were grouped near the birthplace of John, on the eastern shores of the Dead Sea. Abstinence from flesh, wine, and from sexual pleasures was regarded as the novitiate of the prophets. People imagined that the chiefs of any sect should be recluses, having their own rules and institutions, like the founders of religious orders. The teachers of the young were also at times a species of anchorites, resembling to some extent the gourous of Brahminism. In fact, might there not in this be a remote influence of the mounis of India? Perhaps, some of those wandering Buddhist monks who overran the world, as the first Franciscans did in later times, preaching by their actions and converting people who knew not their language, might have turned their steps towards Judæa, as they certainly did towards Syria and Babylon. On this point we have no certainty. Babylon had become for some time a true focus of Buddhism. Boudasp (Bodhisattva) was reputed a wise Chaldean, and the founder of Sabeism. Sabeism was, as its etymology indicates, baptism--that is to say, the religion of many baptisms--the origin of the sect still existing called "Christians of St. John," or Mendaites, which the Arabs call el-

47

Mogtasila, "the Baptists." It is very difficult to unravel these vague analogies. The sects floating between Judaism, Christianity, Baptism, and Sabeism, which we find in the region beyond the Jordan during the first centuries of our era, present to criticism the most singular problem, in consequence of the confused accounts of them which have come down to us. We may believe, at all events, that many of the external practices of John, of the Essenes, and of the Jewish spiritual teachers of this time, were derived from influences then but recently received from the far East. The fundamental practice which gave to the sect of John its character, and which has given him his name, has always had its centre in lower Chaldea, and constitutes a religion which is practised there to this day.

This practice was baptism, or total immersion. Ablutions were already familiar to the Jews, as they were to all the religions of the East. The Essenes had given them a peculiar extension. Baptism had become an ordinary ceremony at the introduction of proselytes into the bosom of the Jewish religion--a sort of initiatory rite. But never before the Baptist's time had there been given to immersion either this form or importance. John had fixed the scene of his labours in that part of the desert of Judæa which borders on the Dead Sea. At the periods when he administered baptism, he betook himself to the banks of the Jordan, either to Bethany or to Bethabara, on the eastern shore, probably opposite Jericho, or to a place called Ænon, or the Fountains, near Salim, where there was much water. There considerable crowds, mainly of the tribe of Judah, hastened to him to be baptized. In a few months he thus became one of the most influential men in Judæa, and all the multitude held him in high estimation.

The people considered him a prophet, and many imagined that he was Elias who had risen from the dead. The belief in such resurrections was widely spread; it was thought that God would raise from their graves certain of the ancient prophets to serve as the leaders of Israel to its final destiny. Others took John for the Messiah himself, although he certainly made no such pretension. The priests and scribes, opposed to this revival of prophetism, and always antagonistic to enthusiasts, despised him. But the popularity of the Baptist awed them, and they dared not speak against him. It was a victory which the feeling of the vulgar gained over the priestly aristocracy. When the chief priests were obliged to explain their exact position on this point, they were much embarrassed.

Baptism, however, was to John nothing more than a sign, destined to make an impression and to prepare men's minds for some great movement. There is no doubt that he was imbued in the highest degree with the Messianic expectations. "Repent," said he, "for the kingdom of heaven is at hand." He announced a "great wrath," that is to say, terrible calamities which were to come, and declared that the axe was already at the root of the tree, and that the tree would soon be cast into the fire. The Messiah he described had a fan in his hand, gathering in the wheat and burning the chaff. Repentance, of which baptism was the type, the giving of alms, and the reformation of manners, were to John's mind the great means of preparation for the coming events. We cannot discover in what light exactly he looked at these events. What we are sure of is that he preached with much power against the same adversaries as Jesus attacked later on, against the rich priests, the Pharisees, the doctors--in one word, against official Judaism; and that, like Jesus, he was specially welcomed by the despised classes. He reduced to a small value the title "son of Abraham," and declared that God could raise up children to Abraham from the stones on the ground. It does not seem that he possessed, even in germ, the great idea which led to the triumph of Jesus--the conception of a pure religion; but he powerfully served this idea by substituting a private rite for those legal ceremonies for which priests were required, just as the Flagellants of the Middle Ages were the precursors of the Reformation, by denying to the official clergy the monopoly of the sacraments and of absolution. The general tone of his sermons was severe and stern. The expressions he used against his adversaries appear to have been very violent. It was a harsh and continuous invective. It is probable that he did not remain a complete stranger to politics. Josephus, who was almost directly brought into connection with John through his teacher Banou, lets us understand this by his ambiguous words, and the catastrophe which put an end to the Baptist's life seems to imply that it was so. His disciples led a very austere life, fasted frequently, and affected a sad and anxious demeanour. We appear sometimes to discover the dawn of the theory of communism in goods--the tenet that the rich man is obliged to share what he possesses with the poor. The poor already appeared as the class who would benefit in the first instance by the kingdom of God.

Although the centre of John's action was Judæa, his fame penetrated quickly to Galilee and reached Jesus, who, by his first discourses, had already gathered round him a little circle of hearers. Enjoying up to this point little authority, and doubtless impelled by the desire to see a teacher whose instructions had so much in them that was in sympathy with his own ideas, Jesus left Galilee and went with his small band of pupils to visit John. The new comers were baptized like every one else. John very warmly welcomed this group of Galilean disciples, and found nothing objectionable in their remaining distinct from his own followers. The two teachers were young; they had many ideas in common; they loved one another and vied with each other before the public in reciprocal kindness of expression. At the first glance, such a fact surprises us in John the Baptist, and we are tempted to call it in question. Humility has never been a feature of strong Jewish minds. It might have been expected that a character so stubborn, a sort of Lamennais, always irritated, would be very passionate, and suffer neither rivalry nor half adhesion. But this manner of viewing things rests upon a false conception of the person of John. We imagine him an old man; he was, on the contrary, of the same age as Jesus, and very young according to the ideas of the time. In mental development, he was the brother rather than the father of Jesus. The two young enthusiasts, full of the same hopes and the same hatreds, were able to make common cause, and mutually to support each other. Certainly an aged teacher, seeing a man without celebrity approach him, and maintain towards him an aspect of independence, would have rebelled; we have scarcely an example of a leader of a school receiving with eagerness his future successor. But youth is capable of all abnegations, and it may be readily admitted that these two young enthusiasts, full of the same hopes and the same hatreds, made common cause and mutually helped each other.

These good relations became afterwards the starting-point of a whole system developed by the evangelists, which consisted in giving John's attestation as the primary basis of the Divine mission of Jesus. Such was the degree of authority attained by the Baptist that men thought it would be impossible to find in the world a better guarantee. But far from the Baptist having abdicated before Jesus, Jesus, during all the time he passed with him, recognised him as his superior, and only developed his own genius with timidity.

It seems, indeed, that, notwithstanding his profound originality, Jesus, during some weeks or months, was the imitator of John. The way before him was yet obscure. At all times, moreover, Jesus yielded much to opinion, and adopted many things which were not in exact accordance with his own ideas, or for which he cared little, merely because they were popular; but these accessories never injured his principal idea, and were always subordinate to it. Baptism had been brought into great favour by John; Jesus thought himself obliged to follow his example; therefore he baptized, and his disciples also. No doubt they accompanied this ceremony with preaching similar to that of John. The river Jordan was thus covered on all sides by Baptists, whose discourses were more or less successful. The disciple soon equalled the master, and his baptism was much prized. There was on this subject some jealousy among the disciples; the pupils of John came to him to complain of the increasing success of the young Galilean, whose baptism would soon, they feared, supplant their own. But the two masters remained superior to these little jealousies. According to a tradition, it was in the school of John where was formed the most celebrated group of the disciples of Jesus. The superiority of John was, besides, too indisputable for Jesus (still little known) to think of contesting it. He desired only to increase under John's shadow, and considered himself obliged, in order to gain the multitude, to employ the external means which in the case of John had produced such astonishing success. When he began to preach again after John's arrest, the first words which are said to have been used by him are nothing but the repetition of one of the familiar phrases of the Baptist. Many other expressions of John are to be found verbally in his discourses. The two schools appear to have lived for a long time with a good mutual understanding, and, after John's death, Jesus, as his trusty friend, was one of the first to be informed of the event.

John, in fact, was soon cut short in his prophetic career. Like the old Jewish prophets, he was, in the highest degree, a censurer of the established authorities. The extreme vivacity with which he expressed himself regarding them could not fail to draw him into an embarrassing position. In Judæa, John does not appear to have been disturbed by Pilate; but, in Perea, beyond the Jordan, he came into the territories of Antipas. This tyrant was uneasy at the political leaven which was thinly veiled by John in his preaching. The great assemblages of men, formed by religious and patriotic enthusiasm, which had gathered round the Baptist, had a suspicious aspect. An entirely personal grievance, besides, was added to these motives of state, and rendered the death of the austere censurer inevitable.

One of the most strongly-marked characters in this tragical family of the Herods was Herodias, grand-daughter of Herod the Great. Violent, ambitious, and passionate, she detested Judaism, and despised its laws. She had been married, probably against her will, to her uncle, Herod, son of Mariamne, whom Herod the Great had disinherited, and who never had assumed any public part. The inferior position of her husband, in comparison with the other members of the family, allowed her no peace of mind; she resolved to be sovereign at any cost. Antipas was the instrument through which she acted. This weak man, having become desperately enamoured of her, promised to marry her and to repudiate his first wife, the daughter of Hâreth, king of Petra, and emir of the neighbouring tribes of Perea. The Arabian princess, having obtained a hint of this purpose, resolved to fly. Concealing her design, she pretended that she wished to make a journey to Machero, in her father's territory, and caused herself to be conducted by the officers of Antipas.

Makaur, or Machero, was a colossal fortress built by Alexander Janneus, and rebuilt by Herod, in one of the most rugged wadys to the east of the Dead Sea. This was a wild and savage country, full of extraordinary legends, and was believed to be haunted by demons. The fortress was just on the boundary of the States of Hâreth and Antipas. At this period it was in the possession of Hâreth. Having been forewarned, the latter had prepared everything for the flight of his daughter, who was reconducted, from tribe to tribe, to Petra.

The almost incestuous union of Antipas and Herodias then took place. The Jewish laws as to marriage were a constant rock of offence between the irreligious family of the Herods and the strict

Jews. The members of this numerous and somewhat isolated dynasty being obliged to intermarry to a large extent, there frequently resulted violations of the limits prescribed by the Law. John was thus the echo of the general feeling when he rebuked Antipas. This was more than sufficient to decide the latter to follow up his suspicions. He caused the Baptist to be arrested and confined in the fortress of Machero, of which he had probably taken possession after the departure of the daughter of Hâreth.

More timid than cruel, Antipas did not wish to put John to death. According to certain reports, he feared popular sedition. According to another version, he had taken pleasure in listening to his prisoner, and these interviews had thrown him into great perplexities. What is certain is, that the detention was prolonged, and that John preserved, even in prison, an extensive influence. He correspnded with his disciples, and we find him still in connection with Jesus. His faith in the near approach of the Messiah only became firmer; he attentively followed the movements outside, and sought to discover the signs that were favourable to the accomplishment of the hopes by which he was sustained.

CHAPTER VII

DEVELOPMENT OF THE IDEAS OF JESUS RELATIVE TO THE KINGDOM OF GOD

Up to the arrest of John, which may be dated approximately in the summer of the year 29, Jesus did not quit the neighbourhood of the Dead Sea and of the Jordan. A sojourn in the desert of Judæa was generally considered as the preparation for great things, as a sort of "retreat" before public acts. Jesus in this respect followed the example of others, and passed forty days in no other society than that of the wild beasts, maintaining a rigorous fast. The minds of the disciples were much exercised in regard to this sojourn. The desert was, according to popular belief, the abode of demons. There are to be found in the world few regions more desolate, more God-forsaken, more shut off from all outward life, than the rocky declivity which forms the western border of the Dead Sea. It was believed that, during the time Jesus passed in this frightful country, he had gone through terrible trials; that Satan had assailed him with his illusions or tempted him by seductive promises, and that finally, to reward him for his victory, angels had come and ministered to him.

It was probably in returning from the desert that Jesus was informed of the arrest of John the Baptist. He had no further reason now to prolong his stay in a country which was comparatively strange to him. Perhaps he feared also being involved in the severities exercised towards John, and did not wish to expose himself at a time in which, seeing the little celebrity he had, his death could in no way serve the advancement of his ideas. He accordingly went back to Galilee, his true fatherland, ripened by an important experience, and having acquired, through contact with a great man very different from himself, a consciousness of his own originality.

On the whole, the influence of John had been more harmful than useful to Jesus. It checked his development; for everything leads us to believe that when he went towards Jordan he had ideas superior to those of John, and it was out of a kind of concession that he inclined for a moment towards baptism. Probably if the Baptist, to whose authority it would have been difficult to submit himself, had remained at liberty, he would not have thought of casting off the yoke of rites and of materialistic practices, and henceforth might have remained an unknown Jewish sectary; for the world had not yet abandoned these practices for others. It is the charm of a religion stripped of all exterior forms that has attracted the most elevated minds to Christianity. The Baptist once imprisoned, his followers became rapidly fewer, and Jesus found himself at liberty to follow his own bent. The only things he was indebted in a sort of way to John for were instruction in the art of preaching and in attracting popularity. From that moment, in fact, he preached with much more force, and awed the multitude with his authority.

It appears also that his close intercourse with John, not so much by the influence of the Baptist as by the natural development of his own mind, matured many of his ideas about the "kingdom of heaven." His watchword henceforth is "glad tidings;" and the announcement that the kingdom of heaven is at hand. Jesus is no longer a delightful moralist merely, aspiring to embody in a few vivid and concise aphorisms sublime lessons; he is a transcendental revolutionary who attempts to renovate the world from its very basis, and to found on earth the ideal which he has conceived. "The kingdom of God" is at hand is to be synonymous with being a disciple of Jesus. The phrase "kingdom of God" or "kingdom of Heaven," as we have already said, had been long familiar to the Jews. Jesus, however, gave to it a moral sense--a social application, that the author of the book of Daniel himself, in his enthusiastic apocalypse, dared hardly venture upon.

In the world, as it is constituted, it is the evil that prevails. Satan is the "king of this world," and everything obeys him. The priests and the doctors do not the things which they order others to do. The just are persecuted, and the sole portion of the good is to weep. The "world" is a species of enemies of God and His saints; but God will reveal Himself and avenge His saints. The day is at hand; for abomination is rampant. The reign of justice is to have its turn.

The advent of the reign of justice is to be a great and unexpected revolution. The world is to be turned upside down; the present state being bad, to represent the future, it is sufficient to conceive as near as may be the contrary of that which exists. The first shall be last. A new order will rule humanity. At present the good and the bad are mixed like wheat and tares in a field. The Master allows them to grow together; but the hour of abrupt separation is to come. The kingdom of God is to be like a great net, which gathers both good and bad fish; we put the good into vessels, and cast the bad away. The beginning of that great revolution will be hardly recognisable. It will be like the grain of mustard seed, which, though the least of all seeds, being cast into the earth, becomes a tree under the leaves of whose branches the birds come and repose; or again, it will be like the leaven, which, put into bread, leavens the whole lump. A series of often obscure parables was designed to express the surprises of that unexpected advent, its apparent injustices, its inevitable and definite character.

Who is to establish this kingdom of God? Let us recall that the first thought of Jesus--a thought so deeply rooted in him that it was probably intuitive forming part of his very being--was that he was the son of God, the bosom friend of his father, the executor of His decrees. The response of Jesus to such a question could not then be doubtful. The persuasion that he should found the kingdom of God took, in the most absolute manner, possession of his mind. He looked upon himself as the universal reformer. Heaven, earth, all nature, depravity, disease, and death are only his instruments. In the glow of his heroic will, he believes himself to be all powerful. If the earth does not lend itself to this complete transformation, it will be broken up, purified by fire and by the breath of God. A new heaven will be created, and the whole earth peopled with the angels of God.

A complete revolution, extending to nature itself --such was the fundamental idea of Jesus. Henceforth, it is certain, he renounced politics; the example of Judas the Gaulonite showed him the uselessness of popular seditions. He never dreamt of revolting against the Romans and the tetrarchs. The wild and anarchical principles of the Gaulonite found no favour with him. His submission to the powers that be, derisive at bottom no doubt, was outwardly complete. He paid tribute to Cæsar, to avoid trouble. Liberty and right do not belong to this world; why then trouble himself with vain susceptibilities? Despising the earth, convinced that the world did not merit solicitude, he sought refuge in his ideal kingdom; he established that great doctrine of transcendent contempt, the true doctrine of the freedom of mind which alone can bring peace. But so far he had not said. "My kingdom is not of this world." Much obscurity was mixed up with his most perfect views. Sometimes singular temptations crossed his mind. In the desert of Judæa, Satan proposed to give him the kingdoms of this world. Not knowing the power of the Roman Empire, he could, with the amount of enthusiasm there was in Judæa, resulting soon after in so terrible a military resistance, he could, I say, considering the daring and the numbers of his partisans, hope to establish a kingdom. Many times, no doubt, this was the supreme thought with him: The kingdom of God, is it to be realised by force or by gentleness, by revolt or by patience? One day, we are told that the common people of Galilee sought to carry him away and make him king; but Jesus fled into the mountains, and remained there for some time alone. His lofty nature shielded him from the error which would make him an agitator or a chief of rebels, a Theudas or a Barkokeba.

The revolution that he sought to bring about was a moral revolution; but he had not yet reached the point of trusting to the angels and the last trumpet for its execution. It was only upon men and through men that he wished to act. A visionary, who had no other idea than the approximateness of the last judgment, would not have had this care for the amelioration of human souls, and would not have laid down the finest moral precepts humanity has ever received. There was no doubt still much vagueness in his ideas; and it was exalted sentiment rather than fixed design which urged him on to the sublime work he had conceived, though in a manner quite different from what he imagined.

It is in fact the kingdom of God, I mean, the kingdom of mind, that he founded, and, if Jesus from the bosom of his father sees his work bearing fruit through the ages, he may indeed truly say: "This is what I wished." That which Jesus founded, and which will remain his to all eternity--deductions being made for the imperfections which enter into everything accomplished by mankind--is the doctrine of freedom of mind. Greece had already exalted ideas on the subject. Several stoics had discovered the means of being free under a tyrant. But, in general, the ancient world only understood liberty as attached to certain political forms; Harmodius and Aristogiton, Brutus and Cassius were concrete examples of such liberty. The true Christian is much more free from all restraints; here below he is a stranger; what boots it to him who is the temporary ruler of this earth, which is not his country? Liberty to him means truth. Jesus was not sufficiently acquainted with history to comprehend how opportune such a doctrine was--the very moment when republican liberty was expiring, and when the small municipal institutions of antiquity were being absorbed in the Roman Empire. But his admirable sound sense and the truly prophetic instinct that he had of his mission, guided him here with marvellous certainty. By these words: "Render unto Cæsar the things which are Cæsar's, and unto God the things which are God's," he originated something unknown to politics--a refuge for souls in the midst of an empire of brute force. To be sure, such a doctrine had its dangers. To establish as a principle that to look at a coin was a symbol of the acknowledgment of legitimate authority, to proclaim that the perfect man contemptuously pays tribute without question, was to annihilate the ancient forms of republicanism and to encourage all kinds of tyranny. Christianity, in this sense, has contributed much to weaken the sense of duty in the citizen, as well as to place the world absolutely in the power of existing circumstances. But in constituting an immense free association, which, during three hundred years, eschewed politics, Christianity amply compensated for the wrong it had done to civic virtue. Thanks to him, the power of the State was limited to terrestrial things; the mind was freed, or at all events, the terrible sceptre of

Roman authority was broken for ever.

The man who is especially preoccupied with the duties of public life does not spare those who place some other object above his party strifes. He especially blames those who subordinate political to social questions, and profess for the former a sort of indifference. In one sense he is right; for exclusiveness is prejudicial to the good government of human affairs. But what have parties done to promote the general morality of our species? If Jesus, instead of founding his heavenly kingdom, had betaken himself to Rome, and had worn his life out in conspiring against Tiberius, or in regretting Germanicus, what would have become of this world? Neither as a stern republican nor as a zealous patriot could he have stemmed the great public current of his age, though in pooh-poohing politics he has revealed to the world the truth that country is not everything, and that the man is anterior and superior to the citizen.

The principles of our positive science have been injured by the dreams embraced in the scheme of Jesus. We know the history of the world. The kind of revolutions expected by Jesus are only produced by geological or astronomical causes, and no one has ever been able to connect them with things moral. But to be just to great originators, they must not be fastened with the prejudices they only shared. Columbus discovered America, though he started out with the most erroneous ideas; Newton believed his silly explanation of the Apocalypse to be as certain as his theory of gravitation. Shall we place a mediocre man of our times above a Francis d'Assisi, a St. Bernard, a Joan of Arc, or a Luther, because he is exempt from the errors that these persons have taught? Ought we to measure men by the correctness of their ideas of physics, and by the more or less exact knowledge they possess of the true natural laws of the universe? Let us understand better the position of Jesus and whence he derived his power. The Deism of the eighteenth century and a certain kind of Protestantism have accustomed us to regard the founder of the Christian faith merely as a great moralist, a benefactor of mankind. We see no more in the gospel than good maxims; we throw a convenient veil over the strange intellectual state whence it had its origin. There are some people who regret even that the French Revolution departed more than once from principle, and that it was not brought about by wise and moderate men. Let us not impose our petty plans and commonplace notions on those extraordinary movements which are so far above our grasp! Let us continue to admire the "morality of the Gospel;" let us suppress in our religious teachings the chimera which was the soul of it, but do not let us imagine that with the simple ideas of happiness or of individual morality we can again move the world. The idea of Jesus was much more profound. His was the most revolutionary idea that human brain ever conceived. But the historian must take it in its entirety, and not with those timid suppressions which strip it of the very thing which has rendered it efficacious for the regeneration of humanity.

At bottom, the ideal is always a Utopia. When we wish at the present time to represent the Christ of the modern conscience, the consoler, the judge of these times, what do we do? That which Jesus himself did over 1800 years ago. We suppose the conditions of the real world quite other than they are; we represent a moral liberator breaking without weapons the chains of the negro, bettering the condition of the common people, delivering oppressed nations. We forget that that implies the subversion of the world, the climate of Virginia and that of the Congo modified, the blood and the race of millions of men changed, our social complications restored to a chimerical simplicity, and the political stratifications of Europe displaced from their natural order. The "restitution of all things" desired by Jesus was not more difficult. That new earth, that new heaven, that new Jerusalem, which comes from above, this cry, "Behold I make all things new," are the characteristics common to reformers. The contrast of the ideal with the sad reality invariably produces in mankind those revolts against cold reason which mediocre minds consider as follies, until the day of their triumph arrives, and then those who have combated them are the first to acknowledge their great wisdom. That there may have been a contradiction between the belief in the approaching end of the world and the general moral system of Jesus, conceived in prospect of a permanent state of humanity, nearly analogous to that which now exists, no one will attempt to deny. It was exactly this contradiction that ensured the success of his work. The millenarian alone would have done nothing lasting; the moralist alone would have done nothing powerful. The millenarian gave the impulse, the moralist ensured the future. Hence Christianity united the two conditions of great success in this world--a revolutionary starting point and the possibility of vitality. Everything which is intended to succeed ought to respond to these two wants; for the world seeks both to change and to endure. Jesus, at the same time that he announced an unparalleled subversion in human affairs, proclaimed the principles upon which society has reposed for eighteen hundred years. That which, in fact, distinguishes Jesus from the agitators of his time and from those of all times is his perfect idealism. In some respects Jesus was an anarchist, for he had no notion of civil government. The latter seemed to him an abuse, pure and simple. He spoke of it in vague terms, after the manner of one of the commonalty who knows nothing of politics. Every magistrate appeared to him a natural enemy of the people of God; and he forewarned his disciples of conflicts with the civil powers without imagining for a moment that there was anything in this to be ashamed of. But the desire to supplant the rich and powerful never manifests itself in him. His aim is to annihilate wealth and power, but not to seize upon them. He prepares his disciples for persecutions and punishments, but in no single instance is the idea of armed resistance foreshadowed. The idea that man is all-powerful through suffering and resignation, that man triumphs over force through purity of heart, is an idea unique with Jesus. Jesus is not a spiritualist; for everything to him had a palpable realisation. But he is a thorough idealist, matter being for him but the symbol of the idea, and the real the vivid expression of that which does not manifest itself.

To whom shall we apply, upon whom shall we rely, to found the kingdom of God? The opinion of Jesus never wavered upon this point. That which is cherished by man is an abomination in the sight of God. The founders of the kingdom of God are the weak and lowly. Neither the rich, the learned, nor the priests; but women, common people, the humble, little children. The grand distinguishing mark of the Messiah is:--"The poor have the gospel preached to them." The idyllic and gentle nature of Jesus here asserted its superiority. A great social revolution, in which rank should be levelled, in which all authority should be brought under, was his dream. The world will not believe him; the world will kill him. But his followers will not be of this world. They will be a small band of the lowly and humble, who will conquer the world by their very humility. The sentiment which made the "world" the antithesis of "Christian" has, in the mind of the Master, its full justification.

CHAPTER VIII

JESUS AT CAPERNAUM

Haunted by a more and more imperious idea, Jesus, with a quiet determination, henceforth follows the path his extraordinary genius and the circumstances in which he lived have traced out for him. Till now, he had only communicated his thoughts to a few persons who had been secretly drawn towards him; henceforward his teaching was public and sought after. He was now about thirty years of age. The small group of hearers who went with him to John was undoubtedly increased, and perhaps he had been joined by some of the disciples of John. It was with this first nucleus of a church, on his return into Galilee, that he boldly proclaimed the "glad tidings of the kingdom of God." This kingdom was at hand; and it was he, Jesus, who was that "Son of Man," whom Daniel in his vision had beheld as the divine herald of the final and supreme revelation.

We must remember that in the Jewish ideas, which were averse to art and mythology, the simple form of man had a superiority over that of Cherubim, and of the fantastic animals which the imagination of the people, since it had been subjected to the influence of Assyria, had ranged around the Divine Majesty. Already in Ezekiel, the Being seated on the supreme throne, far above the monsters of the mysterious chariot, the great revealer of prophetic visions, had the figure of a man. In the book of Daniel, in the midst of the vision of the empires, represented by animals, at the moment when the great judgment commences, and when the books are opened, a Being, "like unto a Son of Man," advances towards the Ancient of days, who confers on him the power to judge the world, and to govern it for eternity. Son of Man, in the Semitic languages, especially in the Aramean dialects, is a simple synonym of man. But this chief passage of Daniel struck the mind; the words, Son of Man, became, at least in certain schools, one of the titles of the Messiah, regarded as judge of the world, and as king of the new era about to be inaugurated. The application which Jesus made of it to himself was therefore the proclamation of his Messiahship, and the affirmation of the coming catastrophe in which he was to figure as judge, clothed with the full powers which had been delegated to him by the Ancient of days.

The success of the teaching of the new prophet was this time decisive. A group of men and women, all characterised by the same spirit of juvenile frankness and of simple innocence, adhered to him and said: "Thou art the Messiah!" As the Messiah was to be the Son of David, he was naturally conceded this appellation, which was synonymous with the former. Jesus accepted it with pleasure, although it might cause him some embarrassment, his origin being so well known. For himself, he preferred the title of "Son of Man," an apparently humble title, but it was connected directly with the Messianic hopes. That was the appellation by which he designated himself, although, in his mouth, the "Son of Man" was a synonym of the pronoun I, which he avoided using. But no one ever thus addressed him, doubtless because the name in question did not quite suit him, until the day of his coming advent.

Jesus' centre of action, at this period of his life, was the little town of Capernaum--situated on the shore of the lake of Gennesareth. The name of Capernaum, into which enters the word caphar, village, seems to denote a small town of the old character, in contradistinction to the great towns built according to the Roman fashion, such as Tiberias. The name was so little known that Josephus, in one place in his writings, takes it for the name of a fountain, the fountain having more celebrity than the village close to it. Like Nazareth, Capernaum had no history, and had not participated in the profane movement favoured by the Herods. Jesus was much attached to this town, and made it a second home. Shortly after his return, he made an unsuccessful experiment upon Nazareth. One of his biographers naïvely remarks that he could work no miracle there. The knowledge that was possessed of his family--a family of little importance--destroyed his authority. People could not regard as the son of David one whose brother, sister, and sister-in-law they were seeing every day. Besides, it is to be remarked that his family were very decidedly opposed to him, refusing point blank to believe in his divine mission. At one time, his mother and his brothers maintained that he had lost his senses, and, treating him as an exalted idiot, attempted to put him under restraint. The Nazarenes, much more violent, desired, it is said, to kill him by throwing him down from a steep rock. Jesus pointedly retorted that this risk was common to all great men, and applied to himself the proverb--"A prophet hath no honour in his own country."

This check was far from discouraging him. He returned to Capernaum, where he found the people much more favourably disposed to him, and from there he organised a series of missions into the small surrounding towns. The people of this beautiful and fertile country rarely assembled together except on the Sabbath. This was the day he selected for his teaching. Each town had then a synagogue or place of meeting. It was a rectangular room, not very large, with a portico, decorated in the Greek style. The Jews, not having any architecture of their own, never attempted to give to those edifices an original design. The remains of many ancient synagogues are still to be seen in Galilee. They have all been constructed of large and good materials; but their appearance is rather paltry, owing to the profusion of floral ornaments, foliage, and network which characterise Jewish edifices. In the interior there were benches, a pulpit for public reading, and a recess for holding the sacred rolls. These edifices, which had nothing of the temple about them, were the centres of Jewish life. There the people assembled on the Sabbath for prayer, and to listen to the reading of the Law and the Prophets. As Judaism, outside of Jerusalem, had, properly speaking, no clergy, the first to arrive stood up and read the lessons, paraschæ et haphtara, of the day, adding thereto an original, a personal midrasch, or commentary, in which he expounded his own views. This was the origin of the "homily," whose finished models we find in the smaller treatises of Philo. The auditors had a right to interrupt and to question the reader; thus, the meeting degenerated quickly into a kind of free discussion assembly. It had a president, "elders," a hazzan--a recognised reader or apparitor, "deputies"-- a sort of secretaries or messengers, who conducted the correspondence between the different synagogues--a shammasch or sacristan. The synagogues were thus really small independent republics; they had an extended jurisdiction, guaranteed enfranchisement, exercised an authority over the enfranchised. Like all the municipal corporations up to an advanced period of the Roman Empire, they issued honorary decrees, which had the force of law in the community, and pronounced sentences of corporal punishment, which were executed ordinarily by the hazzan.

With the marked activity of mind that has always characterised the Jews, such an institution, despite the arbitrary restraints it tolerated, could not fail to give rise to very animated discussions. Thanks to the synagogues, Judaism has been able to pass unscathed through eighteen centuries of persecution. These were so many little separate worlds which at once conserved the national spirit, and offered a ready field for intestine struggles. Within the walls of the synagogues there was vented an enormous amount of passion. Disputes for precedence were keen. To have a reserved seat in the first row was the recompense for great piety, or the privilege of wealth which was the most envied. On the other hand, the liberty accorded to every one, of instituting himself reader and expounder of the sacred text, offered wonderful facilities for the propagation of new ideas. This was one of the great opportunities of Jesus, and the means he most often used in laying down his doctrines. He entered the synagogue and stood up to read; the hazzan gave him the scroll, which he unrolled, and from which he read the lesson of the day. From this reading he evolved some points bearing on his own ideas. As there were few Pharisees in Galilee, the discussion did not assume that degree of animation and that acrimonious tone of opposition which he would have encountered at the very first step at Jerusalem. These good Galileans had never heard a discourse so well adapted to their happy dispositions. They admired him, and they encouraged him; they found that he spoke well, and that his reasonings were convincing. He resolved the hardest questions without any difficulty; the charm of his speech and of his person captivated these ingenuous folk, whose minds had not yet been contaminated by the pedantry of the doctors.

Thus, the authority of the young Master increased daily, and, as a matter of course, the more people believed in him the more he believed in himself. His sphere, however, was limited. It was confined to the basin of the lake of Tiberias, and even here there was one locality which he preferred. The lake is five or six leagues long and three or four broad; though it has the appearance of an all but perfect oval, it forms, from Tiberias to the mouth of the Jordan, a sort of gulf, whose curve measures about three leagues. This was the field in which the seed sown by Jesus found at length a congenial soil. Let us run over it step by step, and endeavour to raise the mantle of aridity and of desolation with which the demon of Islamism has covered it.

The first objects we encounter on leaving Tiberias are steep rocks, a mountain which appears to roll into the sea. The mountains then gradually recede, and a plain (El Ghoueir), almost level with the sea, opens out. It is a charming grove of rich verdure, furrowed by the plentiful waters which issue partly from a great round reservoir of ancient construction (Aïn Medawara). On the verge of this plain, which is, strictly speaking, the country of Gennesareth, we find the miserable village of Medjdel. At the opposite side of the plain (always following the lake) we come upon the site of a town (Khan Minyeh) with charming streams (Aïn-et-Tin), a pretty road, narrow and deep, cut out of the rocks, which Jesus certainly often traversed, and which serves as an outlet into the plain of Gennesareth and to the northern slopes of the lake. A mile from this place the traveller crosses a stream of salt water (Aïn Tabiga), issuing from several large springs a few yards from the lake, and entering it through the middle of a dense mass of verdure. After a further journey of forty minutes over the bare slopes which stretch from Aïn Tabiga to the mouth of the Jordan, we at last find some huts and a collection of monumental ruins, called Tell-Houm.

Five small towns (which will be as long spoken of by mankind as Rome or Athens) were in the time of Jesus scattered about the space which extends from the village of Medjdel to Tell-Houm. Of these five towns, Magdala, Dalmanutha, Capernaum, Bethsaida, and Chorazin, the first alone can to-day be identified with any certainty. The horrible village of Medjdel has doubtless retained the name and the situation of the little town that gave to Jesus his most faithful friend (Mary Magdalene); Dalmanutha is altogether unknown. Possibly Chorazin was a little more inland, on the north side. As for Bethsaida and Capernaum, conjecture has placed them at Tell-Houm, Aïn-et-Tin, Khan Minyeh, and at Aïn Medawara. In topography, as in history, it might indeed be said that a profound design has sought to conceal the traces of the great founder. It is doubtful whether, upon that wofully devastated soil, we shall ever succeed in fixing the spots whence mankind would gladly flock to kiss the imprints of his feet.

The lake, the horizon, the shrubs, the flowers, are all that remain of the little canton, three or four leagues in extent, where Jesus began his Divine work. The trees have totally disappeared. In this country, where the vegetation was formerly so rich that Josephus saw in it a kind of miracle--Nature, according to him, being pleased to bring forth side by side the plants indigenous to cold countries, the products of the torrid zones, the trees of temperate climates, laden all the year round with flowers and fruits--in this country travellers are now obliged to calculate a day beforehand the place where they will on the morrow find a shady nook to sit down to lunch. The lake has become deserted. A solitary, dilapidated barque now ploughs the waves, formerly the scene of so much activity and of happiness. But the waters are still smooth and transparent. The coast, formed of rocks and pebbles, is indeed that of a small sea, not that of a mere pond, like the banks of Lake Huleh. It is clean, neat, mudless, always beaten on the same spot by the gentle waves. There are small clearly-defined promontories, covered with rose laurels, tamarisks, and prickly caper bushes; at two places especially, at the mouth of the Jordan near Tarichea and at the edge of the plain of Gennesareth, there are delightful parterres where the waves ebb and flow over masses of turf and flowers. The Aïn-Tabiga brook forms a little estuary, which is full of pretty shells. Flocks of aquatic birds cover the lake. The sky is dazzling with light. The empyrean blue waters, deeply embedded between glittering rocks, appear, when viewed from the summit of the mountains of Safed, to lie at the bottom of a cup of gold. To the north, the snowy ravines of Hermon are traced in white lines upon the sky; to the west, the high undulating plateaux of Gaulonitis and Peræa, absolutely barren and clothed by the sun with a kind of velvety atmosphere, form one compact mountain, or rather a long high terrace, which runs from Cæsarea-Philippi to the south as far as the eye can reach.

The heat upon the shore is, in summer, very oppressive. The lake occupies a hollow which is over six hundred feet below the level of the Mediterranean, and thus is subjected to the torrid conditions of the Dead Sea. A luxurious vegetation tempered in former times these excessive heats. One can hardly understand that a furnace such as the whole lake basin now is, beginning with the month of May, had ever been the scene of marvellous activity. Josephus, however, found the climate very temperate. Undoubtedly, there has been here, as in the Campagna of Rome, some change of climate, attributable to historical causes. It is Islamism, and, above all, the Mussulman reaction against the crusades, which has withered, as with a blast of death, the region preferred by Jesus. The beautiful country of Gennesareth did not suspect that within the brain of this peaceful wayfarer were concealed its destinies.

A dangerous compatriot indeed! He has ruined the country which had the insuperable honour of giving him birth. Coveted by two rival fanaticisms, after it had become the object of universal love or hate, Galilee, as the price of its glory, has been changed into a desert. But who will say that Jesus would have been happier if he had lived in obscurity in his own village until he had reached the age of mature manhood? and as for the ungrateful Nazarenes, who would ever think of them if one of their number had not, at the risk of compromising the future prosperity of their town, discovered his Father and proclaimed himself the Son of God ?

At the time of which we speak, four or five large villages, situated about half an hour's walk from one another, formed the little world of Jesus. He seems never to have visited Tiberias, a heathen city, peopled for the most part by Pagans, and the permanent residence of Antipas. Sometimes, however, he wandered forth of his favourite region. For instance, he went by boat along the eastern shore to Gergesa. In the north, we find him at Paneas, or Cæsarea-Philippi, at the foot of Mount Hermon. Moreover, he finally made a journey to Tyre and Sidon, a country which at that time must have been in an exceedingly flourishing condition. In all these countries he was surrounded with Paganism. At Cæsarea he saw the celebrated grotto of Panium, which was considered the source of the Jordan, and around which popular belief had entwined many strange legends; he could admire the marble temple that Herod had erected near there in honour of Augustus; he stopped probably before the numerous votive statues erected to Pan, to the Nymphs, to the Echo of the Grotto, which piety had already accumulated in this beautiful spot. The rationalistic Jew, accustomed to look on strange gods for deified men or for demons, had come to consider all these symbolical representations as idols. The attractions of naturalistic worship, which carried away the more sanguine races, did not move him. It is undoubted that he had no knowledge of what the ancient sanctuary of Melkarth at Tyre might still contain of a primitive worship more or less analogous to that of the Jews. Paganism, which, in Phoenicia, had raised on every hill a temple and a sacred grove--outward evidences of great industry and vulgar riches--hardly elicited a smile from him. Monotheism takes away the capacity for understanding Pagan religions. A Mussulman suddenly introduced into polytheistic countries seems to have no eyes. Certainly, Jesus learned little or nothing in these journeys. He always came back to his beloved shores of Gennesareth. His thoughts were centred there, and there he found faith and love.

CHAPTER IX

THE DISCIPLES OF JESUS

In this earthly paradise, which the great historic revolutions had, up till then, affected but little, there lived a people in perfect harmony with the country itself--active, honest, light and tender-hearted. The lake of Tiberias is one of the best fishing-grounds in the world. Very productive fisheries had been established, particularly at Bethsaida and Capernaum, and had created a certain opulence. These fisherman families formed a gentle and peaceable society, extending, by means of numerous ties of relationship, over the whole lake region we have named. Their comparatively idle lives left their imagination quite free. The ideas concerning the kingdom of God found, amongst these small coteries of good people, more credence than anywhere else. Nothing that we call civilisation, in the Greek or worldly sense, had yet penetrated into their midst. Nor had they any of our German and Celtic earnestness; but although their goodness was often, perhaps, wholly superficial, their manners were quiet, and they had a certain amount of intelligence and shrewdness. We can imagine them as being somewhat similar to the better population of the Lebanons, but with the faculty, which the latter lacked, of producing great men. Jesus met there his true kindred. He installed himself as one of them. Capernaum became "his own city," and, in the midst of the little circle which adored him, he forgot his sceptical brothers, ungrateful Nazareth and its mocking incredulity.

One house especially, at Capernaum, offered him an agreeable asylum and devoted disciples. It was that of two brothers, sons of one Jonas, who was probably dead at the time when Jesus came to fix his abode upon the banks of the lake. These two brothers were Simon, surnamed in Syro-Chaldaic Cephas, in Greek Petros, "the Stone," or Peter, and Andrew. Born at Bethsaida, they had established themselves at Capernaum when Jesus entered on public life. Peter was married and had children, and his mother-in-law lived with him in that house, and resided there constantly. Andrew appears to have been a disciple of John the Baptist, and Jesus had probably become acquainted with him on the banks of the Jordan. The two brothers, even at the time when it seemed they were most occupied with their Master, continued always to follow the calling of fishermen. Jesus, who delighted in playing upon words, said sometimes that he would make them fishers of men. In fact, among all his disciples, none of them were more firmly attached to him. It would seem that John, like Andrew, had known Jesus in the school of John the Baptist. The two families of Jonas and Zebedee appear to have been very closely related.

Another family, that of Zabdia or Zebedee, a well-to-do fisherman and the owner of several boats, extended to Jesus a hearty welcome. Zebedee had two sons; James, who was the elder, and a younger son, John, who later on was destined to play so important a part in the history of infant Christianity. Both were zealous disciples. Salome, wife of Zebedee, was also strongly attached to Jesus, and accompanied him till his death.

The women, in fact, received him very gladly. He had in their society those reserved manners which render a very agreeable union of ideas between the two sexes possible. The separation of men and women which has checked all refined development among the peoples of the East was, undoubtedly, then, as in our day, much less rigorous in the country and in the villages than in the large towns. Three or four devoted Galilean women always accompanied the young Master, and disputed among themselves for the pleasure of listening to him and of attending on him in turn. These women imported into the new sect an enthusiastic element, as well as something of the marvellous, the importance of which was already felt. One of them, Mary Magdalene, who has made the name of her poor native town so celebrated in the world, appears to have been a very excitable person. In the language of the time, she had been possessed of seven devils: that is to say, she had been afflicted with nervous and apparently inexplicable maladies. Jesus, by his unspotted and gentle loveliness, soothed that excitable organisation. The Magdalene remained faithful to him even to Golgotha, and on the day but one following his death played a most important part, for, as we shall see later on, she was the principal medium through which was established faith in the resurrection. Joanna, wife of Chuza, one of the attendants of Antipas, Susannah, and others whose names are unknown, accompanied him constantly and ministered unto him. Some of them were rich, and, placing their fortunes at the disposal of the young Prophet, put him in a position to live without having to follow the occupation to which he had been brought up.

There were still many others who followed him habitually and recognised him as their Master:-- one Philip of Bethsaida, Nathaniel, son of Tolmai or Ptolemy, of Cana, perhaps a disciple of the first period; and Matthew, probably the person who was the Xenophon of infant Christianity. He had, according to tradition, been a publican, and, as such, handled with greater facility the kalam than the others. It was then probably that he began to think of writing those memoirs which are the bases of that which we know of the teachings of Jesus. Others of the disciples were Thomas or Didymus, who, though he doubted sometimes, was warm-hearted, and a man of generous impulses; one Lebbæus or Thaddeus; Simon the Zelot, who was, perhaps, a disciple of Judas the Gaulonite, belonging to the party of the Kenaim, which was formed at that time, and which was soon to play so great a part in the affairs of the Jewish nation; lastly Joseph Barsaba, surnamed Justus; Matthias; a personage conjectured to be named Ariston; Judas, son of Simon, of the city of Kerioth, who was the black sheep of the faithful flock, and who acquired such unenviable renown. He was, it appears, the only one of them who was not a Galilean. Kerioth was a town at the extreme south of the tribe of Judah, a day's journey beyond Hebron.

We have seen that the family of Jesus was in general little predisposed towards him. Nevertheless, James and Jude, his cousins, by Mary Cleophas, became from that time his disciples, and Mary Cleophas herself was of the number of those persons who followed him to Calvary. At this period we do not read of his mother being with him. It is only after the death of Jesus that Mary becomes of great importance, and that the disciples seek to attach her to themselves. It is then, too, that the members of the family of the founder, under the appellation of brothers of the Lord, form an influential group, which for long was at the head of the Church at Jerusalem, and which after the sack of the city sought refuge in Batanea. The simple fact of having been on terms of intimacy with him became a decided advantage, just as, after the death of Mahomet, the wives and daughters of the prophet, who were of no account during his life-time, became great authorities.

In this friendly throng Jesus had avowedly his favourites, and a select circle of confidants. The two sons of Zebedee, James and John, appear to have taken the front rank in that small council. They were full of fire and passion. Jesus had uniquely designated them "sons of thunder," on account of their excessive zeal, a zeal which, if it had had the control of the thunder, would have made too frequent use of it. John, in particular, appears to have been on a certain footing of familiarity with Jesus. Perhaps the numerous and active school which later on attached itself to the second of the sons of Zebedee, and who wrote, it appears, his recollections in a manner which did not sufficiently conceal the interests of the school, the records of which are to be found in his recollections (souvenirs), has exaggerated the warm attachment that the Master bore for him. But what is more significant is, that in the synoptical Gospels, Simon Barjona, or Peter, James, son of Zebedee, and John his brother, formed a sort of inner council, which Jesus called together at certain times when he had reason to challenge the faith and the intelligence of the others. It appears, besides, that all three were associated as fishermen. The affection of Jesus for Peter was deep. The character of that disciple --upright, sincere, impulsive--pleased Jesus, who sometimes allowed himself to smile at his eager manner. Peter, who was not much of a mystic, communicated to the Master his simple doubts, his dislikes, his human weaknesses, with an honest unreserve that recalls that of Joinville towards St. Louis. Jesus, full of confidence and esteem, reproved him in a friendly manner. As regards John, his youth, his exquisite tenderness of heart, and his lively imagination, must have possessed a great charm. The individuality of that extraordinary man did not develop itself till afterwards. If he is not the author of the bizarre Gospel which bears his name, and which, although the character of Jesus is misrepresented in it in many particulars, embraces such precious teachings, it is at least possible that he had been the occasion of it. Accustomed to ponder over his recollections with the feverish restlessness of an excited mind, he transformed his Master in wishing to describe him, and has furnished to the skilful forgers the pretext of a narrative in the compilation of which it does not appear that perfect good faith was the guiding principle.

No hierarchy, strictly speaking, existed in this infant sect. They were to call each other "brothers," and Jesus absolutely proscribed titles of superiority, such as rabbi, "master," "father," he alone being Master, and God alone being Father. The greatest was to be the servant of the others. Nevertheless, Simon Barjona distinguished himself among his fellows by a certain personal importance. Jesus lived with him and discoursed from his boat; his house was the head-quarters of evangelical preaching. In public, he was regarded as chief of the band, and it was to him that the superintendent of the tax collectors addressed himself for payment of the taxes due by the sect. Simon was the first to acknowledge Jesus to be the Messiah. In a moment of unpopularity, when Jesus demanded of his disciples: "Will ye also go away?" Simon answered: "Lord, to whom shall we go? Thou hast the words of eternal life." At various times Jesus conferred on him in his Church a certain priority, and interpreted his Syriac surname of Képha (stone), wishing to signify thereby that he would make him the corner-stone of the new building. At one time, he seems to promise him "the keys of the kingdom of Heaven," and to accord him the right of pronouncing upon earth decisions to be ratified always in eternity.

No doubt this preference given to Peter excited not a little jealousy. In view of the future, particularly, was this jealousy kindled--in view of that kingdom of God, in which all the disciples would be seated on thrones, at the right and the left of the Master, in order to judge the twelve tribes of Israel. They demanded of him who should then be the nearest to the "Son of Man," acting in some sort as his first minister and assessor. The two sons of Zebedee aspired to these positions. Filled with such a thought they induced their mother, Salome, who one day took Jesus apart, and solicited him for the two highest places for her sons. Jesus evaded the request by repeating his habitual maxim that he who exalteth himself shall be brought low, and that the kingdom of heaven will be possessed by the meek and lowly. This created some stir in the band: and there was ill-feeling manifested against James and John. The same rivalry is frequently seen in the Gospel of John, in which the writer is never tired of declaring himself to be "the beloved disciple," and the one to whom the Master in dying confided the care of his mother, who seeks to place himself near Simon Peter--nay, sometimes before him--in the important situations in which the older evangelists omitted to mention him.

Among the persons above mentioned, every one of them, of which we know anything, commenced life as a fisherman. In a country of simple manners, in which every one labours, this profession was not so degrading as the declamations of preachers would have us believe, in order the better to magnify the miraculous origins of Christianity. At all events, none of them belonged to a socially elevated class. Matthew or Levi, son of Alphæus, alone had been a publican. But those to whom that name was given in Judæa were not the farmers-general [of taxes], who were men of exalted rank (always Roman patricians), and called at Rome publicani. They were the agents of the farmers-general, subordinate servants, simple customs officers. The great route from Acre to Damascus, one of the most ancient routes in the world, which traversed Galilee skirting the lake, increased greatly the number of this class of employés there. At Capernaum, which was probably on the line of the route, there was a numerous staff. That occupation has never been popular; but amongst the Jews it was regarded as wholly criminal. Taxation, which was new to them, was the symbol of their vassalage. One school, that of Judas the Gaulonite, maintained that to pay taxes was an act of Paganism. The customs officers, moreover, were abhorred by the zealots of the Law. They were only spoken of in conjunction with assassins, highway robbers, and people of infamous character. Jews who accepted such positions were excommunicated and rendered incapable of making a will; their money was accursed, and the casuists forbade its being exchanged. These poor people, placed under the ban of society, lived by themselves apart. Jesus accepted an invitation to dine at the house of Levi, at which were present, according to the language of the times, "many publicans and sinners." That was a great scandal. In those proscribed houses one ran the risk of meeting wicked society. We shall often see him in this position--careless in regard to shocking the prejudices of well-disposed persons, seeking to elevate the ignorant classes by means of the orthodox, and thus exposing himself to the most cutting reproaches of the zealots. Pharisaism, in addition to a sort of external respectability, made infinite observances the test of salvation. The true moralist--who proclaimed only that God required but one thing--to wit, rectitude of sentiment--came to be welcomed by all who were not imbued with the official hypocrisy.

Jesus owed these numerous conquests to an infinite charm of person and of speech. One penetrating word, one look falling upon a simple conscience, which was only waiting to be aroused, made such a one an ardent disciple. Sometimes Jesus made use of an innocent artifice, which was also employed at a later period by Joan of Arc. He pretended to have an intimate knowledge of something affecting the person he wished to gain over, or he would recall some circumstance dear to that person's heart. It was in this manner, it is said, that he touched Nathaniel, Peter, and the Samaritan woman. Dissimulating the real source of his power--I mean his superiority to his surroundings--he allowed it to be believed, in order to satisfy the aspirations of the times--aspirations, moreover, which he fully shared--that a revelation from on high had disclosed to him the secrets and the workings of hearts. Everybody imagined that he moved in a higher sphere than that of mankind. It was said that he spoke with Moses and Elias upon the mountains; it was believed that in those moments of solitude the angels came and ministered unto him, and established a supernatural intercourse between him and heaven.

CHAPTER X

PREACHINGS ON THE LAKE

Such was the group which, on the banks of the Lake of Tiberias, surrounded Jesus. The aristocracy was represented there by a customs-officer and the wife of a steward. The rest were composed of fishermen and common people. They were extremely ignorant; their intellect was feeble. They believed in apparitions and ghosts. Not one particle of Greek culture had penetrated this chief circle. Moreover, their Jewish instruction was very imperfect, but they were full of heart and good will. The beautiful climate of Galilee rendered the existence of these honest fishermen a perpetual enjoyment. They were a true prelude to the kingdom of God--simple, good, happy--rocked gently on their charming little lake, or sleeping at night on its banks. One cannot realise the intoxication of a life which thus glides away under the canopy of heaven; the feelings, now gentle, now ardent, produced by this continual contact with nature; the dreams of those starry nights, under the infinite expanse of the azure dome. It was during such a night that Jacob, with his head resting on a stone, beheld in the stars the promise of an innumerable posterity, and the mysterious ladder reaching from earth to heaven, by which the Elohim ascended and descended. At the time of Jesus heaven was not shut nor the earth grown cold. The cloud still opened above the Son of Man; the angels ascended and descended upon his head; visions of the kingdom of God were reported everywhere, for the reason that man carried them in his heart. The clear and mild eyes of those simple souls contemplated the universe in its mythic origin. The world probably discovered its secret to the divinely enlightened consciences of these happy children, whose purity of heart merited that one day they should see God.

Jesus lived with his disciples almost always in the open air. Sometimes he entered a boat and taught the multitudes assembled on the shore. Sometimes he sat upon the mountains which skirted the lake, where the air was so pure and the sky so luminous. The faithful band led thus a gay and roaming life, receiving the inspirations of the Master fresh from his lips. An innocent doubt was now and then started, some mildly sceptical question raised. A smile or a look from Jesus sufficed to silence the objection. At each step--in the passing cloud, in the sprouting seed, in the ripening corn--they descried a sign of the kingdom which was at hand. They believed they were about to see God, and to become the masters of the world. Tears were turned into joy--it was the advent of "peace on earth" (universelle consolation). "Blessed," said the Master, "are the poor in spirit for theirs is the kingdom of heaven. Blessed are they that mourn: for they shall be comforted. Blessed are the meek: for they shall inherit the earth. Blessed are they which do hunger and thirst after righteousness: for they shall be filled. Blessed are the merciful: for they shall obtain mercy. Blessed are the pure in heart: for they shall see God. Blessed are the peacemakers: for they shall be called the children of God. Blessed are they which, are persecuted for righteousness' sake: for theirs is the kingdom of heaven" (Matt. v. 3-10).

His preaching was unimpassioned and pleasing, redolent of nature and of the perfume of the fields. He loved the flowers, and drew from them his most charming lessons. The birds of the air, the sea, the mountains, the frolics of children, were introduced by turn into his discourses. His style had nothing of the Greek period about it, but resembled much more the turn of the Hebrew parabolists, and in particular the sentences of the Jewish doctors, his contemporaries, which are to be found in the Pirke Aboth. His expositions were not very extended; they formed a species of sorites after the manner of the Koran, which, being put together, constituted later on those long discourses which were written by Matthew. No note of transition linked together these diverse fragments. In general, however, the same inspiration pervaded them all and gave them unity. It was in the parable, especially, that the Master excelled. Nothing in Judaism could have served him as a model for that charming style. It was a creation of his. No doubt there are to be found in Buddhist books some parables precisely of the same tone and of the same form as the Gospel parables. But it is hard to allow that a Buddhist influence had any effect on them. The spirit of meekness and of deep sentiment which animated equally primitive Christianity and Buddhism is sufficient to explain these similarities.

A total indifference to exterior things, and for vain superfluities as regards manners and customs, which our colder climates render imperative, were the outcome of the innocent and sweet lives passed in Galilee. Cold climates, by bringing man and the outer world into perpetual conflict, have caused too much store to be set by researches after comfort and luxury. On the other hand, the climates which awaken fewer desires are the countries of idealism and of poetry. The accessories of life are there insignificant as compared to the pleasure of living. The adornment of dwellings is there superfluous, for people remain within doors as little as possible. The strong and regularly-served food of less generous climates would be looked upon as heavy and disagreeable. And, as for the luxury of clothing, what can equal that which God has given to the earth and to the birds of the air? Labour, in climates of this description, seems useless; what it affords is not worth what it costs. The animals of the field are better clothed than the most opulent of men, and they toil not. This contempt, when it does not proceed from idleness, greatly assists to elevate the souls of men, and inspired Jesus with some charming apologues. "Lay not up for yourselves," said he, "treasures upon earth, where moth and rust doth corrupt, and where thieves break through and steal; for where your treasure is, there will your heart be also. No man can serve two masters; for either he will hate the one and love the other; or else he will hold to the one and despise the other. Ye cannot serve God and Mammon. Therefore I say unto you, Take no thought for your life, what ye shall eat, or what ye shall drink, nor yet for your body, what ye shall put on. Is not the life more than meat, and the body than raiment? Behold the fowls of the air; for they sow not, neither do they reap, nor gather into barns; yet your heavenly Father feedeth them. Are ye not much better than they? Which of you by taking thought can add one cubit unto his stature? And why take ye thought for raiment? Consider the lilies of the field, how they grow; they toil not, neither do they spin: And yet I say unto you, That even Solomon in all his glory was not arrayed like one of these. Wherefore, if God so clothe the grass of the field, which to-day is, and to-morrow is cast into the oven, shall he not much more clothe you, O ye of little faith? Therefore take no thought, saying, What shall we eat? or, What shall we drink? or, Wherewithal shall we be clothed ? (For after all these things do the Gentiles seek): for your heavenly Father knoweth that ye have need of all these things. But seek ye first the kingdom of God, and his righteousness; and all these things shall be added unto you. Take therefore no thought for the morrow: for the morrow shall take thought for the things of itself. Sufficient unto the day is the evil thereof" (Matt. vi. 19-34).

This essentially Galilean sentiment had a decisive influence upon the destinies of the primitive sect. The happy band, trusting to its Heavenly Father to supply its wants, held, as a fundamental principle, the cares of life to be an evil, which extinguished in man the germ of all that was good. Each day it asked of God the bread for the morrow. Wherefore lay up treasure? The kingdom of God is at hand. "Sell that ye have and give alms," said the Master; "provide yourselves bags which wax not old, a treasure in the heavens that faileth not." What more nonsensical than for one to heap up treasures for heirs one shall never see! As an example of human folly, Jesus loved to cite the case of a man who, when he had enlarged his barns and laid up goods for many years, died before having enjoyed them. Brigandage, which was deeply rooted in Galilee, added much force to this point of view. The poor, who could not suffer from it, came to regard themselves as the favoured of God, whilst the rich, whose possessions were so unsafe, were the people actually disinherited. In our communities, established upon a very rigorous idea in regard to property, the position of the poor is wretched; they have not the right to a spot under the sun. There are no flowers, no grass, no shade except for the one who possesses the earth. In the Orient these are the gifts of God, which belong to no one. The landlord has but a slender privilege; nature is the patrimony of all.

Further, primitive Christianity in those things was only following in the footsteps of the Jewish sects who practised the monastic life. A communistic element pervaded all those sects (Essenians, Therapeutæ), which were looked upon with disfavour equally by Pharisees and Sadducees. The Messianic beliefs, which among the orthodox Jews wore a wholly political aspect, had for the two sects just named a purely social meaning. By means of an easy, regulated, and contemplative mode of life, leaving to each individual freedom of action, these small churches, which were supposed (not wrongly, perhaps) to be an imitation of the neo-pythagorian institutes, thought to inaugurate on earth the kingdom of Heaven. Dreams of a blessed life, founded upon the fraternity of man and the worship of the true God, engrossed exalted intellects, which resulted in bold and sincere attempts being made everywhere, but to no purpose.

Jesus, whose relations with the Essenes it is very difficult to make out (resemblances in history do not always imply relations), was in this unquestionably at one with them. Community of goods was for some time the rule in the new society. Avarice was the cardinal sin. Now, it is necessary to remark that the sin of "avarice," against which moral Christianity has been so severe, was then the mere attachment to property. The first condition of being a perfect disciple of Jesus was to sell one's property and give the proceeds to the poor. Those who recoiled from that step were not admitted into the community. Jesus often repeated that he who finds the kingdom of God must buy it at the sacrifice of all his goods, and that in doing so he makes an advantageous exchange. "Again: The kingdom of heaven is like unto treasure hid in a field; the which when a man hath found, he hideth, and for joy thereof goeth and selleth all that he hath, and buyeth that field. Again: The kingdom of heaven is like unto a merchant-man seeking goodly pearls: who, when he hath found one pearl of great price, he went and sold all that he had, and bought it" (Matt. xiii. 44-46). But, alas! The inconveniences of this method were not long in making themselves felt. A treasurer was required. Judas of Kerioth was chosen for the office. Rightly or wrongly, he was accused of stealing from the common purse; a great antipathy was raised against him--he came to a bad end. Sometimes the Master, better versed in things pertaining to Heaven than in those belonging to earth, taught a political economy yet more remarkable. In a fanciful parable, a steward is praised for having made friends amongst the poor at the expense of the rich, so that the poor in turn might introduce him into the kingdom of Heaven. The poor, in fact, having become the dispensers of this kingdom, would not admit anyone to it unless those who had given them something. A discreet man, thinking of the future, had, therefore, to seek to win their favour. "And the Pharisees, also, who were covetous," says the Evangelist, "heard all these things; and they derided him." Did they also hear the remarkable parable which follows?--"There was a certain rich man, which was clothed in purple and fine linen, and fared sumptuously every day: and there was a certain beggar named Lazarus, which was laid at his gate full of sores, and desiring to be fed with the crumbs which fell from the rich man's table; moreover, the dogs came and licked his sores. And it came to pass that the beggar died, and was carried by the angels into Abraham's bosom: the rich man also died, and was buried; and in hell he lifted up his eyes, being in torments, and seeth Abraham afar off, and Lazarus in his bosom: and he cried and said, Father Abraham, have mercy on me, and send Lazarus, that he may dip the tip of his finger in water and cool my tongue; for I am tormented in this flame. But Abraham said, Son, remember that thou in thy lifetime receivedst thy good things, and likewise Lazarus evil things; but now he is comforted, and thou art tormented" (Luke xvi. 19-25). What could be more just? Later on this was denominated the parable of the "wicked rich man." But it is purely and simply the parable of the rich man. He is in hell because he is rich, because he does not give his goods to the poor, because he dines well, whilst others at his door fare badly. Finally, Jesus, in a less extravagant moment, does not insist on the obligation of selling one's goods and of giving them to the poor, except as suggesting perfection; but he nevertheless makes this terrible declaration:--"It is easier for a camel to go through the eye of a needle than for a rich man to enter into the kingdom of God."

In all this a very admirable sentiment dominated the mind of Jesus as well as the minds of the band of joyous children which accompanied him, and made him the true source of the peace of the soul for eternity, and the grand consoler of life. In disengaging men from what he called "the cares of this world," Jesus may have gone to excess, and struck at the conditions essential to human society; but he founded that high spirituality which has during centuries filled souls with joy in passing through this vale of tears. He saw quite clearly that man's inattention, his want of philosophy and morality, proceeded most often from the amusements he indulges in, from the cares which assail him, and which are multiplied beyond measure by civilisation. The Gospel, in some sort, has been the supreme remedy for the weariness of ordinary life, a perpetual sursum corda, a powerful distraction from the miserable cares of the world, a gentle appeal like that of Jesus to the ear of Martha: "Martha, Martha, thou art careful and troubled about many things; but one thing is needful." Thanks to Jesus, existence the most gloomy, the most absorbed by sad and humiliating duties, has been cheered by a glimpse of heaven! In our troublous civilisations, the recollection of the free life led in Galilee is like perfume from another world, like the "dew of Hermon," which has prevented barrenness and vulgarity from pervading entirely the field of God.

CHAPTER XI

THE KINGDOM OF GOD CONCEIVED AS THE INHERITANCE OF THE POOR.

These maxims--good for a country in which life is nurtured by the air and the light, and that delicate communism of a band of children of God, leaning with confidence on the bosom of their Father--might suit a simple sect which was firmly of the belief that its dreams were about to be realised. But it is evident that such principles did not satisfy the whole of the society. Jesus, in fact, soon perceived that the official world would on no account tolerate his kingdom. He therefore took his resolution with extreme boldness. Putting the world, with its unfeeling heart and its narrow prejudices, on one side, he turned towards the common people. A great substitution of one class for another must take place. The kingdom of God is made: first, for children and for those who resemble them; second, for the outcast of this world, victims of that social arrogance which repels the good though humble man; third, for heretics and schismatics, publicans, Samaritans, and Pagans of Tyre and Sidon. A forcible parable explained and justified that appeal to the people. A king prepares a wedding feast, and sends his servants to seek out those that are invited. Each one of the invited excuses himself; some even maltreat the messengers. The king thereupon takes firm measures. The fashionable people have rejected his invitation. Be it so; he will have the first comers instead, the people collected from the highways and byeways, the poor, the beggars, the lame; it matters not; the room must be filled. "I say unto you," said the king, "that none of those men which were bidden shall taste of my supper."

Pure Ebionism, that is to say, the doctrine that the poor (ebionim) alone shall be saved, that the kingdom of the poor is at hand, was, hence, the doctrine of Jesus. "Woe unto you that are rich," said he, "for ye have received your consolation. Woe unto you that are full, for ye shall hunger. Woe unto you that laugh now! for ye shall mourn and weep" (Luke vi. 24, 25). "Then said he also to him that bade him, When thou makest a dinner or a supper, call not thy friends, nor thy brethren, neither thy kinsmen, nor thy rich neighbours; lest they also bid thee again, and a recompense be made thee. But when thou makest a feast, call the poor, the maimed, the lame, the blind: and thou shalt be blessed; for they cannot recompense thee: for thou shalt be recompensed at the resurrection of the just" (Luke xiv. 12-14). It is, in an analogous sense, perhaps, that he often repeated, "Be good bankers"--that is to say, make good investments for the kingdom of God, in giving your wealth to the poor, conformably to the old proverb, "He that hath pity upon the poor lendeth unto the Lord" (Prov. xix. 17).

But this was no new fact. The most exalted democratic movement, the memory of which has been preserved by mankind (the only one, also, that has succeeded, for it alone has maintained itself in the domain of pure thought) had agitated for a long time the Jewish race. The idea that God is the avenger of the poor and of the weak against the rich and powerful is found in every page of the books of the Old Testament. The history of Israel is, of all histories, that in which the popular notions have most certainly predominated. The prophets, the truest, and in a sense the boldest tribunes, had thundered incessantly against the great, and had established a close relation between the terms "rich, impious, violent, wicked," on the one hand, and between "poor, gentle, humble, pious," on the other. Under the Seleucidæ, the aristocracy having almost all apostatised and gone over to Hellenism, these associations of ideas were but strengthened. The Book of Enoch contains even fiercer maledictions against the world, the rich, and the powerful than those of the Gospels. In this book luxury is held up as a crime. "The Son of Man," in that fantastic apocalypse, dethrones kings, tears them away from their voluptuous life and plunges them into hell. The initiation of Judæa into profane life, the recent introduction of an exclusively worldly element of luxury and of comfort, provoked a violent reaction in favour of patriarchal simplicity. "Woe unto you who despise the humble dwelling and inheritance of your fathers? Woe unto you who build your palaces with the sweat of others! Each stone, each brick of which it is built is a sin." The word "poor" (ebion) had become a synonym of "saint," of "friend of God." This was the appellation the Galilean disciples of Jesus loved to give one another: it was for a long time the designation of the Judaising Christians of Batanea, and of the Hauran (Nazarenes, Hebrews) who remained faithful to the language as well as to the earlier teachings of Jesus, and who boasted of having amongst them the descendants of his family. At the end of the second century, these devout sectaries, who had lived outside the path of the great current that had carried away the other churches, were treated as heretics (Ebionites), and in order to explain their name a pretended heresiarch, Ebion, was invented.

We may see, at a glance, that this exaggerated taste for poverty could not be very durable. It was one of those Utopian elements which always mingle in the origin of great movements, and which time rectifies. Thrown into the centre of human society, Christianity very easily consented to receive rich men into her bosom, just as Buddhism, exclusively monastical in its origin, soon began, as conversions multiplied, to admit the laity. But the mark of origin is ever preserved. Although it quickly passed away and was forgotten, Ebionism left a leaven in the whole history of Christian institutions which has not been lost. The collection of the principal Λόγια, or discourses, of Jesus was made in the Ebionitish centre of Batanea. "Poverty" remained an ideal from which the true followers of Jesus were never after separated. To possess nothing was the truly evangelical state; mendicancy became a virtue, a holy condition. The great Umbrian movement of the thirteenth century, which is, among all the attempts at religious construction, that which most resembles the Galilean movement, took place entirely in the name of poverty. Francis d'Assisi, the man who, more than any other, by his exquisite goodness, by his delicate, pure, and tender communion with universal life, most resembled Jesus, was a poor man. The mendicant orders, the innumerable communistic sects of the middle ages (Pauvres de Lyon, Bégards, Bons-Hommes, Fratricelles, Humiliés, Pauvres évangéliques, &c.) grouped under the banner of the "Everlasting Gospel," pretended to be, and in fact were, the true disciples of Jesus. But even in this instance the most impracticable dreams of the new religion were fruitful in results. Pious mendicity, so impatiently borne by our industrial and well-organised communities, was in its day, and in a suitable climate, full of charm. It offered to a multitude of mild and contemplative souls the only condition suited to them. To have made poverty an object of love and desire, to have raised the beggar to the altar, and to have sanctified the coat of the poor man, was a master-stroke which political economy may not appreciate, but in the presence of which the true moralist cannot remain indifferent. Humanity, in order to bear its burden, needs to believe that it is not paid entirely by wages. The greatest service which can be rendered to it is to repeat often that it lives not by bread alone.

Like all great men, Jesus loved the people, and felt himself at home with them. The Gospel, in his idea, is made for the poor; it is to them he brings the glad tidings of salvation. All the despised ones of orthodox Judaism were his favourites. Love of the people and pity for its weakness (the sentiment of the democratic chief, who feels the spirit of the multitude live in him, and recognises him as its natural interpreter) shine forth at each moment in his acts and discourses.

The chosen flock presented, in fact, a very mixed character, and one likely to astonish rigorous moralists. It counted in its fold men with whom a Jew, respecting himself, would not have associated. Perhaps Jesus found in this society, unrestrained by ordinary rules, more mind and heart than in a pedantic and formal middle-class, proud of its apparent morality. The Pharisees, exaggerating the Mosaic prescriptions, had come to believe themselves defiled by contact with men less strict than themselves; in their meals they almost rivalled the senseless distinctions of caste in India. Jesus, despising these miserable aberrations of the religious sentiment, loved to eat with those who suffered on account of them; by his side at table were to be found persons said to lead wicked lives, perhaps solely from the fact that they did not share the follies of the false devotees. The Pharisees and the doctors cried out against the scandal. "See," said they, "with what men he eats!" Jesus returned apt answers, which exasperated the hypocrites: "They that be whole need not a physician." Or again: "What man of you, having an hundred sheep, if he lose one of them, doth not leave the ninety and nine in the wilderness, and go after that which is lost until he find it? And when he hath found it he layeth it on his shoulders rejoicing." Or again, "The Son of man is come to save that which was lost." Or, once more: "I am not come to call the righteous, but sinners." Lastly, that delightful parable of the prodigal son, in which he who has fallen is represented as having a sort of privilege of love over him who has always been just. Weak or guilty women, surprised at so much that was charming, and perceiving, for the first time, the great attractions of contact with virtue, approached him freely. People were astonished that he did not repulse them. "Now when the Pharisee which had bidden him saw it, he spake within himself, saying, This man, if he were a prophet, would have known who and what manner of woman this is that toucheth him: for she is a sinner." Jesus rejoined with the parable of a creditor who forgives his debtors' unequal debts, and he did not hesitate to prefer the lot of him to whom was remitted the greater debt. He appreciated conditions of soul only in proportion to the love contained therein. Women, with sorrowful hearts, and disposed on account of their sins to feelings of humility, were nearer to his kingdom than ordinary natures, who often are deserving of little credit for not having fallen. On the other hand, we can conceive that these tender souls, finding in their conversion to the sect an easy means of rehabilitation, would passionately attach themselves to him.

Far from seeking to allay the murmurs raised by his disdain for the social susceptibilities of the time, he seemed to take pleasure in exciting them. Never did any one avow more loftily this contempt for the "world," which is the first condition of great things and of great originality. He pardoned the rich man only when the rich man, because of some prejudice, was disliked by society. He much preferred people of questionable lives and who had little consideration in the eyes of the orthodox leaders. "The publicans and the harlots go into the kingdom of God before you. For John came unto you and ye believed him not: but the publicans and the harlots believed him." We can understand how galling the reproach of not having followed the good example set by prostitutes would be to men making a profession of seriousness and of rigid morality.

He had no outward affectation or any show of austerity. He did not eschew pleasure; he went willingly to marriage feasts. One of his miracles was performed to enliven a wedding feast at a small town. In the East, weddings take place in the evening. Each person carries a lamp; and the lights coming and going produce a very agreeable effect. Jesus liked these gay and animated scenes and drew parables from them. Such levity, compared with that of John the Baptist, gave offence. One day, when the disciples of John and the Pharisees were observing the fast, it was asked, "Why do the disciples of John and of the Pharisees fast, but thy disciples fast not? And Jesus said unto them, Can the children of the bridechamber fast, while the bridegroom is with them? As long as they have the bridegroom with them they cannot fast. But the days will come when the bridegroom shall be taken away from them, and then they shall fast in those days." His sweet gaiety found expression in lively reflections and amiable pleasantries "But whereunto," said he, "shall I liken this generation? It is like unto children sitting in the markets, and calling unto their fellows, and saying, We have piped unto you, and ye have not danced; we have mourned unto you, and ye have not lamented. For John came neither eating nor drinking, and they say, He hath a devil. The Son of man came eating and drinking, and they say, Behold a man gluttonous, and a winebibber, a friend of publicans and sinners. But Wisdom is justified of her children."

He thus traversed Galilee in the midst of a continual feast. He rode on a mule (which in the East is a good and safe mode of travelling), whose large black eyes, shaded by long eye-lashes, give it an expression of gentleness. His disciples sometimes disposed themselves around him with a kind of rustic pomp, at the expense of their garments, which they used as carpets. They placed them on the mule which carried him, or spread them on the earth in his path. When he entered a house it was considered a joy and a blessing. He halted in the villages and at the large farms, where he received open hospitality. In the East, when a stranger enters a house it becomes at once a public place. All the village assembles there; the children invade it; they are put out by the servants, but always return. Jesus could not suffer these innocent auditors to be treated harshly; he caused them to be brought to him and embraced them. The mothers, encouraged by such treatment, brought him their children in order that he might touch them. Women came to pour oil upon his head, and perfumes on his feet. His disciples sometimes repulsed them as importunates; but Jesus, who loved ancient usages, and everything that indicated simplicity of heart, rectified the ill done by his too zealous friends. He protected those who wished to honour him. In this way children and women came to adore him. The reproach of alienating from their families these gentle creatures, always ready to be led astray, was one of the most frequent charges of his enemies.

The nascent religion was thus in many respects confined to women and children. The latter were like a young guard around Jesus for the inauguration of his innocent royalty, and made him little ovations which much pleased him, calling him "son of David," crying Hosanna, and bearing palms around him. Jesus, like Savonarola, perhaps made them serve as instruments for pious missions; he was very glad to see these young apostles, who did not compromise him, rush to the front and give him titles which he dared not take himself. He let them speak, and when he was asked if he heard, he replied evasively that the praise which fell from young lips was the most agreeable to God.

He lost no opportunity of repeating that the little ones are sacred beings, that the kingdom of God belongs to children, that we must become children to enter there, that we ought to receive it as a child, that the heavenly Father hides his secrets from the wise, and reveals them to babes. The notion of disciples in his mind is almost synonymous with that of children. Once, when they had one of those quarrels for precedence which were not uncommon, Jesus took a little child, placed him in their midst, and said to them, "Whosoever therefore shall humble himself as this little child, the same is greatest in the kingdom of heaven."

It was infancy, in fact, in its divine freshness, in its simple bewilderments of joy, which took possession of the earth. Every one believed that the kingdom so much desired might appear at any moment. Each one already saw himself seated on a throne beside the master. They divided the places amongst themselves; they strove to reckon the precise date of its advent. The latter was called the "Glad Tidings;" the doctrine had no other name. An old word, "paradise," which the Hebrew, like all the languages of the East, had borrowed from the Persian, and which at first designated the parks of the Achæmenidæ kings, summed up the general dream; a delightful garden, in which the charming life led here below would be continued for ever. How long did this intoxication last? We do not know. No one, during the course of this magical apparition, measured time any more than we measure a dream. Duration was suspended; a week was as an age. But, whether it filled years or months, the dream was so beautiful that humanity has lived upon it ever since, and it is still our consolation to gather its weakened perfume. Never did so much joy fill the bosom of man. For one moment humanity, in the most vigorous effort she ever made to rise above the world, forgot the leaden weight which pressed her to earth and the sorrows of the life below. Happy the one who has been able to behold this divine unfolding, and to enjoy, though but for one day, this unexampled illusion! But more happy still, Jesus would say to us, is he who, freed from all illusion, shall reproduce in himself the celestial vision, and, with no millenarian dream, no chimerical paradise, no signs in the heavens, but by the uprightness of his motives and the poetry of his soul, shall be able to create anew in his heart the true kingdom of God!

CHAPTER XII

EMBASSY TO JESUS FROM JOHN IN PRISON--DEATH OF JOHN--THE RELATIONS OF HIS SCHOOL WITH THAT OF JESUS

Whilst joyous Galilee was celebrating in feasts the coming of the well-beloved, the disconsolate John, in his prison of Machero, was pining away with expectation and desire. The success of the young master whom he had seen some months before as his auditor had reached him. It was said that the Messiah predicted by the prophets, he who was to re-establish the kingdom of Israel, had come, and was making known his presence in Galilee by marvellous works. John wished to inquire into the truth of this rumour, and, as he was allowed to communicate freely with his disciples, he chose two of them to go to Jesus in Galilee.

The two disciples found Jesus at the height of his fame. The appearance of happiness which reigned around him surprised them. Accustomed to fasts, to earnest prayer, and to a life full of aspirations, they were astonished to see themselves transported suddenly into the midst of welcome rejoicings. They told Jesus their message: "Art thou he that should come? Or do we look for another?" Jesus, who from that time hesitated no longer respecting his peculiar character as Messiah, enumerated to them the works which ought to characterise the coming of the kingdom of God--such as the healing of the sick, and the glad tidings of a salvation near at hand preached to the poor. He had done all these works. "And blessed is he," said Jesus, "whosoever shall not be offended in me."

We do not know whether this answer reached John the Baptist, or into what temper it threw the austere ascetic. Did he die consoled and certain that he whom he had announced already lived, or did he retain some doubts as to the mission of Jesus? There is nothing to inform us. Seeing, however, that his school continued to exist a considerable time side by side with the Christian churches, we are constrained to believe that, notwithstanding his regard for Jesus, John did not regard him as the one who was to realise the divine promises. Death came, moreover, to end his perplexities. The untamable freedom of the ascetic was to crown his restless and troubled career by the only end which was worthy of it.

The indulgence which Antipas had at first shown towards John was not of long duration. In the conversations which, according to the Christian tradition, John had had with the tetrarch, he did not cease repeating to him that his marriage was unlawful, and that he ought to send Herodias away. We can easily imagine the hatred which the grand-daughter of Herod the Great must have engendered against this importunate counsellor. She only waited an opportunity to ruin him.

Her daughter, Salome, by her first marriage, and like her ambitious and dissolute, entered into her designs. That year (probably the year 30) Antipas was at Machero on the anniversary of his birthday. Herod the Great had caused to be constructed in the interior of the fortress a magnificent palace, in which the tetrarch frequently resided. He gave a great feast there, during which Salome executed one of those character dances which were not considered in Syria as unbecoming a distinguished person. Antipas, being greatly delighted, asked the dancer what she most desired, who, at the instigation of her mother, replied, "Give me here John Baptist's head in a charger." Antipas was sorry, but he could not refuse. A guard took the charger, went and cut off the head of the prisoner, and brought it.

The disciples of the Baptist obtained his body and placed it in a tomb. The people were much offended. Six years later, Hâreth having attacked Antipas, in order to recover Machero and avenge the dishonour of his daughter, Antipas was completely beaten; and his defeat was generally regarded as a punishment for the murder of John.

The news of John's death was brought to Jesus by the disciples of the Baptist. The last step John had taken in regard to Jesus had succeeded in establishing between the two schools the most intimate bonds. Jesus, fearing an increase of ill-will on the part of Antipas, took the precaution to retire to the desert. Many people followed him thence. Thanks to a strict frugality, the holy band succeeded in living there, and in this there was naturally seen a miracle From that time Jesus always spoke of John with redoubled admiration. He declared unhesitatingly that he was more than a prophet, that the Law and the ancient prophets had force only until he came, that he had abrogated them, but that the kingdom of heaven in turn had superseded him. In fine, he assigned him a special place in the economy of the Christian mystery, which constituted him the link of union between the Old Testament and the advent of the new reign.

The prophet Malachi, whose opinion in this matter was soon brought to bear, had persistently declared a precursor of the Messiah, who was to prepare men for the final renovation, a messenger who should come to make straight the paths before the elected of God. This messenger was none other than the prophet Elias, who, according to a widely-spread belief, was soon to descend from heaven, whither he had been carried, in order to prepare men by repentance for the great advent, and to reconcile God with His people. Sometimes they associated with Elias either the patriarch Enoch, to whom for one or two centuries they had been attributing high sanctity; or Jeremiah, whom they regarded as a sort of protecting genius of the people, constantly occupied in praying for them before the throne of God. This idea, of two of the old prophets rising again, to act as precursors to the Messiah, is discovered in so striking a form in the doctrine of the Parsees that we feel much inclined to believe that it comes from that source. Be that as it may, it formed at the time of Jesus an integral portion of the Jewish theories in regard to the Messiah. It was admitted that the appearance of "two faithful witnesses," clothed in garments of repentance, would be the preamble of the great drama about to be unfolded, to the astonishment of the universe.

We can understand that, with these ideas, Jesus and his disciples could not hesitate about the mission of John the Baptist. When the scribes raised the objection that it could not yet be a question of the Messiah, inasmuch as Elias had not yet appeared, they replied that Elias had come, that John was Elias raised from the dead. By his manner of life, by his opposition to the established political authorities, John recalled, in fact, that strange figure in the ancient history of Israel. Nor was Jesus silent in regard to the merits and excellences of his forerunner. He said that among the children of men none greater had been born. He vehemently blamed the Pharisees and the doctors for not having accepted his baptism, and for not being converted at his voice.

The disciples of Jesus were faithful to these principles of their master. Respect for John was an unquestioned tradition during the whole of the first Christian generation. He was supposed to be a relative of Jesus. His baptism was regarded as the most important fact, and, in some sort, as the prefatory obligation of all gospel history. In order to establish the mission of the son of Joseph upon testimony admitted by all, it was stated that John, at the first sight of Jesus, proclaimed him the Messiah; that he recognised himself his inferior, unworthy to unloose the latchets of his shoes; that he refused at first to baptize him, and maintained that it was he who ought to be baptized by Jesus. These were exaggerations, which are sufficiently refuted by the doubtful form of John's last message. But, in a more general sense, John remains in the Christian legend that which he was in reality,--the austere forerunner, the gloomy preacher of repentance before the joy on the arrival of the bridegroom, the prophet who announces the kingdom of God and dies before beholding it. This giant in primitive Christianity, this eater of locusts and wild honey, this rugged redresser of wrongs, was the absinthe which prepared the lip for the sweetness of the kingdom of God. His beheading by Herodias inaugurated the era of Christian martyrs; he was the first witness for the new faith. The worldly, who regarded him their true enemy, could not permit him to live; his mutilated corpse, extended on the threshold of Christianity, indicated the bloody path in which so many others were to follow.

The school of John did not die with its founder. It existed some time distinct from that of Jesus, and from the first on good terms with the latter. Many years after the death of the two masters, people were still baptized with the baptism of John. Certain persons were members of the two schools at the same time,--for example, the celebrated Apollos, the rival of St. Paul (about the year 54), and a goodly number of the Christians of Ephesus. Josephus entered in the year 53 the school of an ascetic named Banou, who presents a striking resemblance to John the Baptist, and who was perhaps of his school. This Banou lived in the desert, and was clothed with the leaves of trees. His only nourishment was wild plants and fruits, and he baptized himself frequently, both day and night, in cold water, in order to purify himself. James, who was called the "brother of the Lord," practised a similar asceticism. Later, about the year 80, Baptism was in conflict with Christianity, especially in Asia Minor. The author of the writings attributed to John the evangelist appears to combat it in an indirect manner. One of the Sibylline poems seems to proceed from this school. As to the sects of Hemerobaptists, Baptists, and Elchasaïtes (Sabiens, Mogtasila of the Arabian writers), who in the second century filled Syria, Palestine, and Babylonia, and whose representatives still exist in our days among the Mendaites, called "Christians of St. John," they had the same origin as the movement of John the Baptist rather than being an authentic descent from him. The true school of John, half Christian in its character, became a small Christian sect, and died out in obscurity. John had distinctly foreseen the destiny of the two schools. If he had yielded to a pitiful rivalry, he would to-day be forgotten in the crowd of sectaries of his time. By his self-abnegation, he has attained a glorious and unique position in the religious pantheon of humanity.

CHAPTER XIII

FIRST ATTEMPTS ON JERUSALEM.

Jesus went almost every year to Jerusalem for the feast of the passover. The particulars of these journeys are meagre, for the synoptics do not speak of them, and the remarks in the fourth Gospel are on this point very confused. It was, it would seem, in the year 31, and certainly after the death of John, that the most important of the visits of Jesus to Jerusalem took place. Several of the disciples followed him. Although Jesus attached at that time little value to the pilgrimage, he conformed himself to it in order not to offend Jewish opinion, with which he had not yet broken. These journeys besides were essential to his design; for he felt already that, in order to play a leading part, he must go from Galilee, and attack Judaism in its stronghold, which was Jerusalem.

The little Galilean community was here by no means at home. Jerusalem was then nearly what it is to-day, a city of pedantry, acrimony, disputes, hatreds, and littleness of mind. Its fanaticism was extreme, and religious seditions were very frequent. The Pharisees were dominant; the study of the Law, pushed to the most insignificant minutiae, and reduced to questions of casuistry, was the only study. This exclusively theological and canonical culture contributed in nowise to refine the intellect. It was something analogous to the barren doctrine of the Mussulman fakir, to that empty science debated round the mosques, which is a great expenditure of time and a pure waste of dialectical skill, without aiding the right discipline of the mind. The theological education of the modern clergy, although very dry, can give us no idea of this, for the Renaissance has introduced into all our teachings, even the most extravagant, something of belles lettres and of method, the consequence of which is that scholasticism has taken a taint, more or less, of the humanities. The science of the Jewish doctor, of the sofer, or scribe, was purely barbarous, absurd beyond measure, and stripped of all moral element. To cap the evil, it filled with ridiculous pride those who had wearied themselves in acquiring it. Proud of the pretended knowledge which had cost him so much trouble, the Jewish scribe had the same contempt for Greek culture as the learned Mussulman of our time has for European civilisation, as the old catholic theologian had for the knowledge of men of the world. The tendency of this scholastic culture was to turn the mind against all that was refined, to create esteem only for those childish difficulties on which they had wasted their lives, and which were regarded as the natural occupation of persons making a profession of seriousness.

This odious society could not but weigh very heavily on the tender and susceptible northern mind. The contempt of the Jerusalemites for the Galileans rendered the separation still more complete. In that beautiful temple, the object of all their desires, they often only experienced insult. A verse of the pilgrim's psalm, "I had rather be a doorkeeper in the house of my God," seemed expressly made for them. A contemptuous priest-hood laughed at their simple devotion, just as formerly in Italy the clergy, familiarised with the sanctuaries, witnessed coldly and almost jestingly the fervour of the pilgrim arriving from afar. The Galileans spoke a rather corrupt dialect, their pronunciation was faulty; they confounded diverse aspirates which led to mistakes that were much laughed at. In religion, they were regarded as ignorant and not very orthodox; the expression "foolish Galileans" had become proverbial. It was believed (not without reason) that they were not of pure Jewish blood, and it was held, as a matter of course, that Galilee could not produce a prophet. Placed thus on the confines of Judaism, nay almost outside of it, the poor Galileans had only one badly interpreted passage in Isaiah on which to build their hopes. "Land of Zebulon, and land of Naphtali, way of the sea, Galilee of the nations! The people that walked in darkness have seen a great light: they that dwell in the land of the shadow of death, upon them hath the light shined." The reputation of the native city of Jesus was particularly bad. It was a popular proverb, "Can there any good thing come out of Nazareth?"

The great barrenness of nature in the neighbourhood of Jerusalem must have added to the dislike Jesus had for the place. The valleys are without water; the soil is arid and stony. Casting the eye into the valley of the Dead Sea, the view is somewhat striking; elsewhere it is monotonous. The hill of Mizpeh, around which clusters the most ancient historical remembrances of Israel, alone relieves the eye. The city presented, at the time of Jesus, nearly the same aspect that it does now. It had very few ancient monuments, for until the time of the Asmoneans the Jews had remained strangers to all the arts. John Hyrcanus had begun to embellish it, and Herod the Great had made it one of the most magnificent cities of the East. The Herodian constructions, by their grand character, perfection of execution, and beauty of material, may dispute superiority with the most finished works of antiquity. A great number of superb tombs, displaying original taste, were erected at the same time in the neighbourhood of Jerusalem. The style of these monuments was Grecian, but appropriate to the customs of the Jews, and considerably modified in accordance with their principles. The ornamental sculptures of the human figure which the Herods had sanctioned, to the great disgust of the purists, were discarded and superseded by floral decorations. The taste of the ancient inhabitants of Phoenicia and Palestine for monoliths cut out of the solid rock seemed to be revived in these singular tombs cut in the rock, and in which Grecian orders are so strangely applied to an architect of troglodytes. Jesus, who regarded works of art as a pompous display of vanity, viewed these monuments with displeasure. His absolute spiritualism, and his settled conviction that the form of the old world was about to pass away, left him only a taste for things belonging to the heart.

The temple, at the time of Jesus, was quite new, while its exterior works were not yet completed. Herod had begun its reconstruction in the year 20 or 21 before the Christian era, in order to make it uniform with his other edifices. The main body of the temple was finished in eighteen months; the porticoes took eight years; and the accessory portions were raised slowly, and were only finished a short time before the taking of Jerusalem. Jesus probably saw the work progressing, not without a degree of secret vexation. These hopes of a long future seemed an insult to his approaching advent. Clearer-sighted than the unbelievers and the fanatics, he foresaw that these superb edifices would have but a short duration.

The temple, nevertheless, formed a marvellously imposing whole, of which the present haram, in spite of its beauty, can scarcely give us any idea. The courts and the porticoes served as the daily rendezvous for a considerable gathering, so much so that this great space was at once temple forum, tribunal, and university. All the religious discussions of the Jewish schools, all the canonical instruction, even the legal processes and civil causes, all the activity of the nation, in short, was concentrated there. It was a place where arguments were perpetually clashing, a battle-field of disputes, resounding with sophisms and subtle questions. The temple thus resembled much a Mahometan mosque. At this period the Romans treated all strange religions with the greatest respect, provided they were kept within proper limits, and carefully refrained from entering the sanctuary; Greek and Latin inscriptions marked the point up to which those who were not Jews were permitted to advance. But the tower of Antonia, the headquarters of the Roman forces, commanded the whole enclosure, and enabled them to see all that passed therein. The guarding of the temple belonged to the Jews; its superintendence was entrusted to a captain, who caused the gates to be opened and shut, prohibited any one from crossing the enclosure with a stick in his hand, or with dusty shoes, or when carrying parcels, or to take a near cut. They were especially scrupulous in watching that no one entered within the inner gates in a state of legal impurity. The women had an entirely separate court.

It was in the temple that Jesus passed his days, whilst he remained at Jerusalem. The period of the feasts attracted to the city extraordinary affluence. Lodged in parties of ten to twenty persons in one chamber, the pilgrims invaded every quarter and lived in that huddled state in which Orientals delight. Jesus was lost in the crowd, and his poor Galileans who grouped around him were of small account. He probably felt that there he was in a hostile world which would receive him only with disdain. Everything he saw he disapproved of. The temple, like all much-frequented places of devotion, presented a not very edifying spectacle. The service of this entailed a multitude of repulsive enough details, especially of mercantile operations, in consequence of which actual shops were established within the sacred enclosure. There people sold beasts for the sacrifices; there one found tables for the exchange of money; at times it seemed as if one were in a bazaar. The inferior officers of the temple fulfilled, doubtless, their functions with the irreligious vulgarity characteristic of the sacristans of all ages. This profane and indifferent air in the handling of holy things wounded the religious sentiment of Jesus, sometimes leading him to excess. He said that they had made the house of prayer a den of thieves. One day, in fact, it is said, that, carried away by his anger, he scourged the vendors with a "scourge of small cords," and overturned their tables. In general, he cared little for the temple. The worship that he had conceived for his Father had nothing to do with scenes of butchery. All these old Jewish institutions displeased him, and he was pained in being obliged to conform to them. Thus, neither the temple nor its site inspired pious sentiments in the bosom of Christianity, except in the case of the Judaising Christians. The true proselytes had an aversion to this ancient sanctuary. Constantine and the first Christian emperors left the Pagan constructions of Hadrian standing there. It was the enemies of Christianity, such as Julian, who remembered the temple. When Omar entered Jerusalem, the site of the temple was designedly polluted in hatred of the Jews. It was Islamism, that is to say, a sort of resurrection of Judaism, in its most Semitic form, which rendered it honours The place has always been antichristian.

The pride of the Jews completed the discontent of Jesus, and rendered his sojourn in Jerusalem painful. In proportion as the great ideas of Israel ripened, the priesthood were debased. The institution of synagogues had given to the interpreter of the Law, to the doctor, a great superiority over the priest. There were no priests except at Jerusalem, and even there, reduced to entirely ritual functions, almost, like our parish priests, excluded from preaching, they were surpassed by the orator of the synagogue, the casuist, the sofer or scribe, though the latter was but a layman. The celebrated men of the Talmud were not priests; they were learned men according to the ideas of the time. The high priesthood of Jerusalem held, it is true, a very elevated rank in the nation; but it was by no means at the head of the religious movement. The sovereign pontiff, whose dignity had already been degraded by Herod, became more and more a Roman functionary, who was frequently removed in order that others might share the profits of the office. Opposed to the Pharisees, who were important lay zealots, the priests were almost all Sadducees, that is to say, members of that unbelieving aristocracy which had been formed around the temple, lived by the altar, though they saw the vanity of it. The sacerdotal caste was separated to such a degree from the national sentiment and from the great religious movement which urged the people on, that the name of "Sadducee" (sadoki), which at first simply designated a member of the sacerdotal family of Sadok, had become synonymous with "Materialist" and with "Epicurean."

An element worse still had begun, since the reign of Herod the Great, to corrupt the high-priesthood. Herod having fallen in love with Mariamne, daughter of a certain Simon, son of Boëthus of Alexandria, and having wished to marry her (about the year 28 J.C.), saw no other means of ennobling his father-in-law and raising him to his own rank than by making him high-priest. This intriguing family remained masters, almost without interruption, of the sovereign pontificate for thirty-five years. Closely allied to the reigning family, it did not lose the office until after the deposition of Archelaus, and recovered it (the year 42 of our era) after Herod Agrippa had for some time recommenced the work of Herod the Great. Under the name of Boëthusim, a new sacerdotal nobility was formed, which was very worldly, being little devotional, and closely allied to the Sadokites. The Boëthusim, in the Talmud and the rabbinical writings, are depicted as a kind of unbelievers, and always reproached as Sadducees. From all this there resulted a kind of "court of Rome" around the temple, living by politics, little carried away by excess of zeal, even rather fearing them, not wishing to hear of holy personages or of innovators, for this "court" derived profit from the established routine. These epicurean priests had not the violence of the Pharisees; they only wished for quietness; it was their moral indifference, their cold irreligion, which revolted Jesus. Although quite distinct, the priests and the Pharisees were thus confounded in his antipathies. But being a stranger, and without influence, he was long compelled to restrain his displeasure within himself, and only to communicate his sentiments to the intimate friends who accompanied him.

Before his last stay, much more protracted than any he had made at Jerusalem, and which was terminated by his death, Jesus endeavoured, however, to make himself heard. He preached; people spoke of him; and they conversed upon certain acts of his which were looked upon as miraculous. But from all that there resulted neither an established church at Jerusalem, nor a group of Jerusalemite disciples. The charming lawgiver, who forgave everyone provided they but loved him, could not find much response in this sanctuary of vain disputes and of obsolete sacrifices. The sole result was that he formed some valuable friendships, the advantage of which he reaped afterwards. He does not appear at that time to have made the acquaintance of the family of Bethany, which, amidst the trials of the latter months of his life, brought him so much consolation. But perhaps he had relations with that Mary, mother of Mark (whose house became some years later the rendezvous of the apostles), and with Mark himself. But very early he attracted the attention of a certain Nicodemus, a rich Pharisee, a member of the Sanhedrim, and a man highly considered in Jerusalem. This man, who appears to have been upright and sincere, felt himself drawn towards the young Galilean. Not wishing to compromise himself, he came to see Jesus by night, and had a long conversation with him. He undoubtedly preserved a favourable impression of him, for later on he defended Jesus against the prejudices of his colleagues, and, at the death of Jesus, we find him tending with pious care the corpse of the master. Nicodemus did not become a Christian; he had too much regard for his position to take part in a revolutionary movement which as yet numbered no men of note amongst its adherents. But he evidently had much friendship for Jesus, and rendered him service, though powerless to rescue him from a death which even at this period was all but decreed.

As to the celebrated doctors of the time, Jesus does not appear to have had any connection with them. Hillel and Shammai were dead; the greatest authority of the day was Gamaliel, grandson of Hillel. He had a liberal mind, was a man of the world, open to secular opinions, and rendered tolerant by his intercourse with good society. Differing from the very strict Pharisees, who walked veiled or with closed eyes, he gazed even upon Pagan women. The sectaries excused this, as well as a knowledge of Greek in him, because he had access to the court. After the death of Jesus he expressed very moderate views in regard to the new sect. St. Paul sat at his feet, but it is highly improbable that Jesus ever entered his school.

One idea, at least, which Jesus carried away from Jerusalem, and which henceforth appeared to be rooted in his mind, was that there was no union possible between him and the ancient Jewish religion.

The abolition of the sacrifices, which had caused him so much disgust, the suppression of an impious and haughty priesthood, and, in a general sense, the abrogation of the Law, appeared to him an absolute necessity! From this moment he is no longer a Jewish reformer, but it is as a destroyer of Judaism that he poses. Some advocates of the Messianic notions had already admitted that the Messiah would bring a new law, which should be common to all people. The Essenes, who were scarcely Jews, appear also to have been indifferent to the temple and to the Mosaic observances. But these were only isolated or unavowed instances of boldness. Jesus was the first who dared to say that from his time, or rather from that of John, the Law was abolished. If sometimes he used more guarded terms it was in order not to shock too violently existing prejudices. When he was driven to extremities he lifted the veil entirely, and declared that the Law had no longer any force. On this subject he used striking comparisons. "No man putteth a piece of new cloth into an old garment, neither do men put new wine into old bottles." Herein lies his chief characteristic as teacher and originator. The temple excluded all except Jews from its enclosure by scornful placards. Jesus did not approve this. That narrow, hard, and uncharitable Law was only made for the children of Abraham. Jesus maintained that every well-disposed man, every man who received and loved him, was a son of Abraham. The pride of blood appeared to him the chief enemy that he had to combat. In other words, Jesus was no longer a Jew. He was in the highest degree revolutionary; he called all men to a worship founded solely on the fact of their being children of God. He proclaimed the rights of man, not the rights of the Jew; the religion of man, not the religion of the Jew; the deliverance of man, not the deliverance of the Jew. Ah! how far removed was this from a Gaulonite Judas or a Matthias Margaloth, preaching revolution in the name of the Law! The religion of humanity was thus established, not upon blood, but upon the heart. Moses was superseded, the temple was rendered useless, and was irrevocably condemned.

CHAPTER XIV

RELATIONS OF JESUS WITH THE PAGANS AND THE SAMARITANS

As a consequence of these principles, Jesus contemned all religion which was not of the heart. The foolish practices of the devotees, the exterior rigorism, which trusted to formality for salvation, had in him a mortal enemy. He cared little for fasting. He preferred forgiving an injury to sacrifice. The love of God, charity and reciprocal forgiveness, were his whole law. Nothing could be less priestly. The priest, by virtue of his office, ever advocates public sacrifice, of which he is the appointed minister; he discourages private prayer, which is a means of dispensing with his office. We should seek in vain in the Gospel for one religious rite recommended by Jesus. Baptism to him was only of secondary importance; and as to prayer, he prescribes nothing, except that it must come from the heart. As is always the case, many thought to substitute the good-will of feeble souls for genuine love of goodness, and imagined they could gain the kingdom of heaven by saying to him, "Rabbi, Rabbi," but he rebuked them, and proclaimed that his religion consisted in doing good. He often quoted the passage in Isaiah, "This people honour me with their lips, but their heart is far from me."

The Sabbath was the principal point upon which was raised the whole edifice of Pharisaic scruples and subtleties. This ancient and excellent institution had become a pretext for the miserable disputes of casuists, and a source of a thousand superstitious beliefs. It was believed that nature observed it; all intermittent sources were accounted "Sabbatical." This was, moreover, the point upon which Jesus most delighted in defying his adversaries. He openly violated the Sabbath, and only replied by subtle raillery to the reproaches that were heaped upon him. For a still stronger reason he despised a host of modern observances, which tradition had added to the Law, and which on that very account were dearer than any other to the devotees. Ablutions, and the too subtle distinctions between things pure and impure, found in him a pitiless opponent. "There is nothing from without a man," said he, "that entering into him can defile him: but the things which come out of him, those are they that defile the man." The Pharisees, who were the propagators of these mummeries, were the target for all his attacks. He accused them of exceeding the Law, of inventing impracticable precepts, in order to create occasions of sin in man: "Blind leaders of the blind," said he, "take care lest ye also fall into the ditch." "O generation of vipers, how can ye, being evil, speak good things for out of the abundance of the heart the mouth speaketh."

He was not sufficiently acquainted with the Gentiles to think of founding anything lasting upon their conversion. Galilee contained a great number of Pagans, but, as it appears, no public and organised worship of false gods. Jesus could see this worship displayed in all its splendour in the country of Tyre and Sidon, at Cæsarea Philippi and in the Decapolis, but he paid little attention to it. In him we never find the wearisome Jewish pedantry of his time, nor those declamations against idolatry so familiar to his co-religionists from the time of Alexander, and which fill, for instance, the book of "Wisdom." That which struck him in the Pagans was not their idolatry, but their servility. The young Jewish democrat agreeing on this point with Judas the Gaulonite, admitting no master but God, was hurt at the honours with which they surrounded the persons of sovereigns, and the mendacious titles frequently given to them. With this exception, in the greater number of instances in which he comes in contact with Pagans, he shows towards them great indulgence; sometimes he professes to conceive more hope of them than of the Jews. The kingdom of God is to be transferred to them. "When the lord, therefore, of the vineyard cometh, what will he do unto these husbandmen? He will miserably destroy those wicked men, and will let out his vine-yard unto other husbandmen, which shall render him the fruits in their seasons." Jesus adhered so much the more to this idea, as the conversion of the Gentiles was, according to Jewish notions, one of the surest signs of the advent of the Messiah. In his kingdom of God he represents, as seated at a feast, by the side of Abraham, Isaac, and Jacob, men come from the four winds of heaven, whilst the lawful heirs of the kingdom are rejected. Sometimes, it is true, there is to be found, in the commands he gives to his disciples, an entirely contrary tendency: he seems to recommend them to preach salvation to the orthodox Jews only; he speaks of Pagans in a manner conformable to the prejudices of the Jews. But we must remember that the disciples, whose narrow minds did not lend themselves to this supreme indifference for the privileges of the sons of Abraham, may have given the instruction of their master the bent of their own ideas. Besides, it is very possible that Jesus may have vacillated on this point; just as Mahomet speaks of the Jews in the Koran, sometimes in the most honourable manner, sometimes with extreme harshness, according as he hoped or not to win their favour. Tradition, in fact, ascribes to Jesus two entirely opposite rules of proselytism, which he may have practised in turn: "He that is not against us is on our part." "He that is not with me is against me." Impassioned contention involves almost necessarily these sorts of contradictions.

It is certain that he numbered amongst his disciples many men whom the Jews designated "Hellenes." This term had in Palestine divers meanings. Sometimes it designated the Pagans; sometimes the Greek-speaking Jews dwelling among the Pagans; sometimes men of Pagan origin converted to Judaism. It was probably in this last category of Hellenes that Jesus found sympathy. The affiliation with Judaism had numerous degrees; but the proselytes always remained in a state of inferiority as compared with the Jew by birth. The former were called "proselytes of the gate," or "men fearing God," and were subject to the precepts of Noah, and not to those of Moses. This very inferiority was unquestionably the cause which drew them to Jesus, and gained them his favour.

It was in the same manner that he treated the Samaritans. Surrounded like a small island, by the two great provinces of Judaism (Judæa and Galilee), Samaria formed in Palestine a kind of enclosure in which was preserved the ancient worship of Gerizim, closely related and rivalling that of Jerusalem. This poor sect, which had neither the genius nor the perfect organisation of Judaism, properly so called, was treated by the Jerusalemites with extreme harshness. They placed them on the same footing with Pagans, but hated them more. Jesus, from a spirit of opposition, was well disposed towards them. He often preferred the Samaritans to the orthodox Jews. If, on the other hand, he seems to forbid his disciples from going to preach to them, reserving his gospel for the Israelites proper, this was no doubt a precept dictated by special circumstances, to which the apostles have attached too absolute a meaning. Sometimes, in fact, the Samaritans received him badly, because they supposed him to be imbued with the prejudices of his co-religionists; in like manner as in our days the European free-thinker is regarded as an enemy by the Mussulman, who always believes him to be a fanatical Christian. Jesus knew how to rise above these misunderstandings. He had many disciples at Shechem, and he passed there at least two days. On one occasion he meets with gratitude and true piety from a Samaritan only. One of his most beautiful parables is that of the man injured on the way to Jericho. A priest passes by and sees him, but goes on his way; a Levite also passes, but does not stop; a Samaritan has compassion on him, approaches, and pours oil into his wounds, and binds them up. Jesus argues hence that true brotherhood is established amongst men by charity, and not by religious tenets. The "neighbour" who in Judaism was limited to the co-religionist was in his estimation the man who has pity on his fellow without distinction of sect. Human brotherhood in its widest sense abounds in all his teaching.

These ideas, which beset Jesus on his leaving Jerusalem, found vivid expression in an anecdote which has been preserved in regard to his return. The route from Jerusalem into Galilee passes Shechem at a distance of about half an hour's walk, at the opening of the valley commanded by Mounts Ebal and Gerizim. This route was in general shunned by the Jewish pilgrims, who preferred journeying by the long detour through Peræa rather than expose themselves to the ill-treatment of the Samaritans, or have to ask anything of them. It was forbidden to eat and drink with them; for it was an axiom of certain casuists that "a piece of Samaritan bread is the flesh of swine." When they followed this route, provisions were always laid up beforehand; yet it was rarely they could avoid scuffles and ill-treatment. Jesus shared neither these scruples nor these fears. Arrived, by this route, at the point whence the valley of Shechem opens on the left, he felt fatigued, and stopped near a well. The Samaritans were then as now in the habit of giving to the different spots of their valley names drawn from patriarchal reminiscences. They called this well the well of Jacob; it was probably the same that is called even up to this day Bir-Iakoub. The disciples entered the valley and went to the city to buy provisions; Jesus sat by the side of the well, having Gerizim in front of him.

It was about noon, and a woman of Shechem came to draw water. Jesus asked of her to drink, which excited great astonishment in the woman, the Jews generally forbidding all intercourse with the Samaritans. Won by the conversation of Jesus, the woman recognising in him a prophet, and anticipating reproaches about her worship, she took up speech first. "Sir," said she, "our fathers worshipped in this mountain, and ye say that in Jerusalem is the place where men ought to worship. Jesus saith unto her, Woman, believe me, the hour cometh when ye shall neither in this mountain, nor yet at Jerusalem, worship the Father. But the hour cometh, and now is, when the true worshippers shall worship the Father in spirit and in truth."

The day on which he uttered this saying, he was in reality Son of God. He uttered for the first time the sentence upon which will repose the edifice of eternal religion. He founded the pure worship, of all ages, of all lands, that which all elevated souls will embrace until the end of time. Not only was his religion on this day the best religion of humanity, it was the absolute religion; and if other planets have inhabitants endowed with reason and morality, their religion cannot be different from that which Jesus proclaimed near Jacob's well. Man has not been able to hold to it; for we can attain the ideal but for a moment. This sentiment of Jesus has been a bright light amidst gross darkness; it has taken eighteen hundred years for the eyes of mankind (I ought rather to say for an infinitely small portion of mankind) to become accustomed to it. But the light will grow into the full day, and, after having traversed all the circles of error, mankind will come back to this sentiment and regard it as the immortal expression of its faith and its hopes.

CHAPTER XV

COMMENCEMENT OF THE LEGEND OF JESUS--HIS OWN IDEA OF HIS SUPERNATURAL CHARACTER

Jesus, having completely lost his Jewish faith, and being filled with revolutionary ardour, returned to Galilee. His ideas are now expressed with perfect clearness. The simple aphorisms of the first part of his prophetic career, borrowed in part from the Jewish rabbis anterior to him, and the beautiful moral teachings of his second period, are discarded for a decided policy. The Law must be abolished; and it is to be abolished by him. The Messiah has come, and he it is who is the Messiah. The kingdom of God is soon to be revealed; and it is he who will reveal it. He knows well that he will suffer for his boldness; but the kingdom of God cannot be conquered without violence; it is by crises and commotions that it is to be established. The Son of man after his death will return in glory, accompanied by legions of angels, and those who have rejected him will be confounded.

The boldness of such a conception ought not to surprise us. Long before this Jesus regarded his relation to God as that of a son to his father. That which in others would be insupportable pride ought not in him to be treated as presumption.

The title of "Son of David" was the first that he accepted, probably without his being implicated in the innocent frauds by which it was sought to secure it to him. The family of David had, as it appears, been long extinct; nor did the Asmoneans, who were of priestly origin, nor Herod, nor the Romans dream for a moment that any representative whatever of the ancient dynasty existed in their midst. But from the close of the Asmonean dynasty the dream of an unknown descendant of the ancient kings, who should avenge the nation of its enemies, worked in every brain. The universal belief was that the Messiah would be son of David, and, like him, would be born at Bethlehem. The first thought of Jesus was not this exactly. The remembrance of David, which was uppermost in the minds of the majority of the Jews, had nothing in common with his heavenly reign. He believed himself the Son of God, and not the son of David. His kingdom, and the deliverance which he meditated, were of quite another order. But opinion on this point made him do himself a sort of violence. The immediate consequence of the proposition, "Jesus is the Messiah," was this other proposition, "Jesus is the son of David." He allowed a title to be given him without which he could not hope for success. And in the end he appears to have taken pleasure in it, inasmuch as he performed most willingly the miracles which were asked of him by those who used this title in addressing him. In this, as in many other circumstances of his life, Jesus yielded to the notions which were current in his time, although they were not precisely his own. He associated with his doctrine of the "kingdom of God" all that could stimulate the heart and the imagination. Hence it is that we have seen him adopt the baptism of John, although it could not be of much importance to him.

One great difficulty presented itself, to wit, his birth at Nazareth, which was of public notoriety. We do not know whether Jesus endeavoured to remove this objection. Perhaps it did not present itself in Galilee, where the idea that the son of David should be a Bethlehemite was less spread. To the Galilean idealist, moreover, the title of "son of David" was sufficiently justified, if he to whom it was given should retrieve the glory of his race, and bring back the great days of Israel. Did Jesus, by his silence, assent to the fictitious genealogies which his partisans invented in order to prove his royal descent? Did he know anything of the legends invented to prove that he was born at Bethlehem; and particularly of the attempt to connect his Bethlehemite origin with the census which had taken place by order of Quirinius, the imperial legate. We cannot tell. The inexactitude and the contradictions of the genealogies lead to the belief that they were the result of popular notions operating at various points, and that none of them was sanctioned by Jesus. Never with his own lips does he designate himself son of David. His disciples, much less enlightened than he, some-times magnified what he said of himself; but very often he knew nothing of these exaggerations. And we must add that, during the first three centuries, considerable portions of Christendom obstinately denied the royal descent of Jesus and the authenticity of the genealogies.

The legend about him was thus the result of a great and entirely spontaneous conspiracy, and began to surround him during his lifetime. There has been no great event in history which has not given rise to a series of fables; and Jesus could not, even had he wished, put a stop to these popular creations.

Doubtless a sagacious observer would have detected in them the germ of the narratives which were to ascribe to him a supernatural birth, either by reason of the idea, very prevalent in ancient times, that the incomparable man could not be born of the ordinary relations of the two sexes; or for the purpose of fulfilling the requirements of an imperfectly understood chapter of Isaiah, which was believed to foretell that the Messiah should be born of a virgin; or, lastly, as the result of a belief that the "breath of God," already regarded as a divine hypostasis, was a principle of fecundity. There was by this time, no doubt, more than one current anecdote regarding his infancy, conceived for the purpose of showing in his biography the accomplishment of the Messianic ideal, or rather the prophetic, that the allegorical exigences of the times reputed to the Messiah. A generally admitted idea was that the Messiah should be announced by a star, that messengers from far countries should come soon after his birth to render him homage, and to bring presents to him. It was alleged that the oracle was accomplished through the pretended Chaldean astrologers who should arrive about that time at Jerusalem. At other times he was connected from his birth with celebrated men, such as John the Baptist, Herod the Great, and two aged persons, Simeon and Anna, who had left memories of great sanctity. A rather loose chronology characterised these combinations, which for the most part were founded on a travesty of real facts. But a singular spirit of gentleness and goodness, an intensely popular sentiment, permeated all these fables, and made them a supplement to his preaching. It was especially after the death of Jesus that such narratives received their development. We can, however, believe that they were circulated during his life even, exciting no more than pious credulity and simple admiration.

That Jesus never dreamt of passing himself for an incarnation of the true God, there can be no doubt. Such an idea was quite foreign to the Jewish mind; and there is no trace of it in the three first gospels; we only find it alluded to in portions of the fourth, which cannot be accepted as reflecting the thoughts of Jesus. Sometimes Jesus even seems to take precautions to repress such a doctrine. The accusation that he made himself God, or the equal of God, is presented, even in the fourth Gospel, as a calumny of the Jews. In the latter Gospel he declares himself less than his Father. Elsewhere he avows that the Father has not revealed everything to him. He believes himself to be more than an ordinary man, but separated from God by an infinite distance. He is Son of God, but all men are or may become so, in divers degrees. Every one each day ought to call God his father; all who are raised again will be sons of God. The divine son-ship was attributed in the Old Testament to beings who, it was by no means pretended, were equal with God. The word "son" has in the Semitic tongues and in the New Testament the widest meaning. Besides, the idea Jesus had of man was not that low idea which a cold Deism has introduced. In his poetic conception of nature, one breath alone pervades the universe: the breath of man is that of God; God dwells in man, and lives by man, the same as man dwells in God, and lives by God. The transcendent idealism of Jesus never permitted him to have a very clear notion of his own personality. He is his Father, his Father is he. He lives in his disciples; he is everywhere with them; his disciples are one, as he and his Father are one. The idea to him is everything; the body, which makes the distinction of individuals, is nothing.

The title "Son of God," or simply "Son," became thus for Jesus a title analogous to "Son of man," with the sole difference that he called himself "Son of man," and does not seem to have made the same use of the phrase, "Son of God." The title, Son of man, expressed his character as judge; that of Son of God, participation in the supreme designs and his power. This power had no limits. His Father had given him all power. He had the right to alter even the Sabbath. No one could know the Father but through him. The Father had delegated to him the right to judge. Nature obeyed him: but she obeys also all who believe and pray, for faith can do everything.

We must bear in mind that no idea of the laws of nature marked, either in his own mind or in that of his hearers, the limit of the impossible. The witnesses of his miracles thanked God "for having given such power unto men." He pardoned sins; he is superior to David, to Abraham, to Solomon, to the prophets. We do not know in what form, nor to what extent, these affirmations of himself were made. Jesus ought not to be judged by the rule governing our petty conventionalities. The admiration of his disciples overwhelmed and carried him away. It is evident that the title of Rabbi, with which he was at first contented, no longer satisfied him; the title even of prophet or messenger of God responded no longer to his ideas. The position which he assigned himself was that of a superhuman being, and he wished to be regarded as having a higher relationship with God than other men. But it must be observed that these words, "superhuman" and "supernatural," borrowed from our pitiful theology, had no meaning in the exalted religious consciousness of Jesus. To him nature and the development of humanity were not limited kingdoms outside of God--paltry realities subject to the laws of a desperate rigorism. There was no supernatural for him, for the reason that there was no nature. Intoxicated with infinite love, he forgot the heavy chain which holds the spirit captive; he cleared at one bound the abyss, impossible to most, which the weakness of the human faculties has formed between God and man.

We cannot mistake in these affirmations of Jesus the germ of the doctrine which was, later on, to make of him a divine hypostasis, in identifying him with the Word, or "second God," or eldest Son of God, or Angel Metathronas, which Jewish theology created apart from him. A sort of necessity produced this theology, in order to correct the extreme rigour of the old Monotheism, to place near God a vicegerent, to whom the eternal Father is supposed to delegate the government of the universe. The belief that certain men are incarnations of divine faculties or "powers" was wide-spread; the Samaritans possessed about the same time a thaumaturgus, which they identified with the "great power of God." For nearly two centuries, the speculative minds of Judaism had yielded to the tendency of personifying the divine attributes, and certain expressions which were connected with the Divinity. Thus, the "breath of God," which is often referred to in the Old Testament, is considered as a separate being, the "Holy Spirit" In like manner, the "Wisdom of God" and the "Word of God" became distinct existing entities. This was the germ of the process which has engendered the Sephiroth of the Cabbala, the Æons of Gnosticism, the hypostasis of Christianity, and all that dry mythology, consisting of personified abstractions, to which Monotheism is obliged to resort when it wishes to pluralise the Deity.

Jesus appears to have remained a stranger to these hair-splittings of theology, which were soon to fill the world with barren disputes. The meta-physical theory of the Word, such as we find it in the writings of his contemporary Philo, in the Chaldæan Targums, and even in the book of "Wisdom," is neither seen in the Λόγια of Matthew, nor in general in the synoptics, the most authentic interpreters of the words of Jesus. The doctrine of the Word, in fact, had nothing in common with Messianism. The "Word" of Philo, and of the Targums, is in no sense the Messiah. It was later that Jesus came to be identified with the Word, and when, in starting from that principle, there was created quite a new theology, very different from that of the "kingdom of God." The essential character of the Word was that of Creator and of Providence. Now, Jesus never pretended to have created the world, nor to govern it. His office was to judge it, to renovate it. The position of president at the final assizes of humanity, was the function which Jesus attached to himself, and the office which all the first Christians attributed to him. Until the great day he sits at the right hand of God, as His Metathronos, His first minister, and His future avenger. The superhuman Christ of the Byzantine absides, seated as judge of the world, in the midst of the apostles in the same rank with him, and superior to the angels who only assist and serve, is the identical representation of that conception of the "Son of man" of which we find the first features so strongly indicated in the book of Daniel.

In any case, the rigour of scholastic rejection had no place in such a world. All the collection of ideas we have just stated formed in the mind of the disciples a theological system so little settled that the Son of God, this kind of duplication of the Divinity, is made to act purely as man. He is tempted--he is ignorant of many things--he corrects himself--he changes his opinion--he is cast down, discouraged--he asks his Father to spare him trials--he is submissive to God as a son. He who must judge the world does not know the date of the day of judgment. He takes precautions for his safety. Immediately after his birth he has to be concealed to escape from powerful men who wish to kill him. All this is simply the work of a messenger of God--of a man protected and favoured by God. We must not ask here for logic or sequence. The need Jesus had of obtaining credence, and the enthusiasm of his disciples, piled up contradictory notions. To those who believed in the coming of the Messiah, and to the enthusiastic readers of the books of Daniel and of Enoch, he was the Son of man; to the Jews holding the common faith, and to the readers of Isaiah and Micah, he was the Son of David; to the disciples he was the Son of God, or simply the Son. Others, without being blamed by the disciples, took him for John the Baptist risen from the dead, for Elias, for Jeremiah, conformable to the popular belief that the ancient prophets were about to reappear, in order to prepare the way of the Messiah.

An absolute conviction, or rather the enthusiasm which freed him from the possibility of doubt, shrouded all this boldness. We, with our cold and scrupulous natures, little understand how any one can be so entirely possessed by the idea of which he has made himself the apostle. To us, the deeply earnest races, conviction signifies to be sincere with one's self. But sincerity to one's self has not much meaning to Oriental peoples, little accustomed to the subtleties of the critical spirit. Honesty and imposture are words which, in our rigid consciences, are opposed as two irreconcilable terms. In the East they are connected by a thousand subtle links and windings. The authors of the Apocryphal books (of "Daniel" and of "Enoch" for instance), men highly exalted, in order to aid their cause, committed, without a shadow of scruple, an act which we should term a fraud. The literal truth has little value to the Oriental; he sees everything through the medium of his ideas, his interests, and his passions.

History is impossible if we do not fully admit that there are many standards of sincerity. Faith knows no other law than the interest in that which it believes to be true. The aim which it pursues being for it, absolutely holy, it makes no scruple about introducing bad arguments into a thesis where good ones do not succeed. If such a proof is not sound, how many others are? If such a prodigy is not real, how many others have been so? How many pious men, convinced of the truth of their religion, have sought to conquer the obstinacy of other men, by the use of means the weakness of which they could clearly apprehend? How many stigmatics, fanatics, and occupants of convents have been carried away by the influence of the world in which they lived, and by their individual beliefs in feigned acts, either for the purpose of not being considered as beneath others, or to sustain the cause when in danger! All great things are done through the people; now we can only lead the people by adapting ourselves to their ideas. The philosopher who, knowing this, isolates and intrenches himself in his nobleness, is highly praiseworthy. But he who takes humanity with its illusions, and seeks to act with it and upon it, cannot be blamed. Cæsar knew well that he was not the son of Venus; France would not be what it is if it had not for a thousand years believed in the Holy Ampulla of Rheims. It is, of course, easy for us, who are so powerless, to call this falsehood, and, proud of our feeble honesty, to treat with contempt the heroes who have accepted the battle of life under other conditions. When we have effected by our scruples what they accomplished by their falsehoods, we shall have the right to be severe upon them. At least, we must make a marked distinction between societies like our own, where everything takes place in the full light of reflection, and simple and credulous societies, in which the beliefs that have governed ages have been born. Nothing great has been established which does not rest on a legend. The only culprit in such cases is the humanity which is willing to be deceived.

CHAPTER XVI

MIRACLES

Two means of proof, miracles and the accomplishment of prophecies, could alone, in the opinion of the contemporaries of Jesus, establish a supernatural mission. Jesus, and above all his disciples, employed these two processes of demonstration in perfect good faith. For a long time Jesus had been convinced that the prophets had written only in reference to him. He recognised himself in their sacred oracles; he regarded himself as the mirror in which all the prophetic spirit of Israel had read the future. The Christian school, perhaps even in the lifetime of its founder, endeavoured to prove that Jesus answered perfectly to all that the prophets had predicted of the Messiah. In many cases these comparisons were quite superficial, and are hardly appreciable by us. They were most frequently fortuitous or insignificant circumstances in the life of the master which recalled to the disciples certain passages of the Psalms and the Prophets, in which, in consequence of their constant preoccupation, they saw images of what was passing before their eyes. The exegesis of the time consisted thus almost entirely in a play upon words, and in quotations made in an artificial and arbitrary manner. The synagogue had no officially settled list of the passages which related to the future reign. The Messianic references were very freely applied, and constituted artifices of style rather than serious argument.

As to miracles, at that time they were regarded as the indispensable mark of the divine, and as the sign of the prophetic vocation. The legends of Elijah and Elisha were full of them. It was understood that the Messiah would perform many. In Samaria, a few leagues from where Jesus was, there was a magician named Simon, who acquired an almost divine character by his illusions. Afterwards, when it was sought to establish the reputation of Apollonius of Tyana, and to prove that his life had been the sojourn of a god upon the earth, it was not thought possible to succeed therein except by inventing a vast cycle of miracles. The Alexandrian philosophers themselves, Plotinus and others, were supposed to have performed several. Jesus was, therefore, obliged to choose between these two alternatives--either to renounce his mission or to become a thaumaturgist. It must be borne in mind that all antiquity, with the exception of the great scientific schools of Greece and their Roman disciples, believed in miracles; and that Jesus not only believed in them, but also had not the least idea of an order of nature regulated by laws. His knowledge on this point was not at all superior to that of his contemporaries. Nay, more, one of his most deeply rooted opinions was that by faith and prayer man had entire power over nature. The faculty of performing miracles was held to be a privilege regularly conferred by God upon men, and there was nothing surprising in it.

The lapse of time has changed that which constituted the power of the great founder of Christianity into something offensive to our ideas, and, if ever the worship of Jesus loses its hold upon humanity, it will be precisely on account of those acts which originally inspired belief in him. Criticism experiences no embarrassment in presence of this kind of historical phenomenon. A thaumaturgist of our days, unless of an extreme simplicity, like that manifested by certain stigmatics of Germany, is odious; for he performs miracles without believing in them; he is a mere charlatan. But, if we take a Francis d'Assisi, the question becomes altogether different; the cycle of miracles attending the origin of the order of St. Francis, far from offending us, affords us real pleasure. The founders of Christianity lived in at least as complete a state of poetic ignorance as did St. Clair and the tres socii. The disciples deemed it quite natural that their master should have interviews with Moses and Elias, that he should command the elements, and that he should heal the sick. We must remember, besides, that every idea loses something of its purity as soon as it aspires to realise itself. Success is never attained without some injury being done to the sensibility of the soul. Such is the feebleness of the human mind that the best causes are ordinarily gained only by bad arguments. The demonstrations of the primitive apologists of Christianity were based upon very poor reasonings. Moses, Christopher Columbus, Mahomet, have only triumphed over obstacles by constantly making allowance for the weakness of men, and by not always giving the true reasons for the truth. It is probable that those about Jesus were more struck by his miracles than by his eminently divine discourses. Let us add that doubtless popular rumour, both before and after the death of Jesus, enormously exaggerated the number of occurrences of this kind. The types of the gospel miracles, in fact, do not present much variety; they are repetitions of each other, and seem fashioned from a very small number of models, accommodated to the taste of the country.

It is impossible, amongst the miraculous narratives so tediously enumerated in the Gospels, to distinguish the miracles attributed by common consent to Jesus from those in which he consented to play an active part. It is especially impossible to ascertain whether the offensive circumstances attending them, the groanings, the strugglings, and other features savouring of jugglery, are really historical, or whether they are the fruit of the belief of the compilers, strongly prepossessed with theurgy, and living, in this connection, in a world analogous to that of the spiritualists of our days. Popular opinion, in fact, insisted that the divine virtue was in man thus an epileptic and convulsive principle. Almost all the miracles that Jesus believed he performed appear to have been miracles of healing. Medicine was at that period in Judæa what it still is in the East, that is to say, far from being scientific, and absolutely dependent upon individual inspiration. The scientific school of medicine, founded by Greece five centuries before, was at the time of Jesus unknown to the Jews of Palestine. In such a state of knowledge, the presence of a superior man, treating the sick with gentleness, and giving him by some tangible signs the assurance of his recovery, is often a decisive remedy. Who would dare to say that in many cases, excepting, of course, certain peculiar injuries, the touch of a superior being is not equal to all the resources of pharmacy? The mere pleasure of seeing such a one, cured. He gives what he can--a smile, a hope, and these are not in vain.

Jesus had no more idea than the majority of his countrymen of a rational medical science; he shared the general belief that healing was to be effected by religious practices, and such a belief was perfectly consistent. From the moment that disease was regarded as the punishment of sin, or as the act of a demon, and in no way as the result of physical causes, the best physician was the holy man who had power in the supernatural world. Healing was regarded as a moral act; Jesus, who was conscious of moral power, would believe himself specially gifted to heal. Convinced that the touching of his robe, the imposition of his hands, the application of his saliva, benefited the sick, he would have been hard-hearted if he had refused to those who suffered, a solace which it was in his power to bestow. The healing of the sick was considered as one of the signs of the kingdom of God, and was always associated with the emancipation of the poor. Both were the signs of the great revolution that was to culminate in the relief of all infirmities. The Essenians, who had so many ties of relationship with Jesus, passed also for very powerful spiritual physicians.

One of the species of cure which Jesus most frequently performed was exorcism, or the casting out of devils. A strange disposition to believe in demons pervaded all minds. It was a universal opinion, not only in Judæa, but everywhere, that demons took possession of the bodies of certain persons and made them act contrary to their will. A Persian div, often named in the Avesta, Aeschmadaëva, the "div of concupiscence," adopted by the Jews under the name of Asmodeus, became the cause of all the hysterical afflictions of women. Epilepsy, in mental and nervous maladies, when the patient seems no longer to belong to himself, and in infirmities the cause of which is not apparent, such as deafness and dumbness, were explained in the same manner. The admirable treatise, "On Sacred Disease," by Hippocrates, which set forth the true principles of medicine on this subject, four centuries and a half before Jesus, had not banished from the world so great an error. It was supposed that there were processes more or less efficacious for driving away the demons; and the occupation of exorcist was a regular profession like that of physician. There is no doubt that Jesus had in his lifetime the reputation of possessing the greatest secrets of this art. There were then many lunatics in Judæa, doubtless the result of the great mental excitement. These fools, who were permitted to roam about, as they still are in the same districts, inhabited the abandoned sepulchral caves, which were the ordinary retreat of vagrants. Jesus had much control over these unfortunates. A thousand singular stories are related in connexion with his cures, in which the credulity of the time had full scope. Nevertheless these difficulties must not be exaggerated. The disorders which were regarded as "possessions" were often very slight. In our times, in Syria, people are regarded as mad or possessed by a demon (these two ideas were expressed by the same word, medjnoun) who are only somewhat eccentric. A gentle word often suffices in such cases to drive away the demon. Such were doubtless the means employed by Jesus. Who knows if his celebrity as an exorcist was not spread almost without his own knowledge? Persons who reside in the East are occasionally surprised to find themselves, after some time, in possession of a great reputation, as doctors, sorcerers, or discoverers of treasures, without being able to account to themselves for the facts which have given rise to these fancies.

Many circumstances, moreover, seem to indicate that Jesus only became a thaumaturgist late in life and against his inclination. He often performs his miracles only after he has been besought to do so, and with a degree of reluctance, reproaching those who asked them for their hardness of heart. One singularity, apparently inexplicable, is the care he takes to perform his miracles in secret, and the request he addresses to those whom he heals to tell no one. When the demons wish to proclaim him the Son of God, he forbids them to open their mouths; but they recognise him in spite of himself. These traits are especially prominent in Mark, who is pre-eminently the evangelist of miracles and exorcisms. It seems that the disciple, who has furnished the fundamental teachings of this Gospel, importuned Jesus with his admiration for prodigies, and that the master, wearied of a reputation which weighed upon him, had often said to him, "See thou say nothing to any man." Once this discordance evoked a singular outburst, a fit of impatience, in which the annoyance of these perpetual demands of weak minds caused Jesus to break forth. One would say, at times, that the character of thaumaturgist was disagreeable to him, and that he sought to give as little publicity as possible to the marvels which, in a manner, grew under his feet. When his enemies asked a miracle of him, especially a celestial miracle, a "sign from heaven," he obstinately refused. It is, therefore, permissible to believe that his reputation of thaumaturgist was imposed upon him, that he did not resist it much, but also that he did nothing to aid it, and that, at all events, he felt the vanity of public opinion on this point.

We should be lacking in historical method if we listened here too much to our repugnances. The essential condition of the true critic is to comprehend the diversity of times, and to divest himself of instinctive habits, which are the results of a purely rational education. In order to meet the objections which might be raised against the character of Jesus, we must not suppress facts which, in the eyes of his contemporaries, were considered of the greatest importance, It would be convenient to say that these are the additions of disciples much inferior to their Master, who, not being able to conceive his true grandeur, have sought to magnify him by illusions unworthy of him. But the four narrators of the life of Jesus are unanimous in extolling his miracles; one of them, Mark, interpreter of the Apostle Peter, insists so much on this point that, if we trace the character of Christ only according to this Gospel, we should represent Jesus as an exorcist in possession of charms of rare efficacy, as a very potent sorcerer, who inspired fear, and whom the people wished to get rid of. We will admit, then, without hesitation, that acts which would now be considered as acts of illusion or folly held a large place in the life of Jesus. Must we sacrifice to these uninviting features the sublimity of such a life? God forbid. A mere sorcerer would not have brought about a moral revolution like that effected by Jesus. If the thaumaturgist had effaced in Jesus the moralist and the religious reformer, there would have proceeded from him a school of theurgy, and not Christianity.

The problem, moreover, presents itself in the same manner with respect to all saints and religious founders. Things now considered morbid, such as epileptic visions, were formerly principles of power and greatness. Physicians know the name of the disease which made the fortune of Mahomet. Almost in our own day, the men who have done the most for their kind (the excellent Vincent de Paul himself!) were, whether they wished it or not, thaumaturgists. If we set out with the principle that every historical personage to whom acts have been attributed, which we in the nineteenth century hold to be irrational or savouring of quackery, was either a madman or a charlatan, all criticism is falsified. The school of Alexandria was a noble school, but, nevertheless, it gave itself up to the practices of an extravagant theurgy. Socrates and Pascal were not exempt from hallucinations. Facts ought to explain themselves by proportionate causes. The weaknesses of the human mind only engender weakness; great things have always great causes in the nature of man, although they are often produced amidst a crowd of littlenesses which, to superficial minds, eclipse their grandeur.

In a general sense, it is therefore true to say that Jesus was only thaumaturgist and exorcist in spite of himself. Miracles are ordinarily the work of the public much more than of him to whom they are attributed. Jesus persistently shunned the performance of the prodigies which the multitude would have created for him; the greatest miracle would have been his refusal to perform any; never would the laws of history and popular psychology have suffered so great a derogation. He was no more able than St. Bernard, or Francis d'Assisi, to moderate the avidity of the multitude and of his own disciples for the marvellous. The miracles of Jesus were a violence done to him by his age, a concession forced from him by a passing necessity. The exorcist and the thaumaturgist have alike passed away; but the religious reformer will live eternally.

Even those who did not believe in him were struck with these acts, and sought to be witnesses of them. The Pagans, and persons unacquainted with him, experienced a sentiment of fear, and sought to remove him from their district. Many thought perhaps to abuse his name by connecting it with seditious movements. But the purely moral and in no respect political tendency of the character of Jesus saved him from these entanglements. His kingdom was in the circle of disciples, whom a like freshness of imagination and the same foretaste of heaven had grouped and retained around him.

CHAPTER XVII

DEFINITE FORM OF THE IDEAS OF JESUS IN RESPECT OF THE KINGDOM OF GOD

We suppose that this last phase of the activity of Jesus continued about eighteen months, reckoning from the time of his return from the Passover of the year 31 to his journey to the feast of tabernacles of the year 32. During that interval the mind of Jesus does not appear to have been enriched by any new element; but all that was in him developed and grew with ever-increasing power and boldness.

The fundamental idea of Jesus from the first was the establishment of the kingdom of God. But this kingdom of God, as we have already said, appears to have been understood by Jesus in very different senses. At times he might be taken for a democratic leader desiring only the reign of the poor and the disinherited. At other times the kingdom of God is the literal accomplishment of the apocalyptic visions of Daniel and Enoch. Finally, the kingdom of God is often a spiritual kingdom, and the near deliverance is a deliverance of the spirit. The revolution then desired by Jesus was that which has actually taken place; the establishment of a new worship, purer than that of Moses. All these thoughts appear to have been coexistent in the mind of Jesus. The first, however--that of a temporal revolution-- does not appear to have had much hold on him; Jesus never regarded the earth or the riches of the earth, or material power as a thing worth caring for. He had no exterior ambition. Sometimes, by a natural consequence, his great religious importance was on the point of being changed into mere social importance. Men came requesting him to judge and arbitrate on questions which affected their interests. Jesus rejected these proposals with scorn, treating them as insults. Full of his heavenly ideal, he never abandoned his disdainful poverty. As to the other two conceptions of the kingdom of God, Jesus appears always to have held them simultaneously. If he had been only an enthusiast, led away by the apocalypses on which the popular imagination fed, he would have remained an obscure sectary, inferior to those whose ideas he followed. If he had been only a puritan, a sort of Channing or "Savoyard vicar," he would undoubtedly have been unsuccessful. The two parts of his system, or, rather, his two conceptions of the kingdom of God, rest one on the other, and this reciprocal support has been the cause of his incomparable success. The first Christians were visionaries living in a circle of ideas which we should term reveries; but, at the same time, they were the heroes of that social war which has resulted in the enfranchisement of the conscience, and in the establishment of a religion from which the pure worship, proclaimed by the founder, will eventually proceed.

The apocalyptic ideas of Jesus, in their most complete form, may thus be summed up:

The existing order of humanity is approaching its termination. This termination will be an immense revolution, "an anguish" similar to the pains of child-birth; a palingenesis, or, in the words of Jesus himself, a "new birth," preceded by dark calamities and heralded by strange phenomena. In the great day there will appear in the heavens the sign of the Son of man; it will be a startling and luminous vision like that of Sinai, a great storm rending the clouds, a fiery meteor flashing rapidly from east to west. The Messiah will appear in the clouds, clothed in glory and majesty, to the sound of trumpets and surrounded by angels. His disciples will sit by his side upon thrones. The dead will then arise, and the Messiah will proceed to judgment.

At this judgment men will be divided into two classes according to their works. The angels will be the executors of the sentences. The elect will enter into a delightful abode which has been prepared for them from the foundation of the world; there they will be seated, clothed with light, at a feast presided over by Abraham, the patriarchs, and the prophets. They will be the smaller number. The rest will depart into Gehenna. Gehenna was the western valley of Jerusalem. There the worship of fire had been practised at various times, and the place had become a kind of sewer. Gehenna was, therefore, in the mind of Jesus a gloomy, filthy valley, full of fire. Those excluded from the kingdom will there be burnt and eaten by the never-dying worm, in company with Satan and his rebel angels. There, there will be wailing and gnashing of teeth. The kingdom of heaven will be as a closed room, lighted from within, in the midst of a world of darkness and torments.

This new order of things will be eternal. Paradise and Gehenna will have no end. An impassable abyss separates the one from the other. The Son of man, seated on the right hand of God, will preside over this final condition of the world and of humanity.

That all this was taken literally by the disciples and by the master himself at certain moments appears clearly evident from the writings of the time. If the first Christian generation had one profound and constant belief, it was that the world was near its end, and that the great "revelation" of Christ was soon to take place. The startling proclamation, "The time is at hand," which commences and closes the Apocalypse; the incessantly reiterated appeal, "He that hath ears to hear let him hear!" were the cries of hope and encouragement for the whole apostolic age. A Syrian expression, Maranatha, "Our Lord cometh!" became a sort of password, which the believers used amongst themselves in order to strengthen their faith and their hope. The Apocalypse, written in the year 68 of our era, fixed the end at three years and a half. The "Ascension of Isaiah" adopts a calculation closely approaching this.

Jesus never indulged in such precision. When he was interrogated as to the time of his advent he always refused to reply; once even he declared that the date of this great day was known only by the Father, who had revealed it neither to the angels nor to the Son. He said that the time when the kingdom of God was most anxiously expected was just that in which it would not appear. He constantly repeated that it would be a surprise, as in the times of Noah and of Lot; that we must be on our guard, always ready to depart; that each one must watch and keep his lamp trimmed as for a wedding procession, which arrives unforeseen; that the Son of man would come like a thief, at an hour when he would not be expected; that he would appear as a flash of lightning, running from one end of the heavens to the other. But his declarations as to the proximity of the catastrophe leave no room for any equivocation. "This generation," said he, "shall not pass till all these things be fulfilled. There be some standing here which shall not taste of death till they see the Son of man coming in his kingdom." He reproaches those who do not believe in him for not being able to read the signs of the future kingdom. "When it is evening, ye say, It will be fair weather; for the sky is red. And in the morning, It will be foul weather to-day; for the sky is red and lowering. O ye hypocrites, ye can discern the face of the sky; but can ye not discern the signs of the times?" By an illusion common to all great reformers, Jesus imagined the end to be much nearer than it really was; he did not take into account the slowness of the movements of humanity; he thought to realise in one day that which, eighteen centuries later, has still to be accomplished.

These formal declarations preoccupied the Christian family for nearly seventy years. It was believed that some of the disciples would see the day of the final revelation before dying. John, in particular, was considered as being of this number; many believed that he would never die. Perhaps this was a later opinion suggested towards the end of the first century, by the advanced age which John seems to have reached; this age having given occasion to the belief that God wished to prolong his life indefinitely until the great day, in order to realise the words of Jesus. When he died in turn, the faith of many was shaken, and his disciples attached to the prediction of Christ a more subdued meaning.

At the same time that Jesus fully admitted the Apocalyptic beliefs, such as we find them in the apocryphal Jewish books, he admitted the dogma which is the complement, or rather the condition of them all, namely, the resurrection of the dead. This doctrine, as we have already said, was still somewhat new in Israel; a number of people either did not know it, or did not believe in it. It was the faith of the Pharisees, and of the fervent adherents of the Messianic beliefs. Jesus accepted it unreservedly, but always in the most idealistic sense. Many imagined that in the resuscitated world they would eat, drink, and marry. Jesus, indeed, admits into his kingdom a new passover, a table, and a new wine; but he expressly excludes marriage from it. The Sadducees had on this subject an apparently gross argument, but at bottom quite conformable with the old theology. It will be remembered that, according to the ancient sages, man survived only in his children. The Mosaic code had consecrated this patriarchal theory by a strange institution, the levitical law. The Sadducees drew thence subtle deductions against the resurrection. Jesus escaped them by formally declaring that in the life eternal there would no longer exist differences of sex, and that men would be like the angels. Sometimes he seems to promise resurrection only to the just, the punishment of the wicked consisting in complete annihilation. Oftener, however, Jesus declares that the resurrection shall bring eternal confusion to the wicked.

It will be seen that nothing in all these theories was absolutely new. The Gospels and the writings of the apostles scarcely contain anything as regards apocalyptics but what might be found already in "Daniel," "Enoch," the "Sibylline Oracles," and the assumption of Moses, which are of Jewish origin. Jesus accepted these ideas, which were generally received among his contemporaries. He made them his basis of action, or rather one of his bases; for he had too profound an idea of his true work to establish it solely upon such fragile principles, so liable to receive from facts a crushing refutation.

It is evident, indeed, that such a doctrine, taken by itself in a literal manner, had no future. The world, in continuing to endure, entirely disproves it. One generation of man at the most, was reserved for it. The faith of the first Christian generation is intelligible, but the faith of the second generation is no longer so. After the death of John, or of the last survivor, whoever he might be, of the group which had seen the master, the word of Jesus was convicted of falsehood. If the doctrine of Jesus had been simply belief in an approaching end of the world, it would certainly now be sleeping in oblivion. What is it, then, that has saved it? The great breadth of the Gospel conceptions, which has permitted doctrines suited to very different intellectual conditions to be found under the same creed. The world has not ended, as Jesus announced, and as his disciples believed. But it has been renewed, and in one sense renewed as Jesus desired. It is because his thought was two-sided that it has been fruitful. His chimera has not had the fate of so many others which have crossed the human mind, because it concealed a germ of life which having been introduced, thanks to a covering of fable, into the bosom of humanity, has thus brought forth eternal fruits.

And let us not say that this is a benevolent interpretation, imagined in order to clear the honour of our great master from the cruel contradiction inflicted on his dreams by reality. No, no; this true kingdom of God, this kingdom of the spirit, which makes each one, king and priest; this kingdom which, like the grain of mustard-seed, has become a tree which overshadows the world, and under whose branches the birds have their nests, was understood, wished for, and founded by Jesus. By the side of the false, cold, and impossible idea of an ostentatious advent, he conceived the real city of God, the true "renaissance," the Sermon on the Mount, the apotheosis of the weak, the love of the people, regard for the poor, and the re-establishment of all that is humble, true, and simple. This rehabilitation he has depicted as an incomparable artist, by features which will last eternally. Each of us owes that which is best in himself to him. Let us pardon him his hope of a vain apocalypse, of a second coming in great triumph upon the clouds of heaven. Perhaps these were the errors of others rather than his own; and if it be true that he himself shared the general illusion, what matters it, since his dream rendered him strong against death, and sustained him in a struggle to which he might otherwise have been unequal? We must, then, attach several meanings to the divine city conceived by Jesus. If his only thought had been that the end of time was near, and that we must prepare for it, he would not have surpassed John the Baptist. To renounce a world ready to crumble, to detach one's self gradually from the present life, and to aspire to the kingdom about to come; such would have been the essence of his preaching. The teaching of Jesus had always a much larger scope. He proposed to himself to create a new state of humanity, and not merely to prepare the end of that which did exist. Elias or Jeremiah, reappearing in order to prepare men for the supreme crisis, would not have preached as he did. This is so true that this morality, attributed to the latter days, is found to be the eternal morality, that which has saved humanity. Jesus himself in many cases makes use of modes of speech which do not enter at all into a material kingdom. He often declares that the kingdom of God has already begun; that every man bears it within himself, and can, if he be worthy, enjoy it; that each one silently creates this kingdom by the true conversion of the heart. The kingdom of God at such times is only the highest form of good; a better order of things than that which exists, the reign of justice, which the faithful, according to their ability, ought to help in establishing; or, again, the liberty of the soul, something analogous to the Buddhist "deliverance," the result of isolation. These truths, which to us are pure abstractions, were living realities to Jesus. Everything in his mind was concrete and substantial. Jesus was the man who believed most thoroughly in the reality of the ideal.

In accepting the Utopias of his time and his race, Jesus, thanks to the fruitful misconceptions of their import, thus knew how to elevate them into great truths. His kingdom of God was no doubt the approaching apocalypse, which was about to be unfolded in the heavens. But it was still, and probably above all, the kingdom of the soul, founded on liberty and on the filial sentiment which the virtuous man feels when resting on the bosom of his Father. It was a pure religion, without forms, without temple and without priest; it was the moral judgment of the world, delegated to the conscience of the just man, and to the arm of the people. This is what was destined to live; this is what has lived. When, at the end of a century of vain expectation, the materialistic hope of a near end of the world was exhausted, the true kingdom of God became apparent. Complaisant explanations drew a veil over the real kingdom, which did not come. The Apocalypse of John, the first book, properly speaking, of the New Testament, being too formally tied to the idea of an immediate catastrophe, was rejected by the second plan, held to be unintelligible, and tortured in a thousand ways. At least, its accomplishment was adjourned to an indefinite future. Some poor benighted ones who, in a fully enlightened age, still preserved the hopes of the first disciples, became heretics (Ebionites, Millenarians) lost in the shallows of Christianity. Mankind had passed to another kingdom of God. The degree of truth contained in the thought of Jesus had prevailed over the chimera which obscured it.

Let us not, however, despise this chimera, which has been the thick rind of the sacred fruit on which we live. This fantastic kingdom of heaven, this endless pursuit after a city of God, which has constantly preoccupied Christianity during its long career, has been the principle of that great instinct of futurity which has animated all reformers, persistent believers in the Apocalypse, from Joachim of Flora down to the Protestant sectary of our days. This impotent effort to establish a perfect society has been the source of the extraordinary tension which has always made the true Christian an athlete struggling against the present. The idea of the "kingdom of God," and the Apocalypse, which is the complete image of it, are thus, in a sense, the highest and most poetic expressions of human progress. No doubt they must also have given rise to great errors. The end of the world, suspended as a perpetual menace over mankind, was, by the periodical panics which it caused during centuries, a great hindrance to all secular development. Society, being no longer certain of its existence, contracted therefrom a degree of trepidation, and those habits of servile humility which rendered the Middle Ages so inferior to ancient and modern times. A profound change had also taken place in the mode of regarding the coming of Christ. When it was first announced to mankind that the end of the world was at hand, like the infant which receives death with a smile, it experienced the greatest access of joy that it has ever felt. But in growing old, the world became attached to life. The day of grace, so long expected by the simple souls of Galilee, became to these iron ages a day of wrath: Dies iræ, dies illa! But even in the midst of barbarism, the idea of the kingdom of God continued fruitful. "At the approach of the end of the world . . . "are the charters of enfranchisement. In spite of the feudal church, of sects, and of religious orders, holy persons continued to protest, in the name of the Gospel, against the iniquity of the world. Even in our days, troubled days, in which Jesus has no more authentic followers than those who seem to deny him, the dreams of an ideal organisation of society, which have so much analogy with the aspirations of the primitive Christian sects, are only in one sense the blossoming of the same idea, one of the branches of that immense tree in which germinates all thought of a future, and of which the "kingdom of God" will be eternally the root and stem. All the social revolutions of humanity will be grafted on this phrase. But, tainted by a coarse materialism, and aspiring to the impossible, that is to say, to found universal happiness upon political and economical measures, the "socialist" attempts of our time will remain unfruitful, until they take as their rule the true spirit of Jesus; I mean absolute idealism--the principle that in order to possess the world we must renounce it.

The phrase "kingdom of God," on the other hand, expresses also very happily the want which the soul experiences of a supplementary destiny, of a compensation for the present life. Those who do not accept the definition of man as a compound of two substances, and who regard the deistical dogma of the immortality of the soul as in contradiction with physiology, love to fall back upon the hope of a final reparation, which under an unknown form shall satisfy the wants of the heart of man. Who knows if the highest term of progress after millions of ages may not evoke the absolute conscience of the universe, and in this conscience the awakening of all that has lived? A sleep of a million of years is not longer than the sleep of an hour. St. Paul, on this hypothesis, was right in saying, In ictu oculi! It is certain that moral and virtuous humanity will have its reward, that one day the ideas of the poor but honest man will judge the world, and that on that day the ideal figure of Jesus will be the confusion of the frivolous man who has not believed in virtue and of the egotist who has not been able to attain to it. The favourite phrase of Jesus continues, therefore, full of an eternal beauty. A sort of grandiose divinity seems in this to have guided the incomparable master, and to have held him in a vague sublimity, embracing at the same time various orders of truths.

CHAPTER XVIII

INSTITUTIONS OF JESUS

That which proves, moreover, that Jesus was never entirely absorbed in his apocalyptic ideas is that, at the very time he was most preoccupied with them, he laid with rare foresight the basis of a church destined to endure. It is scarcely possible to doubt that he himself only chose from among his disciples those who were pre-eminently called the "apostles," or the "twelve," since on the day after his death we find them forming a distinct body, and filling up by election the vacancies that had been produced in their midst. They were the two sons of Jonas; the two sons of Zebedee; James, son of Alphæus; Philip; Nathaniel bar-Tolmai; Thomas; Matthew; Simon Zelotes; Thaddeus or Lebbæus; and Judas of Kerioth. It is probable that the idea of the twelve tribes of Israel had had something to do with the choice of this number. The "twelve," at all events, formed a group of privileged disciples, among whom Peter maintained a fraternal priority, and to them Jesus confided the propagation of his work. There was nothing, however, which suggested a regularly organised sacerdotal school. The lists of the "twelve," which have been preserved, present many uncertainties and contradictions; two or three of those who figure in them have remained completely obscure. Two, at least, Peter and Philip, were married and had children.

Jesus evidently confided secrets to the twelve, which he forbade them to communicate to the world. It seems sometimes as if his intentions had been to surround his person with some mystery, to postpone the most important testimony till after his death, and to reveal himself clearly only to his disciples, confiding to them the care of demonstrating him afterwards to the world. "What I tell you in darkness, that speak ye in light; and what ye hear in the ear, that preach ye upon the housetops." He was thus spared the necessity of too precise declarations, and created a kind of medium between the public and himself. What is certain is that there were teachings reserved to the apostles, and that he explained many parables to them, the meaning of which was ambiguous to the multitude. An enigmatical form and a degree of oddness in connecting ideas were customary in the teachings of the doctors, as may be seen in the sentences of the Pirké Aboth. Jesus explained to his disciples whatever was peculiar in his apothegms or in his apologues, and showed them his meaning stripped of the wealth of illustration which sometimes obscured it. Many of these explanations appear to have been carefully preserved.

During the lifetime of Jesus the apostles preached, but without ever departing far from him. Their preaching, moreover, was confined to the announcement of the speedy coming of the kingdom of God. They went from town to town, receiving hospitality, or rather taking it themselves, according to custom. The guest in the East has much authority; he is superior to the master of the house; the latter places the greatest confidence in him. This fireside preaching is well suited to the propagation of new doctrines. The hidden treasure is communicated, and payment is thus made for what is received; politeness and good feeling lend their aid; the household is touched and converted. Remove Oriental hospitality, and it would be impossible to explain the propagation of Christianity. Jesus, who adhered strongly to the good old customs, encouraged his disciples to make no scruple of profiting by this ancient public right, probably abolished already in the great towns where there were hostelries. "The labourer," said he, "is worthy of his hire!" Once installed in the house of any one they were to remain there, eating and drinking what was offered them as long as their mission lasted.

Jesus desired that, by imitating his example, the messengers of the glad tidings should render their preaching agreeable by kindly and polished manners. He directed that, on entering a house, they should give the host the salaam--wish him happiness. Some hesitated; the salaam being then, as now, in the East, a sign of religious communion, which is not risked with persons of a doubtful faith. "Fear nothing," said Jesus; "if no one in the house is worthy of your salute, it will return unto you." Sometimes, in fact, the apostles of the kingdom of God were badly received, and came to complain to Jesus, who generally sought to conciliate them. Some of them, persuaded of the omnipotence of their master, were hurt at this forbearance. The sons of Zebedee wanted him to call down fire from heaven upon the inhospitable towns. Jesus answered these outbursts with a fine irony, and stopped them by saying, " The Son of man is not come to destroy men's lives, but to save them."

He sought in every way to establish as a principle that his apostles were as himself. It was believed that he had communicated his marvellous virtues to them. They cast out demons, prophesied, and formed a school of renowned exorcists, although certain cases were beyond their power. They also made cures, either by the imposition of hands or by the unction of oil, one of the fundamental processes of Oriental medicine. Lastly, like the Psylli, they could handle serpents and drink with impunity deadly potions. The further we get from Jesus this theurgy becomes more and more offensive. But there is no doubt that it was a common practice in the primitive Church, and that it held a chief place in the estimation of the world around. Charlatans, as generally happens, exploited this movement of popular credulity. Even in the lifetime of Jesus many, without being his disciples, cast out demons in his name. The true disciples were much hurt at this, and sought to prevent them. Jesus, who saw in this a homage to his renown, did not manifest much severity towards them. It must be observed, moreover, that these supernatural gifts had, if I may say so, become a trade. Carrying the logic of absurdity to the extreme, certain men cast out demons by Beelzebub, the prince of demons. They imagined that this sovereign of the infernal regions must have entire authority over his subordinates, and that in acting through him they were certain to make the intruding spirit depart. Some even sought to buy from the disciples of Jesus the secret of the miraculous powers which had been conferred upon them.

The germ of a church began from this time to appear. This fertile idea of the power of men in association (ecclesia) seemed indeed an idea of Jesus. Full of the purely idealistic doctrine that it is the union of love which brings souls together, he declared that whenever men assembled in his name, he would be in their midst. He confided to the Church the right to bind and to unbind (that is to say, to render certain things lawful or unlawful), to remit sins, to reprimand, to warn with authority, and to pray with the certainty of being heard. It is possible that many of these sayings may have been attributed to the master, so as to give a foundation to the collective authority by which subsequently it was sought to replace that of Jesus. At all events, it was only after his death that particular churches were seen to be constituted, and even this first constitution was made purely and simply on the model of the synagogues. Many personages who had loved Jesus much, and had founded great hopes upon him, such as Joseph of Arimathea, Lazarus, Mary Magdalen, and Nicodemus, did not, it seems, enter these churches, but clung to the tender or respectful memory which they had preserved of him.

Moreover, there is no trace, in the teaching of Jesus, of an applied morality or of a canonical law, ever so slightly defined. Once only, respecting marriage, he spoke with decision, and forbade divorce. Neither was there any theology or creed. There were hardly any opinions respecting the Father, the Son, and the Spirit, from which, afterwards, were drawn the Trinity and the Incarnation, but they still remained in a state of indeterminate imagery. The later books of the Jewish canon recognised already in the Holy Spirit a sort of divine hypostasis, sometimes identified with Wisdom or the Word. Jesus insisted upon this point, and pretended to give to his disciples a baptism by fire and by the Spirit, as much preferable to that of John. For Jesus, this Holy Spirit, was not distinct from the inspiration emanating from God the Father in a continuous manner. People then speculated. It was pretended that Jesus had promised his disciples to send them after his death, to replace him, a Spirit who should teach them all things and bear witness to the truths he himself had promulgated. One day the apostles believed they had received the baptism of this spirit in the form of a great wind and tongues of fire. In order to designate this Spirit, people made use of the word Paraklit, which the Syro-Chaldaic had borrowed from the Greek (παρακλητος), and which appears to have had in this case the meaning of "advocate," "counsellor," and sometimes that of "interpreter of celestial truths," and of "teacher charged to reveal to men the hitherto hidden mysteries." It is very doubtful whether Jesus made use of this word. It was in this case an application of the process which the Jewish and Christian theologies would follow during centuries, and which was to produce a whole series of divine assessors, the Metathronos, the συναδελφος or Syndelphon, and all the personifications of the Cabala. Still, in Judaism, these creations were to remain free and individual speculations, whilst in Christianity, commencing with the fourth century, they were to form the very essence of orthodoxy and of the universal dogma.

It is needless to remark how remote from the thought of Jesus was the idea of a religious book, containing a code and articles of faith. Not only did he not write, but it was contrary to the spirit of the nascent sect to produce sacred books. They believed themselves on the eve of the great final catastrophe. The Messiah came to put the seal upon the Law and the Prophets, not to promulgate new texts. Further, with the exception of the Apocalypse, which was in one sense the only revealed book of the primitive Christianity, the writings of the apostolic age were works arising from circumstances, making no pretentions to furnish a completely dogmatic whole. The Gospels had at first an entirely personal character, and much less authority than tradition.

Had not the sect, however, some sacrament, some rite, some rallying point? It had the one which all tradition ascribes to Jesus. One of the favourite notions of the master was that he was the new bread, a bread very superior to manna, and on which mankind was to live. This notion, the germ of the Eucharist, took in his mouth at times singularly concrete forms. On one occasion especially, in the synagogue of Capernaum, he took a bold step, which cost him several of his disciples. "Verily, verily, I say unto you, Moses gave you not that bread from heaven; but my Father giveth you the true bread from heaven." And he added, "I am the bread of life: he that cometh to me shall never hunger, and he that believeth on me shall never thirst." These words excited deep murmurings. The Jews then murmured at him because he said, "I am the bread which came down from heaven. And they said, is not this Jesus the son of Joseph, whose father and mother we know? how is it then that he saith, I came down from heaven?" But Jesus, insisting with still more force, said, "I am that bread of life; your fathers did eat manna in the wilderness and are dead. This is the bread which cometh down from heaven, that a man may eat thereof and not die. I am the living bread which came down from heaven; if any man eat of this bread, he shall live for ever; and the bread that I will give is my flesh, which I will give for the life of the world." The ill-feeling was now at its height: "How can this man give us his flesh to eat?" Jesus, going still further, said, "Verily, verily, I say unto you, Except ye eat the flesh of the Son of man, and drink his blood, ye have no life in you. Whoso eateth my flesh and drinketh my blood hath eternal life, and I will raise him up at the last day. For my flesh is meat indeed, and my blood is drink indeed. He that eateth my flesh and drinketh my blood dwelleth in me, and I in him. As the living Father has sent me, and I live by the Father: so he that eateth me, even he shall live by me. This is that bread which came down from heaven: not as your fathers did eat manna, and are dead: he that eateth of this bread shall live for ever." Such paradoxical obstinacy offended several of his disciples, who ceased to follow him. Jesus did not retract; he only added: "It is the spirit that quickeneth; the flesh profiteth nothing. The words that I speak unto you, they are spirit, and they are life." The twelve remained faithful, despite this odd preaching. It gave to Cephas, in particular, an opportunity of showing his absolute devotion and of proclaiming once more, "Thou art that Christ, the Son of the living God."

It is probable that henceforward in the common repasts of the sect, there was established some custom which from the discourse was badly received by the men of Capernaum. But the apostolic traditions on this subject are very divergent and probably intentionally incomplete. The synoptical gospels, whose account is confirmed by St. Paul, suppose that a unique sacramental act served as basis to the mysterious rite, and refer it to "the last supper." The fourth gospel, which has accurately preserved to us the incident at the synagogue of Capernaum, does not speak of such an act, although it describes the last supper at great length. Elsewhere we see Jesus recognised in the breaking of bread, as if this act had been to those who associated with him the most characteristic of his person. When he was dead, the form under which he appeared to the pious memory of his disciples was that of chairman of a mysterious banquet, taking the bread, blessing it, breaking and giving it to those present. It is probable that this was one of his habits, and that at such times he was particularly amiable and tender. One material circumstance, the presence of fish upon the table (a striking indication, which proves that the rite was instituted on the shore of Lake Tiberias), was itself almost sacramental, and became a necessary part of the conceptions of the sacred feast.

Their repasts had become the sweetest moments of the infant community. At these times they all assembled; the master spoke to each one, and kept up a charming and lively conversation. Jesus loved these seasons, and was pleased to see his spiritual family thus grouped around him. The participation of the same bread was considered as a kind of communion, a reciprocal bond. The master used, in this respect, extremely strong terms, which were afterwards taken in a very literal sense. Jesus was, at once, very idealistic in his conceptions and very materialistic in his expression of them. Wishing to express the thought that the believer lives only by him, that altogether (body, blood, and soul) he was the life of the truly faithful, he said to his disciples, "I am your nourishment,"--a phrase which, turned in figurative style, became, "My flesh is your bread, my blood your drink." Then the modes of speech employed by Jesus, always strongly subjective, carried him yet further. At table, pointing to the food, he said, "I am here," holding the bread; "this is my body; holding up the wine, "This is my blood,"--all modes of speech which were equivalent to, "I am your nourishment."

This mysterious rite obtained in the lifetime of Jesus great importance. It was probably established some time before the last journey to Jerusalem, and it was the result of a general doctrine much more than a determinate act. After the death of Jesus, it became the great symbol of Christian communion, and it is to the most solemn moment of the life of the Saviour that its establishment is referred. It was wished to be shown in the consecration of bread and wine, a farewell memorial which Jesus, at the moment of quitting life, had left to his disciples. They recognised Jesus himself in this sacrament. The wholly spiritual idea of the presence of souls, which was one of the most familiar to the master, which made him say, for instance, that he was personally with his disciples when they were assembled in his name, rendered this easily admissible. Jesus, we have already said, never had a very clear idea of that which constitutes individuality. In the degree of exaltation to which he had attained, the ideal surpassed everything to such an extent that the body counted for nothing. We are one when we love one another, when we live in dependence on each other; it was thus that he and his disciples were one. His disciples adopted the same language. Those who for years had lived with him had seen him constantly take the bread and the cup "between his holy and venerable hands," and thus offer himself to them. It was he whom they ate and drank; he became the true passover, the former one having been abrogated by his blood. It is impossible to translate into our essentially hard and fast tongue, in which a rigorous distinction between the material and the metaphorical must always be observed, habits of style whose essential character is to attribute to metaphor, or rather to the idea it represents, a complete reality.

CHAPTER XIX

INCREASING PROGRESSION OF ENTHUSIASM AND OF EXALTATION

It is clear that such a religious society, founded exclusively on the expectation of the kingdom of God, must be in itself very incomplete. The first Christian generation lived almost entirely upon expectations and dreams. On the eve of seeing the world come to an end, it regarded as useless everything which served but to prolong the world. The desire to possess property was regarded as reprehensible. Everything which attaches man to earth, everything which draws him aside from heaven, was to be avoided. Although several of the disciples were married, there was, it seems, to be no more marriage after one became a member of the sect. The celibate was greatly preferred. At one time the master seems to approve of those who should mutilate themselves in view of the kingdom of God. In this he acted up to his precept. "If thy hand or thy foot offend thee, cut them off, and cast them from thee; it is better for thee to enter into life halt or maimed, rather than having two hands or two feet to be cast into everlasting fire. And if thine eye offend thee, pluck it out, and cast it from thee; it is better for thee to enter into life with one eye, rather than having two eyes to be cast into hell-fire." The cessation of generation was often considered as the symbol and condition of the kingdom of God.

We can perceive that this primitive Church never could have formed a durable society but for the great variety of germs embraced in the teaching of Jesus. It required more than another century for the true Christian Church--that which has converted the world--to disengage itself from this small sect of "latter-day saints," and to become a framework applicable to the whole of human society. The same thing, moreover, took place in Buddhism, which at first was founded only for monks. The same thing would have happened in the order of St. Francis, if that order had succeeded in its attempt to become the rule of the whole of human society. Being Utopian in their origin, and succeeding by their very exaggeration, the great systems of which we have just been speaking have only spread over the world after being profoundly modified, and after abandoning their excesses. Jesus did not overstep this first and entirely monachal period, in which it was believed that the impossible could be attempted with impunity. He did not make any concession to necessity. He boldly preached war against nature and a total rupture with the ties of blood. "Verily I say unto you," said he, "there is no man that hath left house, or parents, or brethren, or wife, or children, for the kingdom of God's sake, who shall not receive manifold more in this present time, and in the world to come life everlasting."

The instruction which Jesus is alleged to have given to his disciples breathes the same exaltation. He who was so lenient with the outside world, he who contented himself sometimes with formal adhesions, exercised towards his own an extreme rigour. He would have no "all buts." We should call it an "order," founded upon the most austere rules. Wrapped up in his idea that the cares of life trouble and debase man, Jesus required of his companions a complete detachment from the earth, an absolute devotion to his work. They ought not to carry with them either money or provisions for the way, not even a scrip, or a change of raiment. They ought to practise absolute poverty, live on alms and hospitality. "Freely ye have received, freely give," said he, in his beautiful language. Arrested and arraigned before the judges, they were not to prepare their defence; the heavenly advocate would inspire them as to what they should say. The Father would confer upon them His spirit from on high. This spirit would regulate all their acts, direct their thoughts, and guide them through the world. If chased from one town, they were to cast at it the dust from their shoes, and that none might plead ignorance, declaring always the proximity of the religion of God. "Ye shall not have gone over the cities of Israel," added he, "till the Son of man shall have appeared."

A strange ardour animates all these discourses, which may in part be the creation of the enthusiasm of his disciples, but which even in that case came indirectly from Jesus, since such enthusiasm was his work. Jesus informed those who wanted to follow him that they would be subjected to severe persecutions and the hatred of mankind. He sent them forth as lambs in the midst of wolves. They would be scourged in the synagogues, and dragged to prison. Brother should deliver up brother to death, the father the son. When they were persecuted in one country, they were to flee to another. "The disciple," said he, "is not above his master, nor the servant above his lord. Fear not them which kill the body, but are not able to kill the soul. Are not two sparrows sold for a farthing? and one of them shall not fall to the ground without your Father. But the very hairs of your head are all numbered. Fear ye not therefore, ye are of more value than many sparrows." "Whosoever, therefore," continued he, "shall confess me before men, him will I confess also before my Father which is in heaven. But whosoever shall deny me before men, him will I also deny before my Father which is in heaven."

In these fits of severity he went the length of suppressing the desires of the flesh. His requirements had no longer any bounds. Despising the healthy limits of man's nature, he demanded that the latter should exist only for him, that he should love him alone. "If any man come to me," said he, "and hate not his father, and mother, and wife, and children, and brethren, and sisters, and his own life also, he cannot be my disciple. So likewise, whosoever he be of you that forsaketh not all that he hath, he cannot be my disciple." There was something strange and more than human thus mixed up in his speech; it was like a fire consuming light to its root, and reducing everything to a frightful wilderness. The harsh and gloomy sentiment of distaste for the world, and of the excessive self-abnegation which characterises Christian perfection, was for the founders not the refined and cheerful moralist of his earlier days, but the sombre giant whom a kind of presentiment was withdrawing, more and more without the pale of humanity. We should even say that, in these moments, when warring against the most legitimate cravings of the heart, Jesus had forgotten the pleasure of living, of loving, of seeing, and of feeling. Employing more unmeasured language, he dared to say, "If any man will come after me, let him deny himself and follow me. He that loveth father or mother more than me is not worthy of me; and he that loveth son or daughter more than me is not worthy of me. He that findeth his life shall lose it, and he that loseth his life for my sake and the Gospel's shall find it. What is a man profited if he shall gain the whole world, and lose his own soul?" Two anecdotes of the kind we cannot accept as historical, which were intended to be an exaggeration of a trait of character, clearly illustrating this defiance of nature. He said to one man, "Follow me!"-- But he said, "Lord, suffer me first to go and bury my father." Jesus answered, "Let the dead bury their dead: but go thou and preach the kingdom of God." Another said to him, "Lord I will follow thee; but let me first go bid them farewell, which are at home at my house." Jesus replied, "No man, having put his hand to the plough and looking back, is fit for the kingdom of God." An extraordinary assurance, and at times accents of singular sweetness, reversing all our ideas of him, made these exaggerations acceptable. "Come unto me," cried he, "all ye that labour and are heavy laden, and I will give you rest. Take my yoke upon you, and learn of me: for I am meek and lowly in heart: and ye shall find rest unto your souls. For my yoke is easy, and my burden is light."

A great danger might result in the future from this exalted memory, which was expressed in hyperbolical language and with a terrible energy. By thus detaching man from earth, the ties of life were severed. The Christian would be praised for being a bad son, or a bad patriot, if it was for Christ that he resisted his father and fought against his country. The ancient city, the parent republic, the state, or the law common to all, were thus placed in hostility with the kingdom of God. A fatal germ of theocracy was introduced into the world.

From this point another consequence may be perceived. This morality, invented for a time of crisis, being transported into a peaceful country, into the bosom of a society assured of its own duration, must seem impossible. The Gospel was thus destined to become for Christians a Utopia, which very few would give themselves the trouble to inquire into. These terrible maxims, for the greater number sunk into profound oblivion, were encouraged by the clergy itself; the Gospel man was a dangerous man. The most selfish, proud, hard, and worldly of all human beings, a Louis XIV., for instance, found priests to persuade him, in spite of the Gospel, that he was a Christian. But, on the other hand, there have always been holy men who accepted the sublime paradoxes of Jesus literally. Perfection being placed beyond the ordinary conditions of society, a complete Gospel life could only be led away from the world, and thus the principle of asceticism and of monasticism was established. Christian societies would have two moral rules; the one moderately heroic for common men, the other exalted in the extreme for the perfect man; and the perfect man would be the monk, subjected to rules which professed to realise the Gospel ideal. It is certain that this ideal, were it only on account of the celibacy and poverty it imposed, could not become the common law. The monk would thus, in some respects, be the only true Christian. Ordinary common sense revolts at these excesses; and to believe in the latter is to believe that the impossible is a mark of weakness and error. But ordinary common sense is a bad judge where the question at issue has reference to great things. To obtain little from humanity, we must ask much. The immense moral progress due the Gospel is the result of its exaggerations. It is thus that it has been, like stoicism, but with infinitely greater fulness, a living argument for the divine powers, which are, in man, an exalted monument of the potency of the will.

We may readily imagine that to Jesus, at this period of his life, everything which did not belong to the kingdom of God had absolutely disappeared. He was, if we may say so, totally outside nature: family, friendship, country, had no longer any meaning for him. He, no doubt, from this moment, had already sacrificed his life. At times, we are tempted to believe that, seeing in his own death a means of founding his kingdom, he conceived the purpose of allowing himself to be killed. At other times, although such a thought was only afterwards erected into a doctrine, death presented itself to him as a sacrifice, destined to appease his Father and to save mankind. A singular taste for persecution and torments possessed him. His blood appeared to him as the water of a second baptism with which he ought to be saturated, and he seemed possessed by a strange haste to anticipate this baptism, which alone could quench his thirst.

The grandeur of his views upon the future was at times surprising. He did not deceive himself as to the terrible storm he was about to cause in the world. "Think not," said he, boldly and beautifully, "that I am come to send peace on earth: I came not to send peace, but a sword. There shall be five in one house divided, three against two, and two against three. I am come to set a man at variance against his father, and the daughter against her mother, and the daughter-in-law against her mother-in-law. And a man's foes shall be they of his own household." "I am come to send fire on the earth; and what will I, if it be already kindled?" "They shall put you out of the synagogues," he continued; "yea, the time cometh, that whosoever killeth you will think that he doeth God service." "If the world hate you, ye know that it hated me before it hated you. Remember the word that I said unto you: The servant is not greater than his lord. If they have persecuted me, they will also persecute you."

Carried away by this fearfully increasing enthusiasm, and governed by the necessities of a preaching more and more exalted, Jesus was no longer free; he belonged to his mission, and, in one sense, to mankind. Sometimes it might have been averred that his reason was disturbed. He suffered great mental anguish and agitation. The great vision of the kingdom of God, dangling constantly before his eyes, bewildered him. It must be remembered that, at times, those about him believed him to be mad, while his enemies declared him to be possessed. His excessively impassioned temperament carried him incessantly beyond the bounds of human nature. His work not being a work of the reason, jeering at all the laws of the human mind, that which he most imperiously required was "faith." This was the word most frequently repeated in the little guest-chamber. It is the watchword of all popular movements. It is clear that none of these movements would take place, if it were necessary that their author should gain his disciples one by one by force of logic. Reflection leads only to doubt, and if the authors of the French Revolution, for instance, had had to be previously convinced by lengthened meditations, they would all have become old without accomplishing anything. Jesus, in like manner, aimed less at convincing his hearers than at exciting their enthusiasm. Urgent and imperative, he suffered no opposition: men must be converted, nothing less would satisfy him. His natural gentleness seemed to have abandoned him; he was sometimes harsh and capricious. His disciples at times did not understand him, and experienced in his presence a feeling akin to fear. Sometimes his displeasure at the slightest opposition led him to commit inexplicable and apparently absurd acts.

It was not that his virtue deteriorated; but his struggle in the cause of the ideal against the reality became insupportable. Contact with the world pained and revolted him. Obstacles irritated him. His notion of the Son of God became disturbed and exaggerated. One is such at certain times, through sudden illuminations, and is lost in the midst of long obscurities. Divinity has its intermittencies; one is not the Son of God all his life and in consecutive manner. The fatal law which condemns an idea to decay as soon as it seeks to convert men, was applicable to Jesus. Contact with men degraded him to their level. The tone he had adopted could not be sustained beyond a few months; it was time that death came to liberate him from an endurance strained to the utmost, to remove him from the impossibilities of an interminable path, and by delivering him from a trial in danger of being too prolonged, introduce him henceforth sinless into celestial peace.

CHAPTER XX

OPPOSITION TO JESUS

During the early period of his career, Jesus does not appear to have encountered any serious opposition. His preaching, thanks to the extreme liberty which was enjoyed in Galilee, and to the great number of teachers who arose on all sides, made no noise outside a somewhat restricted circle of persons. But when Jesus entered upon a career brilliant with prodigies and public successes, the storm began to howl. More than once he was obliged to conceal himself and fly. Antipas, however, never interfered with him, although Jesus expressed himself sometimes very severely respecting him. At Tiberias, his usual residence, the Tetrarch was only one or two leagues distant from the district chosen by Jesus for the field of his activity; he was told of his miracles, which he doubtless took to be clever tricks, and desired to see them. The incredulous were at that time very curious about this sort of illusions. With his ordinary tact, Jesus refused to gratify him. He took care not to be led astray by an irreligious world, which wished to extort from him some idle amusement; he aspired only to gain the people; he reserved for the simple, means suitable to them alone.

Once the report was spread that Jesus was no other than John the Baptist risen from the dead. Antipas became anxious and uneasy; he employed artifice to rid his dominions of the new prophet. Certain Pharisees, under the pretence of being interested in Jesus, came to tell him that Antipas was seeking to kill him. Jesus, despite his great simplicity, saw the snare, and did not depart. His wholly pacific attractions, and his remoteness from popular agitation, ultimately reassured the Tetrarch and dissipated the danger.

The new doctrine was by no means received with equal favour in all the towns of Galilee. Not only did incredulous Nazareth continue to reject him who was to become her glory; not only did his brothers persist in not believing in him, but also the cities of the lake themselves, in general well-disposed, were not wholly converted. Jesus often complained of the incredulity and hardness of heart which he encountered, and although it is natural in such reproaches to make allowance for a certain kind of exaggeration of the preacher, although we are sensible of that kind of convicium seculi which Jesus affected in imitation of John the Baptist, it is clear that the country was far from yielding itself entirely to the kingdom of God. "Woe unto thee, Chorazin! woe unto thee, Bethsaida!" cried he; "for if the mighty works, which were done in you, had been done in Tyre and Sidon, they would have repented long ago in sackcloth and ashes. But I say unto you, It shall be more tolerable for Tyre and Sidon at the day of judgment than for you. And thou, Capernaum, which art exalted unto heaven, shalt be brought down to hell; for if the mighty works, which have been done in thee, had been done in Sodom, it would have remained until this day. But I say unto you, That it shall be more tolerable for the land of Sodom in the day of judgment than for thee." "The queen of the south," added he, "shall rise up in the judgment against the men of this generation, and shall condemn it; for she came from the uttermost parts of the earth to hear the wisdom of Solomon; and behold, a greater than Solomon is here. The men of Nineveh shall rise in judgment with this generation, and shall condemn it: because they repented at the preaching of Jonas; and behold, a greater than Jonas is here." His roaming life, at first so full of charm, now began to weigh upon him. "The foxes," said he, "have holes, and the birds of the air have nests; but the Son of man hath not where to lay his head." He accused unbelievers of not yielding to evidence.

Jesus, in fact, could not withstand opposition with the coolness of the philosopher, who, understanding the reason of the various opinions which divide the world, finds it quite natural that all should not be of his opinion. One of the principal defects of the Jewish race is its harshness in controversy, and the abusive tone which it almost always infuses into it. There never were in the world such bitter quarrels as those of the Jews among themselves. It is the sentiment of nice discernment which makes the polished and moderate man. Now, the lack of this feeling is one of the most constant features of the Semitic mind. Refined works, such as the dialogues of Plato, for example, are altogether foreign to these nations. Jesus, who was exempt from almost all the defects of his race, and whose dominant quality was precisely an infinite delicacy, was led in spite of himself to make use of the general style in polemics. Like John the Baptist, he employed very harsh terms against his adversaries. Of an exquisite gentleness with the simple, he was irritated in presence of incredulity, however little aggressive. He was no longer the mild teacher who delivered the "Sermon on the Mount," who as yet had met with neither resistance nor difficulty. The passion that underlay his character led him to make use of the keenest invectives. This singular mixture ought not to surprise us. A man of our own times, M. de Lamennais, has forcibly presented the same contrast. In his beautiful book, "The Words of a Believer," the most immoderate anger and the sweetest relentings alternate, as in a mirage. This man, who was extremely kind in the intercourse of life, became foolishly intractable toward those who did not think as he did. Jesus, in like manner, applied to himself, not without reason, the passage from Isaiah: "He shall not strive, nor cry; neither shall any man hear his voice in the streets. A bruised reed shall he not break, and smoking flax shall he not quench." And yet many of the recommendations which he addressed to his disciples contain the germs of a real fanaticism, germs which the Middle Ages were to develop in a cruel manner. Must we reproach him for this? No revolution can be effected without some harshness. If Luther, or the actors in the French Revolution, had had to observe the rules of politeness, neither the Reformation nor the Revolution would have taken place. Let us congratulate ourselves in like manner that Jesus encountered no law which punished the outrageous denunciation of one class of citizens. The Pharisees in such a case would have been inviolate. All the great things of humanity have been accomplished in the name of absolute principles. A critical philosopher would have said to his disciples: Respect the opinion of others, and believe that no one is so completely right that his adversary is completely wrong. But the action of Jesus has nothing in common with the disinterested speculation of the philosopher. To say that we have touched the ideal for a moment, and have been deterred by the wickedness of a few, is a thought insupportable to an ardent soul. What must it have been for the founder of a new world?

The invincible obstacle to the designs of Jesus came in particular from orthodox Judaism, represented by the Pharisees. Jesus drifted away more and more from the ancient Law. Now, the Pharisees were the backbone of Judaism. Although this party had its centre at Jerusalem, it had, nevertheless, adherents either established in Galilee or who often came to the North. They were, in general, men of a narrow mind, giving much attention to externals; with a devoutness that was haughty, formal, and self-satisfied. Their manners were ridiculous, and excited the smiles of even those who respected them. The epithets which the people gave them, and which savour of caricature, prove this. There was the "bandy-legged Pharisee" (Nikfi), who walked in the streets dragging his feet and knocking them against the stones; the "bloody-browed Pharisee" (Kizai), who went with his eyes shut in order not to see the women, and dashed his head so much against the walls that it was always bloody; the "pestle Pharisee" (Medoukia), who kept himself bent double like the handle of a pestle; the "Pharisee of strong shoulders" (Schikmi), who walked with his back bent as if he carried on his shoulders the whole burden of the Law; the "What-is-there-to-do?-I-do-it Pharisee," always on the outlook for a precept to fulfil. To these we must add the "dyed Pharisee," whose whole outward devotion was but a varnish of hypocrisy. This rigourism was, in fact, often only apparent, and concealed in reality great moral laxity. The people, nevertheless, were duped by it. The people, whose instinct is always right, even when it goes furthest astray on the question of individuals, is very easily deceived by false devotees. That which it loves in them is good and worthy of being loved; but it has not sufficient penetration to distinguish the appearance from the reality.

The antipathy which, in such an impassioned state of society, would necessarily break out between Jesus and persons of this character is easy to understand. Jesus sought only the religion of the heart; the religion of the Pharisees consisted almost exclusively in observances. Jesus sought after the humble and all kinds of outcasts; the Pharisees saw in this an insult to their religion of respectability. The Pharisee was an infallible and impeccable man, a pedant always certain of being in the right, taking the first place in the synagogue, praying in the street, giving alms to the sound of a trumpet, and watching to see whether people saluted him. Jesus maintained that each one ought to await the judgment of God with fear and trembling. The bad religious tendency represented by Pharisaism by no means reigned without opposition. Many men before or during the time of Jesus, such as Jesus, son of Sirach (one of the real ancestors of Jesus of Nazareth), Gamaliel, Antigonus of Soco, and especially the gentle and noble Hillel, had taught much more elevated and almost Gospel doctrines. But these good seeds had been choked. The beautiful maxims of Hillel, summing up the whole Law as equity, and those of Jesus, son of Sirach, making worship consist in the pursuit of the good, were forgotten or anathematised. Shammai, with his narrow and exclusive mind, had prevailed. An enormous mass of "traditions" had stifled the Law, under the pretext of protecting and interpreting it. No doubt these conservative measures had their useful side; it is well that the Jewish people loved its Law even to madness, inasmuch as this frantic love in saving Mosaism under Antiochus Epiphanes and under Herod, preserved the leaven necessary for the production of Christianity. But taken by themselves, these obsolete precautions we speak of were only puerile. The synagogue, which was the depository of them, was no more than a parent of error. Its reign was ended; and yet to ask for its abdication was to ask for that which an established power has never done or been able to do.

The conflicts of Jesus with official hypocrisy were continual. The ordinary tactics of the reformers who appeared in the religious state which we have just described, and which might be called "traditional formalism," were to oppose the "text" of the sacred books to "traditions." Religious zeal is always an innovator, even when it pretends to be in the highest degree conservative. Just as the neo-Catholics of our days are getting further and further away from the Gospel, so the Pharisees, at each step, got further away from the Bible. This is why the Puritan reformer is as a rule essentially "biblical," setting out with the unchangeable text in order to criticise the current theology, which has changed from generation to generation. Thus acted later the Karaites and the Protestants. Jesus applied the axe to the root of the tree much more energetically. True, we see him sometimes quoting texts against the false masores or traditions of the Pharisees. But, in general, he set little store by exegesis; it was the conscience to which he appealed. With the same stroke he cut through both text and commentaries. He showed indeed to the Pharisees that by their traditions they seriously perverted Mosaism, but he by no means pretended himself to return to Mosaism. His goal was the future, not the past. Jesus was more than the reformer of an obsolete religion; he was the founder of the eternal religion of humanity.

Disputes broke out, especially in regard to a number of external practices introduced by tradition, a tradition which neither Jesus nor his disciples observed. The Pharisees reproached him sharply for this. When he dined with them he scandalised them greatly by not going through the customary ablutions. "Give alms," said he, "of such things as ye have; and behold, all things are clean unto you." That which in the highest degree wounded his sensitive nature was the air of assurance which the Pharisees carried into religious matters; their contemptible devotion which ended in a vain seeking after precedents and titles, and not the improvement of their hearts. An admirable parable expressed this thought with infinite charm and justice. "Two men," said he, "went up into the temple to pray; the one a Pharisee, and the other a publican. The Pharisee stood and prayed thus with himself, God, I thank thee that I am not as other men are, extortioners, unjust, adulterers, or even as this publican. I fast twice in the week, I give tithes of all that I possess.' And the publican, standing afar off, would not lift up so much as his eyes unto heaven, but smote upon his breast, saying, God be merciful to me a sinner. I tell you this man went down to his house justified rather than the other."

A hatred which death alone could assuage was the consequence of these struggles. John the Baptist had previously provoked enmities of the same kind. But the aristocrats of Jerusalem, who despised him, had allowed simple men to regard him as a prophet. In this case, however, the war was to the death. It was a new spirit that had appeared in the world, which shattered all that had preceded it. John the Baptist was a thorough Jew: Jesus was scarcely one at all. Jesus always addressed himself to refined moral sentiment. He was only a disputant when he argued against the Pharisees, his opponents forcing him, as almost always happens, to adopt their tone. His exquisite irony, his stinging remarks, always went to the heart. They were everlasting stings, and have remained festering in the wound. This Nessus-shirt of ridicule which the Jew, son of the Pharisees, has dragged in tatters after him during eighteen centuries, was woven by Jesus with a divine skill. Masterpieces of fine raillery, their features are written in lines of fire upon the flesh of the hypocrite and the false devotee. Incomparable traits worthy of a Son of God! A god alone knows how to kill in this way. Socrates and Molière only grazed the skin. The former carried fire and rage to the very marrow.

But it was also just that this great master of irony should pay for his triumph with his life. Even in Galilee the Pharisees sought to kill him, and employed against him the manoeuvre which ultimately succeeded at Jerusalem. They endeavoured to interest in their quarrel the partisans of the new political order which was established. The facilities Jesus found for escaping into Galilee, and the weakness of the government of Antipas, baffled these attempts. He exposed himself to danger of his own free will. He saw clearly that his action, if he remained interned in Galilee, was necessarily limited. Judea attracted him as by a charm; he wished to put forth a last effort to gain over the rebellious city, and seemed anxious to undertake the task of fulfilling the proverb--that a prophet must not die outside Jerusalem.

CHAPTER XXI

LAST JOURNEY OF JESUS TO JERUSALEM

For a long time Jesus had been conscious of the dangers which surrounded him. During a period which we may estimate at eighteen months, he avoided going on a pilgrimage to the holy city. At the feast of Tabernacles of the year 32 (according to the hypothesis we have adopted), his relations, always malevolent and incredulous, persuaded him to go there. The evangelist seems to insinuate that there was some hidden project to ruin him in this invitation. "Depart hence, and go into Judea, that thy disciples also may see the works that thou doest. For there is no man that doeth anything in secret, and he himself seeketh to be known openly. If thou do these things, show thyself to the world." Jesus, suspecting some treachery, at first refused; but when the caravan of pilgrims had set out, he started on the journey, unknown to every one, and almost alone. It was the last farewell which he bade to Galilee. The feast of Tabernacles fell at the autumnal equinox. Six months had still to run before the fatal denouement. But, during this interval, Jesus did not again see his beloved provinces of the north. The pleasant days are passed; he must now traverse, step by step, the sorrowful path which will terminate in the anguish of death.

His disciples and the pious women who ministered to him found him again in Judea. But how much everything else was changed for him! Jesus was a stranger at Jerusalem. He felt that there was a wall of resistance he could not pierce. Surrounded by snares and obstacles, he was unceasingly pursued by the ill-will of the Pharisees. In place of that illimitable faculty of belief, the happy gift of youthful natures, which he found in Galilee--instead of those good and gentle people, amongst whom opposition (always the fruit to some extent of ill-will and indocility) had no existence, he encountered there at each step an obstinate incredulity, upon which the policy that had succeeded so well in the north had little effect. His disciples were despised as being Galileans. Nicodemus, who, on one of his former journeys, had had a conversation with him by night, almost compromised himself with the Sanhedrim, by having sought to defend him. "Art thou also of Galilee they said to him. "Search and look: for out of Galilee ariseth no prophet."

The city, as we have already said, was disliked by Jesus. Until then he had always eschewed great centres, preferring to pursue his avocation in the country and the towns of small importance. Many of the precepts which he had given to his apostles were absolutely inapplicable outside a simple society of humble men. Having no idea of the world, and accustomed to the amiable communism of Galilee, remarks continually escaped him, the simplicity of which at Jerusalem would appear very singular. His imagination and his love of nature found themselves restrained within these walls. True religion does not proceed from the tumult of towns, but from the tranquil serenity of the fields.

The arrogance of the priests rendered the precincts of the temple disagreeable to him. One day some of his disciples, who were better acquainted with Jerusalem than he, wished to draw his attention to the beauty of the buildings of the temple, the admirable choice of materials, and the richness of the votive offerings that covered the walls. "Seest thou these buildings?" said he; "there shall not be left one stone upon another." He refused to admire anything, unless it was a poor widow who passed at that moment, and threw a small coin into the box. "She has cast in more than they all," said he; "for all these have of their abundance cast in unto the offerings of God: but she of her penury hath cast in all the living that she had." This manner of regarding critically all that was going on at Jerusalem, of extolling the poor who gave little, of slighting the rich who gave much, and of blaming the opulent priesthood who did nothing for the good of the people, naturally exasperated the sacerdotal caste. The seat of a conservative aristocracy, the temple, like the Mussulman karam which succeeded it, was the last place in the world whence revolution could succeed. Imagine for a moment an innovator in our days going to preach the overturning of Islamism round the mosque of Omar! Jerusalem, however, was the centre of the Jewish life, the point where it was necessary to conquer or die. On this Calvary, where Jesus certainly suffered more than at Golgotha, his days passed away in disputation and bitterness, in the midst of tedious controversies as to canonical law and exegesis, for which his great moral elevation served him to little purpose--nay, placed him rather at a disadvantage.

In the midst of this troubled life, the sensitive and kindly heart of Jesus succeeded in creating a refuge, where he enjoyed much soft contentment. After having passed the day disputing in the temple, towards evening Jesus descended into the valley of Kedron, and took a little repose in the orchard of a farming establishment (probably for the making of oil) named Gethsemane (which was used as a pleasure resort by the inhabitants), after which he proceeded to pass the night upon the Mount of Olives, which limits on the east the horizon of the city. This side is the only one, in the environs of Jerusalem, which presents an aspect somewhat pleasing and verdant. The plantations of olives, figs, and palms were numerous around the villages, farms, or enclosures of Bethphage, Gethsemane, and Bethany. There were upon the Mount of Olives two great cedars, the recollection of which was long preserved amongst the dispersed Jews; their branches served as an asylum to clouds of doves, and under their shade were established small bazaars. All this precinct was in a manner the abode of Jesus and his disciples; we can see that they knew it almost field by field and house by house.

The village of Bethany, in particular, situated at the summit of the hill, upon the incline which commands the Dead Sea and the Jordan, at a journey of an hour and a half from Jerusalem, was the place preferred by Jesus. He made there the acquaintance of a family consisting of three persons, two sisters and a third member, whose friendship had a great charm for him. Of the two sisters, the one, named Martha, was an obliging, kind, and bustling person; the other, named Mary, on the contrary, pleased Jesus by a sort of languor, and by her strongly-developed speculative instincts. Often, when seated at the feet of Jesus, she forgot, in listening to him, the duties of real life. Her sister, upon whom fell all the duty at such times, gently complained. "Martha, Martha," said Jesus to her, "thou art troubled, and carest about many things; now, one thing only is needful. Mary has chosen the better part, which will not be taken away." A certain Simon, the leper, who was the owner of the house, appears to have been the brother of Martha and Mary, or, at least, to have formed part of the family. It was there, in the midst of a pious friendship, that Jesus forgot the vexations of public life. In this tranquil abode he consoled himself for the bickerings with which the Pharisees and the scribes unceasingly irritated him. He often sat on the Mount of Olives, facing Mount Moriah, having beneath his view the splendid perspective of the terraces of the temple, and its roofs covered with glittering plates of metal. This view struck strangers with admiration. At the rising of the sun, especially, the sacred mountain dazzled the eyes, and appeared like a mass of snow and of gold. But a profound feeling of sadness poisoned for Jesus the spectacle that filled all other Israelites with joy and pride. "O Jerusalem, Jerusalem, thou that killest the prophets, and stonest them which are sent unto thee, how often would I have gathered thy children together, even as a hen gathereth her chickens under her wings, and ye would not."

It was not that many good people here, as in Galilee, were not touched. But such was the power of the dominant orthodoxy that very few dared to confess it. They feared to discredit themselves in the eyes of the Jerusalemites by placing themselves in the school of a Galilean. They would have risked being driven from the synagogue, which, in a mean and bigoted society, was the greatest affront. Excommunication, besides, carried with it the confiscation of all possessions. By ceasing to be a Jew a man did not become a Roman; he remained without protection in the power of a theocratic legislation of the most atrocious severity. One day the inferior officers of the temple, who had assisted at one of the discourses of Jesus, and had been enchanted with it, came to confide their doubts to the priests. "Have any of the rulers or of the Pharisees believed on him?" was the reply to them; " but this people who knoweth not the Law are cursed." Jesus remained thus at Jerusalem, a provincial, admired by provincials like himself, but spurned by all the aristocracy of the nation. The chiefs of the school were too numerous for any one to be stirred by seeing one more appear. His voice made little noise in Jerusalem. The prejudices of race and of sect, the direct enemies of the spirit of the Gospel, were too deeply rooted there.

The teaching of Jesus in this new world necessarily became much modified. His beautiful discourses, the effect of which was always calculated upon when addressed to youthful imaginations and consciences morally pure, here fell upon stone. He who was so much at his ease on the shores of his charming little lake felt constrained and not at home in the company of pedants. His perpetual self-assertion appeared somewhat fastidious. He was obliged to become controversialist, jurist, exegetist, and theologian. His conversations, generally so full of charm, became a rolling fire of disputes, an interminable train of scholastic battles. His harmonious genius was wasted in insipid argumentations upon the Law and the prophets, in which case we should have preferred not seeing him sometimes play the part of aggressor. He lent himself with a condescension which wounds us to the captious criticisms to which the merciless cavillers subjected him. In general, he extricated himself from difficulties with much finesse. His reasonings, it is true, were often subtle (simplicity of mind and subtlety touch each other; when simplicity reasons, it is often a little sophistical); we find that sometimes he courted misconceptions, and prolonged them intentionally; his argumentation, judged according to the rules of Aristotelian logic, was very feeble. But when the unequalled charm of his mind could be displayed, he was triumphant. One day it was intended to embarrass him by presenting to him an adulteress and asking him what was to be done to her. We know the admirable answer of Jesus. The fine raillery of a man of the world, tempered by a divine goodness, could not be expressed in a more exquisite manner. But the wit which is allied to moral grandeur is that which fools forgive the least. In pronouncing this sentence of so just and pure a taste, "He that is without sin among you, let him first cast a stone at her." Jesus pierced hypocrisy to the heart, and with the same stroke sealed his own death-warrant.

It is probable, in fact, that but for the exasperation caused by so many bitter retorts, Jesus might long have remained unnoticed, and have been lost in the dreadful storm which was soon about to overwhelm the whole Jewish nation. The high priesthood and Sadducees treated him rather with disdain than hatred. The great sacerdotal families, the Boethusim, the family of Hanan, were only fanatical in their conservatism. The Sadducees, like Jesus, rejected the "traditions" of the Pharisees. By a very strange singularity, it was these unbelievers who, denying the resurrection, the oral Law, and the existence of angels, were the true Jews. Or rather, as the old Law in its simplicity no longer satisfied the religious wants of the time, those who strictly adhered to it, and rejected modern inventions, were regarded by the devotees as impious, just as an evangelical Protestant of the present day is regarded as an unbeliever in orthodox countries. At all events, from such a party no very strong reaction against Jesus could proceed. The official priesthood, with its eyes turned towards political power, and intimately connected with it, did not comprehend these enthusiastic movements. It was the middle-class Pharisees, the innumerable soferim, or scribes, living on the science of "traditions," who took the alarm, and whose prejudices and interests were in reality threatened by the doctrine of the new teacher.

One of the most constant efforts of the Pharisees was to draw Jesus into the discussion of political questions, and to compromise him as being connected with the party of Judas the Gaulonite. Their tactics were clever; for it required all the great ingenuity of Jesus to avoid conflict with the Roman authority, whilst he was proclaiming the kingdom of God. They sought to break through this ambiguity, and compel him to explain himself. One day, a group of Pharisees, and of those politicians named "Herodians" (probably some of the Boethusim), approached him, and, under pretence of pious zeal, said unto him, "Master, we know that thou art true, and teachest the way of God in truth, neither carest thou for any man. Tell us, therefore, what thinkest thou? Is it lawful to give tribute unto Cæsar, or not?" They hoped for an answer, which would give them a pretext for delivering him up to Pilate. The reply of Jesus was admirable. He made them show him the image of the coin. "Render," said he, "unto Cæsar the things which are Cæsar's; and unto God the things that are God's." Sage words, which have decided the future of Christianity! Words of a perfected spiritualism, and of marvellous justness, which have established the separation between the spiritual and the temporal, and laid the basis of true liberalism and true civilisation!

His gentle and penetrating genius inspired him when he was alone with his disciples, with accents full of tenderness! "Verily, verily, I say unto you, he that entereth not by the door into the sheepfold, but climbeth up some other way, the same is a thief and a robber. But he that entereth in by the door is the shepherd of the sheep. The sheep hear his voice: and he calleth his own sheep by name, and leadeth them out. He goeth before them, and the sheep follow him; for they know his voice. The thief cometh not, but for to steal, and to kill, and to destroy. But he that is an hireling, and not the shepherd, whose own the sheep are not, seeth the wolf coming, and leaveth the sheep, and fleeth. I am the good shepherd, and know my sheep, and am known of mine; and I lay down my life for the sheep." The idea that the crisis of humanity was close at hand frequently recurred to him. "Now," said he, "learn a parable of the fig-tree: When his branch is yet tender, and putteth forth leaves, ye know that summer is nigh. Lift up your eyes, and look on the fields; for they are white already to harvest."

His powerful eloquence found expression always when contending with hypocrisy. "The scribes and Pharisees sit in Moses' seat. All, therefore, whatsoever they bid you observe, that observe and do; but do not ye after their works: for they say and do not. For they bind heavy burdens and grievous to be borne, and lay them on men's shoulders; but they themselves will not move them with one of their fingers.

"But all their works they do to be seen of men; they make broad their phylacteries, enlarge the borders of their garments, and love the uppermost rooms at feasts, and the chief seats in the synagogues, and greetings in the markets, and to be called of men, Rabbi, Rabbi. Woe unto them! . . . . . .

"Woe unto you, scribes and Pharisees, hypocrites! for ye have taken away the key of knowledge, shut up the kingdom of heaven against men! For ye neither go in yourselves, neither suffer ye them that are entering to go in. Woe unto you, for ye devour widows' houses, and for a pretence, make long prayers: therefore ye shall receive the greater damnation. Woe unto you, for ye compass sea and land to make one proselyte; and when he is made, ye make him twofold more the child of hell than yourselves! Woe unto you, for ye are as graves which appear not; and the men that walk over them are not aware of them.

"Ye fools, and blind! for ye pay tithe of mint and anise and cummin, and have omitted the weightier matters of the Law, judgment, mercy, and faith: these ought ye to have done, and not to leave the other undone. Ye blind guides, which strain at a gnat, and swallow a camel! Woe unto you!

"Woe unto you, scribes and Pharisees, hypocrites! for ye make clean the outside of the cup and of the platter; but within they are full of extortion and excess. Thou blind Pharisee, cleanse first that which is within the cup and platter, that the outside of them may be clean also.

"Woe unto you, scribes and Pharisees, hypocrites! for ye are like unto whited sepulchres, which indeed appear beautiful outward, but are within full of dead men's bones and of all uncleannesss. Even so ye also outwardly appear righteous unto men, but within ye are full of hypocrisy and iniquity.

Woe unto you, scribes and Pharisees, hypocrites! because ye build the tombs of the prophets, and garnish the sepulchres of the righteous, and say, If we had been in the days of our fathers, we would not have been partakers with them in the blood of the prophets.' Wherefore, ye be witnesses unto yourselves, that ye are the children of them which killed the prophets. Fill ye up then the measure of your fathers. Therefore, also,' said the Wisdom of God, I will send unto you prophets, and wise men, and scribes; and some of them ye shall kill and crucify; and some of them shall ye scourge in your synagogues, and persecute them from city to city. That upon you may come all the righteous blood shed upon the earth, from the blood of righteous Abel unto the blood of Zacharias, son of Bacharias, whom ye slew between the temple and the altar.' Verily, I say unto you, all these things shall come upon this generation."

His terrible dogma of the substitution of the Gentiles,--the idea that the kingdom of God was going to be transferred to others, because those for whom it was destined would not receive it, is used as a fearful menace against the aristocracy, and his title "Son of God," which he openly assumed in striking parables, wherein his enemies appeared as murderers of the heavenly messengers, was an open defiance of legal Judaism. The bold appeal he addressed to the poor was still more seditious. He declared that he had "come that they which see not might see, and that they which see might be made blind." One day, his dislike of the temple forced from him an imprudent speech: "I will destroy this temple that is made with hands, and within three days I will build another made without hands." We do not know what meaning Jesus attached to this phrase, in which his disciples sought for allegories. But as only a pretext was wanted, this sentence was quickly laid hold of. It reappeared in the preamble of his death-warrant, and rang in the ears amidst his last agonies of Golgotha. These irritating discussions always ended in tumult. The Pharisees threw stones at him; in doing which they only fulfilled an article of the Law, which commanded that every prophet, even a thaumaturgist, who should turn the people from the ancient worship, be stoned without a hearing. At other times they called him mad, possessed, Samaritan, or even sought to kill him. These words were taken note of in order to invoke against him the laws of an intolerant theocracy, which the Roman government had not yet abrogated.

CHAPTER XXII

MACHINATIONS OF THE ENEMIES OF JESUS

Jesus passed the autumn and a part of the winter at Jerusalem. This season is there rather cold. The portico of Solomon, with its covered aisles, was the place where he habitually walked. This portico, the only portion of the ancient temple which remained, consisted of two galleries, formed by two rows of columns, by the wall which overlooked the valley of Kedron, which was doubtless less covered with debris than it is at the present time. The depth of the ravine could not be measured from the height of the portico; and it seemed, in consequence of the angle of the slopes, as if an abyss opened immediately beneath the wall. The other side of the valley even at that time was adorned with sumptuous tombs. Some of the monuments, which may be seen at the present day, were perhaps those cenotaphs in honour of ancient prophets which Jesus pointed out, when, seated under the portico, he denounced the official classes, who covered their hypocrisy or their vanity by these colossal piles.

At the end of the month of December he celebrated at Jerusalem the feast established by Judas Maccabeus in memory of the purification of the temple after the sacrileges of Antiochus Epiphanes. It was also called the "Feast of Lights," because, during the eight days of the feast, lamps were kept lighted in the houses. Jesus soon after undertook a journey into Perea and to the banks of the Jordan, -- that is to say, into the same country he had visited some years previously, when he belonged to the school of John, and where he himself had administered baptism. He seems to have reaped some consolation from this journey, specially at Jericho. This city, either as the terminus of several important routes, or on account of its gardens of spices and its rich cultivation, was a customs station of some importance. The chief receiver, Zaccheus, a rich man, desired to see Jesus. As he was of small stature, he mounted a sycamore tree near the road which the procession had to pass. Jesus was touched with this condescension in a person of consideration, and at the risk of giving offence he went to the house of Zaccheus. There was much murmuring at his thus honouring the house of a sinner by a visit. In parting, Jesus described his host as a good son of Abraham; and, as if to add to the vexation of the orthodox, Zaccheus became a Christian; he gave, it is said, the half of his goods to the poor, and restored fourfold to those whom he might have wronged. Further, this was not the only pleasure Jesus experienced there. On leaving the town, the beggar Bartimeus pleased him much by persistently calling him "son of David," although he was enjoined to be silent. The cycle of Galilean miracles appeared for a time to recommence in this country, a country similar in many respects to the provinces of the north. The delightful oasis of Jericho, at that time well watered, must have been one of the most beautiful places in Syria. Josephus speaks of it with the same admiration as of Galilee, and calls it, like the latter province, a "divine country."

After Jesus had completed this kind of pilgrimage to the scenes of his earliest prophetic activity, he returned to his beloved abode in Bethany. That which most pained the faithful Galileans at Jerusalem was that he had not done any miracles there. Grieved at the cold reception which the kingdom of God found in the capital, the friends of Jesus wished, it seems, for a great miracle which should strike powerfully the incredulity of the Jerusalemites. A resurrection of a man known at Jerusalem appeared to them the most likely to carry conviction. It is to be supposed that Martha and Mary had spoken to Jesus on the subject. We must bear in mind that the essential condition of true criticism is to understand the diversity of times, and to rid ourselves of the instinctive repugnances which are the fruit of a purely rational education. We must also remember that in this dull and impure city of Jerusalem Jesus was no longer himself. Not by any fault of his own, but by that of others, his conscience had lost something of its originate purity. Desperate, and driven to extremity, he was no longer his own master. His mission overwhelmed him, and he yielded to the torrent. As always happens in the lives of great and inspired men, he suffered the miracles opinion demanded of him rather than performed them. At this distance of time, and with only a single text, bearing evident traces of artifices of composition, it is impossible to decide whether in this instance the whole is fiction, or whether a real fact which happened at Bethany has served as basis to the rumours which were spread about it. It must be acknowledged, however, that the way John narrates the incident differs widely from those descriptions of miracles, the offspring of the popular imagination, which fill the synoptics. Let us add that John is the only evangelist who has a precise knowledge of the relations of Jesus with the family of Bethany, and that it is impossible to believe that a mere creation of the popular mind could exist in a collection of remembrances so entirely personal. "If one was raised from the dead, perhaps the living would repent," was no doubt the remark made by the pious sisters. "No," was the response of Jesus; "even though one rose from the dead, they would not be persuaded;" recalling next a story which was familiar to him--that of the pious beggar, covered with sores, who died and was carried by angels to Abraham's bosom. "Even should Lazarus return," he might have added, "they would not be persuaded." Later on this subject was treated with singular levity. The hypothesis became a fact. People spoke of the resurrected Lazarus, and of the unpardonable obstinacy which could resist such testimony. The "sores" of Lazarus and the "leprosy" of Simon the leper were confounded, and it was admitted in one part of the tradition that Mary and Martha had a brother named Lazarus, whom Jesus had raised from the dead. When we know that such inaccuracies, such cock-and-bull stories, form the gossip of an Eastern city, we cannot regard it as impossible that a rumour of that kind had spread to Jerusalem of the life of Jesus, and the consequences of which were fatal to him.

Certain notable indications, in fact, lead us to the belief that some of the reports received from Bethany had the effect of hastening the death of Jesus. At times we are led to suppose that the family of Bethany were guilty of some indiscretions or plunged into an excess of zeal. It was probably the ardent desire of closing the mouth of those who vigorously denied the divine mission of their friend which carried these passionate persons beyond all reasonable limits. It must be remembered that in this impure and inanimate city of Jerusalem Jesus was not quite himself His conscience, through a fault of the people and not his own, had lost something of his primordial sincerity. Desperate and pressed to extremes, he no longer was master of himself. His mission had been imposed on him, and he pursued it fearlessly. Death would in a few days restore him his divine liberty, and wrench him away from the fatal necessities of a position which each day was becoming more exacting and more difficult to sustain.

The contrast between his always increasing exaltation and the indifference of the Jews became more and more marked. The power of the State, at the same time, became more bitter against him. From the beginning of February to the commencement of March a council had been assembled by the chief priests, and in that council the question had been pointedly put, "Can Jesus and Judaism exist together?" To raise the question was to reserve it; and, without being a prophet, as thought by the evangelist, the high priest could easily pronounce his cruel axiom, "It is expedient that one man should die for the people."

"The high priest of that same year," to use an expression of the fourth Gospel, which shows clearly the state of abasement to which the sovereign pontificate was reduced, was Joseph Kaïapha, appointed by Valerius Gratus, and entirely devoted to the Romans. From the time that Jerusalem had been under procurators, the office of high priest had been a temporary one; removals had taken place nearly every year. Kaïapha, however, held it longer than any one else. He had assumed his office in the year 25, and he did not lose it till the year 36. We know nothing of his character; but many circumstances lead to the belief that his power was only nominal. Another personage is always seen in conjunction with him, who appears to have exercised at the decisive moment we have now reached, a preponderating power.

This personage was Hanan or Annas, son of Seth, and father-in-law of Kaïpha, who was formerly the high priest, and had in reality preserved amidst the numerous changes of the pontificate all the authority of the office. Hanan had received the high priesthood from the legate Quirinius, in the year 7 of our era. He lost his function in the year 14, on the accession of Tiberius; but he continued to be much respected. He was still called "high priest," although he was out of office, and was consulted upon all important matters. During fifty years the pontificate continued in his family almost uninterruptedly; five of his sons successively sustained this dignity, without counting Kaïapha, who was his son-in-law. His was called the "priestly family," as if the priesthood had become hereditary in it. The chief offices of the temple almost all devolved upon them. Another family, that of Boëthus, alternated, it is true, with that of Hanan's in the pontificate. But the Boethusim, whose fortunes were of not very honourable origin, were much less esteemed by the pious middle class. Hanan was then in reality the chief of the sacerdotal party. Kaïapha did nothing without him; it was the custom to associate their names, and Hanan's was always put first. It will be understood, in fact, that under this régime of an annual pontificate, changed according to the caprice of the procurators, an old high priest, who had preserved the secret of the traditions, who had seen many younger than himself succeed each other, and who had retained sufficient influence to get the office delegated to persons who were subordinate to him in family rank, must have been a very important personage. Like all the aristocracy of the temple, he was a Sadducee, "a sect," says Josephus, "particularly severe in its judgments." All his sons were moreover violent persecutors. One of them, named like his father, Hanan, caused James, the brother of the Lord, to be stoned, under circumstances not unlike those connected with the death of Jesus. The temper of the family was haughty, bold, and cruel; it had that particular kind of proud and sullen wickedness which characterises Jewish politicians. Thus, upon this Hanan and his family must rest the responsibility of all the acts which followed. It was Hanan (or if you like the party he represented) who killed Jesus. Hanan was the principal actor in the terrible drama, and far more than Kaïapha, far more than Pilate, ought to bear the weight of the maledictions of mankind.

It is in the mouth of Kaïapha that the evangelist puts the decisive words which led to the sentence of death being passed on Jesus. It was supposed that the high priest possessed a certain gift of prophecy; his words thus became an oracle full of profound meaning to the Christian community. But such a sentence, whoever he might be that pronounced it, expressed the feeling of the whole sacerdotal party. This party was much opposed to popular seditions. It sought to put down religious enthusiasts, rightly foreseeing that by their excited preachings they would lead to the total ruin of the nation. Although the excitement created by Jesus had nothing temporal about it, the priests saw, as an ultimate consequence of this agitation, an aggravation of the Roman yoke and the overturning of the temple, the source of their riches and honours. Certainly the causes which, thirty-seven years after, were to effect the ruin of Jerusalem, did not proceed from infant Christianity. We cannot, say, however, that the motive alleged in this circumstance by the priests was so improbable that we must necessarily regard it as insincere. In a general sense, Jesus, if he had succeeded, would have really effected the ruin of the Jewish nation. According to the principles universally admitted by all ancient polity, Hanan and Kaïapha were right in saying, "Better the death of one man than the ruin of a people!" In our opinion this reasoning is detestable. But his reasoning has been that of conservative parties from the commencement of all human society. The "party of order" (I use this expression in its mean and narrow sense) has ever been the same. Deeming the highest duty of government to be the prevention of popular disturbances, it believes it performs an act of patriotism in preventing, by judicial murder, the tumultuous effusion of blood. Little thoughtful of the future, it does not dream that by declaring war against all innovations, it incurs the risk of crushing ideas destined one day to triumph. The death of Jesus was one of the thousand illustrations of this policy. The movement he directed was entirely spiritual, but it was still a movement; hence the men of order, persuaded that it was essential for humanity not to be disturbed, felt themselves bound to prevent the new movement from extending itself. Never was seen a more striking example of how much such conduct defeats its own object. Left alone, Jesus would have exhausted himself in a desperate struggle with the impossible. The unintelligent hate of his enemies determined the success of his work, and sealed his divinity.

The death of Jesus was thus resolved upon in the month of February or March. But he escaped yet for a short time. He withdrew to a town called Ephraim or Ephron, in the direction of Bethel, a short day's journey from Jerusalem near the border of the desert. He spent a few days there with his disciples, allowing the storm to pass over. But the order to arrest him as soon as he appeared at Jerusalem was given. The solemnity of the Passover was drawing nigh, and it was thought that Jesus, according to his custom, would come to celebrate it at Jerusalem.

CHAPTER XXIII

LAST WEEK OF JESUS

Jesus set out in fact, in the train of his disciples, to see again, and for the last time, the unbelieving city. The hopes of his followers were more and more exalted. All believed that in his going up to Jerusalem, the kingdom of God was about to be manifested there. The impiety of men was at its height, and this was regarded as a great sign that the consummation was near. The belief in this was such that they already disputed for precedence in the kingdom. This was, it is said, the moment chosen by Salome to demand on behalf of her sons the two seats on the right and left of the Son of man. The master, for his part, was beset by grave thoughts. Sometimes he allowed a gloomy resentment against his enemies to appear; he related the parable of a nobleman, who went to take possession of a kingdom in a far country; but hardly had he set out when his fellow-citizens wished to rid themselves of him. The king returned, and commanded that those who had conspired against him should be brought before him, and he had them all put to death. At other times he peremptorily destroyed the illusions of the disciples. As they walked along the stony roads to the north of Jerusalem, Jesus pensively preceded the group of his companions. All regarded him in silence, experiencing a sentiment of fear, and not daring to interrogate him. He had already spoken to them on various occasions of his future sufferings, and they had listened reluctantly. Jesus at length spoke out, and, no longer concealing from them his presentiments, discoursed on his approaching end. There was great sadness in the whole band. The disciples were expecting soon to see the sign appear in the clouds. The inaugural cry of the kingdom of God, "Blessed is he that cometh in the name of the Lord," resounded already in joyous accents through the company of Jesus. The sanguinary prospect troubled them. At each step of the fatal road, the kingdom of God became nearer or more remote in the mirage of their dreams. For himself, he was confirmed in the idea that he was about to die, but that his death would save the world. The misunderstanding between him and his disciples became more intense at each moment.

The custom was to go Jerusalem several days before the Passover, in order to prepare for the feast. Jesus was the last to arrive, and at one time his enemies believed they were frustrated in the hope that they had formed of seizing him. The sixth day before the feast (Saturday, 8th of Nisan, the 28th of March) he at length reached Bethany. He entered, according to his custom, the house of Lazarus, Martha, and Mary, or of Simon the leper, thence they gave him a grand reception. There was a dinner at Simon the leper's, at which many persons assembled, attracted by the desire of seeing him, and also, it is said, of seeing Lazarus. Simon the leper, who was seated at the table, passed already, perhaps, in the eyes of many, as the person who had been resurrected, and attracted much attention. Martha, as was her wont, served. It seems that they sought, by an increased show of respect, to overcome the coolness of the public, and to assert strongly the high dignity of the guest whom they received. Mary, in order to give to the feast a greater appearance of festivity, entered during the dinner, carrying a vase of perfume, which she poured upon the feet of Jesus. She afterwards broke the vase, following an ancient custom of breaking the vessel that had been used in the entertainment of a stranger of distinction. Finally, pushing the evidences of her cult to a point hitherto unheard of, she prostrated herself, and wiped with her long hair the feet of the master. The house was filled with the odour of the perfume, to the great delight of every one except the avaricious Judas of Kerioth. If we consider the economical habits of the community, this was certainly prodigality. The greedy treasurer reckoned up immediately how much the perfume might have been sold for, and what it would have realised for the poor-box. This not very affectionate feeling, which seemed to place something above him, dissatisfied Jesus. He loved honours, for honours furthered his aim and established his title of Son of David. So, when they spoke to him of the poor, he replied somewhat sharply, "Ye have the poor always with you; but me ye have not always." And, rising to the occasion, he promised immortality to the woman who in this critical moment gave him a token of love.

The next day (Sunday, 9th of Nizan) Jesus descended from Bethany to Jerusalem. When, at a bend of the road, upon the summit of the Mount of Olives, he saw the city spread out before him, it is said he wept over it, and addressed to it a last appeal. At the base of the mountain, a few steps from the gate, on entering the adjoining portion of the eastern wall of the city, which was called Bethphage, on account, no doubt, of the fig-trees with which it was planted, Jesus had once more a moment of human satisfaction. His arrival was noised abroad. The Galileans who had came to the feast were highly elated, and prepared a little triumph for him. An ass was brought to him, followed, according to custom, by its colt. The Galileans spread their finest garments upon the back of this humble animal as saddle-cloths, and seated him thereon. Others, however, spread their garments upon the road, and strewed it with green branches. The multitude which preceded and followed him, carrying palms, cried, "Hosanna to the son of David! Blessed is he that cometh in the name of the Lord!" Some persons even gave him the title of king of Israel. "Master, rebuke thy disciples," said the Pharisees to him. "If these should hold their peace, the stones would immediately cry out," replied Jesus, and he entered into the city. The Jerusalemites, who hardly knew him, asked who he was. "It is Jesus, the prophet of Nazareth, in Galilee," was the reply. Jerusalem was a city of about 50,000 souls. A trifling event, like the entrance of a stranger, however little celebrated, or the arrival of a band of provincials, or a movement of people to the avenues of the city, could not fail, under ordinary circumstances, to be quickly noised about. But at the time of the feast the confusion was extreme. Jerusalem on these occasions was taken possession of by strangers. Again, it was amongst the latter that the excitement appears to have been most lively. Some Greek-speaking proselytes, who had come to the feast, were piqued with curiosity, and wished to see Jesus. They addressed themselves to his disciples; but we do not know much of the result of the interview. Jesus, according to his custom, went to pass the night at his beloved village of Bethany. The three following days (Monday, Tuesday, and Wednesday) he descended regularly to Jerusalem; after the setting of the sun he reascended either to Bethany or to the farms on the western side of the Mount of Olives, where he had many friends.

A deep melancholy appears during these last days to have filled his soul, which was generally so gay and so serene. All the narratives agree in attributing to him before his arrest that he had a short experience of doubt and trouble; a kind of anticipated agony. According to some, he cried out suddenly, "Now is my soul troubled. O Father, save me from this hour." It was believed that a voice from heaven was heard at this moment; others said that an angel came to console him. According to one widely-spread version this occurred to him in the garden of Gethsemane. Jesus, it was said, went about a stone's throw from his sleeping disciples, taking with him only Peter and the two sons of Zebedee, then fell on his face and prayed. His soul was sad almost to death; a terrible anguish pressed upon him; but resignation to the divine will sustained him. This scene, owing to the instinctive art which regulated the compilation of the synoptics, and often led them in the arrangement of the narrative to study adaptability and effect, has been given as occurring on the last night of the life of Jesus, and at the precise moment of his arrest. If such a version be the true one, we should scarcely understand why John, who had been the intimate witness of so touching an episode, should not mention it to his disciples, and that the compiler of the fourth Gospel should not allude to it in the very circumstantial narrative which he has furnished of the evening of the Thursday. That which is certain is that, during his last days, the enormous weight of the mission he had undertaken pressed cruelly upon Jesus. Human nature asserted itself for a time. Perhaps he began to hesitate about his work. Terror and doubt seized upon him, and threw him into a state of exhaustion worse than death. The man who sacrifices his repose, and the legitimate rewards of life, to a great idea, always experiences a moment of sad revulsion when the image of death presents itself to him for the first time, and seeks to persuade him that everything is vanity. Perhaps some of those touching reminiscences which the strongest souls retain, and which at times pierce like a sword, seized upon him at this moment. Did he recall the clear fountains of Galilee, where he might have refreshed himself; the vine and the fig-tree under which he sat down, and the young maidens who, perhaps, might have consented to love him? Did he curse the hard destiny which had denied him the joys conceded to all others? Did he regret his too lofty nature, and (a victim of his greatness) did he grieve that he had not remained a simple artizan of Nazareth? We do not know, for all these internal troubles were evidently to his disciples a sealed letter. They understood nothing of them, supplying by simple conjectures that which, in the great soul of their Master, was obscure to them. It is certain, at least, that his divine nature soon regained its supremacy. He might still have avoided death; but he would not. Love for his work prevailed. He elected to drink the cup even to the dregs. Henceforth in fact we find Jesus entirely himself, wholly unclouded. The subtleties of the polemic, the credulity of the thaumaturgist and of the exorcist, are forgotten. There remains only the incomparable hero of the Passion, the founder of the rights of free conscience, and the perfect model which all suffering souls will contemplate in order to fortify and console themselves.

The triumph of Bethphage, that audacious act of the provincials in celebrating at the very gates of Jerusalem the advent of their Messiah-King, completed the exasperation of the Pharisees and the aristocracy of the temple. A new council was held on the Wednesday (12th of Nisan) at the house of Joseph Kaïapha. The immediate arrest of Jesus was resolved upon. A great idea of order and of conservative policy presided over all their plans. The question was how to avoid a scene. As the feast of the Passover, which commenced that year on the Friday evening, was a time of bustle and excitement, it was resolved to anticipate it. Jesus was popular; they feared an outbreak. Although it was customary to relieve the solemnities in which the whole nation joined by the execution of individual rebels to the priestly authorities--a species of religious murder designed to inculcate on the people a religious terror-- it was, however, arranged that such executions should not fall upon the holy days. The arrest was therefore fixed for the next day, Thursday. It was resolved, further, not to seize him in the temple, where he came every day, but to observe his habits, in order to capture him in some retired place. The agents of the priests sounded his disciples, hoping to obtain some information by playing upon their weakness or their simplicity. They found what they sought in Judas of Kerioth. This wretched creature, from motives impossible to explain, betrayed his Master, gave all the particulars necessary, and even undertook himself (although such an excess of baseness is hardly credible) to conduct the force which was to make the arrest. The recollection of horror which the folly or the wickedness of this man has left in the Christian tradition must have been the cause of some exaggeration on this point. Judas up to this time had been a disciple like the others; he had even the title of apostle; he had driven out demons. Legend, which always employs highly coloured language, will not admit in the supper-room more than eleven saints and one reprobate. Reality does not proceed by such absolute categories. Avarice, which the synoptics give as the motive of the crime in question, does not suffice to explain it. It would be singular if a man who kept the purse, and who knew what he would lose by the death of his chief, were to exchange the profits of his occupation for a very small sum of money. Had the self-love of Judas been wounded by the rebuff he received at the dinner at Bethany? Even that would not suffice to explain his conduct. The fourth evangelist would like to make him out a thief, an unbeliever from the beginning, for which, however, there is no justification. We would prefer to attribute it to some feeling of jealousy, or to some intestine dissension. The peculiar hatred which is manifested towards Judas in the gospel attributed to John confirms this hypothesis. Less pure in heart than the others, Judas had imbibed, without knowing it, the narrow-mindedness of his office. By a caprice very common in active life he had come to regard the interests of the purse as superior even to those of the work for which it was destined. The administrator had overcome the apostle. The murmurings which escaped him at Bethany seem to suggest that sometimes he considered that the Master cost his spiritual family too much. No doubt this mean economy had been the occasion of many other collisions in the little society.

Without denying that Judas of Kerioth may have contributed to the arrest of his Master, we yet believe that the curses with which he is loaded are somewhat unjust. There was, perhaps, in what he did more awkwardness than perversity. The moral conscience of the man of the people is quick and correct, but unstable and inconsequent. It cannot resist the impulse of the moment. The secret societies of the republican party were characterised by much earnestness and sincerity, and yet their denouncers were very numerous. A trifling spite sufficed to convert a partisan into a traitor. But, if the foolish desire for a few pieces of silver turned the head of poor Judas, he does not seem to have lost the moral sentiment completely, since, on seeing the consequences of his fault, he repented, and, it is said, killed himself.

Each minute, at this crisis, was solemn, and counted more than whole ages in the history of humanity. We have reached Thursday, 13th of Nisan (2nd April). The evening of the next day was the beginning of the festival of the Passover, begun by the feast at which the Paschal lamb was eaten. The feast continued for seven days, during which unleavened bread was eaten. The first and the last of these seven days were of a peculiarly solemn character. The disciples were already occupied with preparations for the feast. As for Jesus, we are led to believe that he was cognisant of the treachery of Judas, and that he was suspicious of the fate that awaited him. In the evening he took with his disciples his last repast. It was not the ritual feast of the Passover, as was afterwards supposed, owing to an error of a day in reckoning; but for the primitive church this supper of the Thursday was the true Passover, the seal of the new covenant. Each disciple connected with it his most cherished recollections, and a multitude of touching traits of the Master which each one preserved were associated with this repast, which became the cornerstone of Christian piety, and the starting-point of the most important institutions.

Doubtless the tender love which filled the heart of Jesus for the little church which surrounded him overflowed at this moment. His serene and strong soul became gay under the weight of the gloomy preoccupations that beset him. He had a word for each of his friends; John and Peter especially were the objects of tender marks of attachment. John reclined on the divan, by the side of Jesus, with his head resting upon the breast of the Master. Towards the end of the repast, the secret which weighed upon the heart of Jesus nearly escaped him: he said, "Verily I say unto you that one of you shall betray me." This was for these simple men a moment of anguish; they looked at each other, and each questioned himself. Judas was present; perhaps Jesus, who had had for some time reasons to distrust him, sought by this remark to draw from his looks or from his embarrassed manner the avowal of his fault. But the unfaithful disciple did not lose countenance; he even dared, it is said, to ask with the others, "Master, is it I ?"

Meanwhile, the good and upright soul of Peter was in torture. He made a sign to John to endeavour to ascertain of whom the Master was speaking. John, who could converse with Jesus without being heard, asked him the meaning of this enigma. Jesus, having only suspicions, did not wish to give any name: he only told John to observe him to whom he was going to offer the unleavened bread. At the same time he soaked a mouthful and offered it to Judas. John and Peter alone were cognisant of the fact. Jesus addressed to Judas some words containing a bitter reproach, which were not understood by those present. They thought that Jesus was simply giving him orders for the morrow's feast, and he left the room.

At the time this repast struck no one; and apart from the apprehensions which the Master confided to his disciples, who only half understood them, nothing extraordinary took place. But after the death of Jesus they attached to this evening a singularly solemn meaning, and the imagination of believers spread over it a colouring of sweet mysticism. The last hours of a dear friend are those we best remember. By an inevitable illusion, we attribute to the conversations we have then had with him a sense that death only gives to them; we concentrate into a few hours the memories of many years. The majority of the disciples did not after the supper of which we have just spoken see their Master again. It was the farewell banquet. In this repast, as well as in many others, Jesus practised his mysterious rite of the breaking of bread. As it was believed from the earliest years of the Church that the repast in question took place on the day of the Passover, and was the Paschal feast, the idea naturally arose that the Eucharistic institution was established at this supreme moment. Starting from the hypothesis that Jesus knew in advance the precise moment of his death, the disciples were led to suppose that he reserved for his last hours a number of important acts. As, moreover, one of the fundamental ideas of the first Christians was that the death of Jesus had been a sacrifice, replacing all those of the ancient Law, the "Last Supper," which was supposed to have taken place, once for all, on the eve of the Passion, became the chief sacrifice, the act which constituted the new alliance, the sign of the blood shed for the salvation of all. The bread and wine, placed in juxtaposition with death itself, were thus the image of the new testament that Jesus had sealed with his sufferings, the commemoration of the sacrifice of Christ until his advent.

Very early this mystery was incorporated into a small sacramental narrative, which we possess under four forms, very similar to one another. The fourth Evangelist, preoccupied with the Eucharistic ideas, and who narrates the Last Supper with so much prolixity, connecting it with so many circumstances and discourses, does not mention this narrative. This is a proof that he did not regard the Eucharist as a peculiarity of the Lord's Supper. To the fourth Evangelist the rite of the Last Supper was the washing of feet. It is probable that in certain primitive Christian families this latter rite obtained an importance which it has since lost. No doubt Jesus, on some occasions, had practised it to give his disciples an example of brotherly humility. It was connected with the eve of his death, in consequence of the tendency to group around the Last Supper all the great moral and ritual recommendations of Jesus.

A high sentiment of love, of concord, of charity, and of mutual deference, animated, moreover, the remembrances which were believed to surround the last hours of Jesus. It is always the unity of his Church, constituted by him or by his Spirit, which is the essence of the symbols and of the discourses which Christian tradition referred to this sacred moment. "A new commandment I give unto you," said he, " that ye love one another; as I have loved you, that ye also love one another. By this shall all men know that ye are my disciples, if ye have love one to another. Henceforth I call you not servants; for the servant knoweth not what his lord doeth: but I have called you friends; for all things that I have heard of my Father I have made known unto you. These things I command you, that ye love one another." At this last sacred moment several rivalries and struggles for precedence again took place. Jesus remarked that if he, the Master, had been in the midst of his disciples as their servant, how much more ought they to submit themselves to one another. According to some, in drinking the wine, he said, "I will not drink henceforth of this fruit of the vine until that day when I drink it anew with you in my Father's kingdom." According to others, he promised them soon a celestial feast, at which they would be seated on thrones at his side.

It seems that, towards the close of the evening, the presentiments of Jesus took hold of the disciples. All felt that a very serious danger threatened the Master, and that they were verging on a crisis. At one time Jesus thought of precautions, and spoke of swords. There were two in the company. "It is enough," said he. He did not, however, follow out this idea; he saw clearly that timid provincials could not stand up before the armed force of the great powers of Jerusalem. Cephas, full of zeal and self-confidence, swore that he would go with him to prison and to death. Jesus, with his usual astuteness, expressed doubts concerning him. According to a tradition, which probably originated with Peter himself, Jesus gave him till cock-crowing. Like Peter, they all swore that they would not yield.

CHAPTER XXIV

ARREST AND TRIAL OF JESUS

It was quite dark when they left the room. Jesus, as was his wont, passed through the valley of Kedron; and, accompanied by his disciples, went to the garden of Gethsemane, at the foot of the Mount of Olives. He sat down there. Overawing his friends by his great superiority, he watched and prayed. They were sleeping near him, when suddenly an armed troop appeared bearing lighted torches. It was the guards of the temple, armed with staves, a kind of brigade of police under the control of the priests; they were supported by a detachment of Roman soldiers with their swords; the order for the arrest emanated from the high priest and the Sanhedrim. Judas, knowing the habits of Jesus, had indicated this place as that where he might most easily be surprised. According to the unanimous tradition of the earliest times, Judas accompanied the detachment himself; according to some, he carried his hateful conduct even to the length of betraying him with a kiss. Be that as it may, certain it is that there was some show of resistance on the part of the disciples. One of them (Peter, according to eye-witnesses) drew his sword, and wounded one of the servants of the high priest, named Malchus, on the ear. Jesus put a stop to this resistance, and surrendered himself to the soldiers. Weak and incapable of acting with effect, especially against authorities with so much prestige, the disciples took to flight and became dispersed. Peter and John alone did not lose sight of their Master. Another unknown young man (probably Mark), wrapped in a light garment, followed him. The authorities sought to arrest him, but the young man fled, leaving his tunic in the hands of the guards.

The course which the priests had resolved to pursue in regard to Jesus was quite in conformity with the established law. The procedure against the "corrupter" (mésith), who sought to attaint the purity of religion, is explained in the Talmud, with details the naïve impudence of which provokes a smile. A judicial ambush is therein erected into an essential part of the examination of criminals. When a man was accused of being a "corrupter," two witnesses were suborned who were concealed behind a partition. It was arranged to bring the accused into a contiguous room, where he could be heard by these two witnesses without his perceiving them. Two candles were lighted near him, in order that it might be satisfactorily proved that the witnesses "saw him." He was then made to repeat his blasphemy; next, urged to retract it. If he persisted, the witnesses who had heard him conducted him to the tribunal, and he was stoned to death. The Talmud adds that this was the manner in which they treated Jesus; that he was condemned on the faith of two witnesses who had been suborned, and that the crime of "corruption" is, moreover, the only one for which the witnesses are thus prepared.

In fact, the disciples of Jesus inform us that the crime with which their Master was charged was that of "corruption;" and, apart from some minutiæ, the offspring of the rabbinical imagination, the narrative of the Gospels corresponds exactly with the procedure described by the Talmud. The plan of the enemies of Jesus was to convict him, by the testimony of witnesses and by his own avowals, of blasphemy and of outrage against the Mosaic religion, to condemn him to death according to law, and then to get the condemnation sanctioned by Pilate. The priestly authority, as we have already seen, was in reality entirely in the hands of Hanan. The order for the arrest in all probability emanated from him. It was to the residence of this powerful personage that Jesus was first taken. Hanan questioned him in regard to his doctrine and his disciples. Jesus, with justifiable pride, declined to enter into long explanations. He referred Hanan to his teachings, which had been public; he maintained that he had never held any secret doctrine; and requested the ex high priest to interrogate those who had listened to him. This was a perfectly natural response; but the idolatrous respect which surrounded the old priest made it appear audacious; and one of those present replied to it, it is said, by a blow.

Peter and John had followed their Master to the residence of Hanan. John, who was known in the house, was admitted without difficulty; but Peter was stopped at the entrance, and John was obliged to beg the porter to let him pass. The night was cold. Peter remained in the antechamber, and approached a brazier, around which the servants were warming themselves. He was soon recognised as a disciple of the accused. The unfortunate man, betrayed by his Galilean accent, and pursued by questions from the servants, one of whom was a kinsman of Malchus and had seen him at Gethsemane, denied thrice that he had ever had the slightest connection with Jesus. He imagined that Jesus could not hear him, and never dreamt that this dissimulated cowardice was exceedingly dishonourable. But his better nature soon revealed to him the fault he had committed. A fortuitous circumstance, the crowing of the cock, recalled to him a remark that Jesus had made. Touched to the heart, he went out and wept bitterly.

Hanan, although the real author of the judicial murder about to be committed, had not power to pronounce sentence upon Jesus, so he sent him to his son-in-law, Kaïapha, who bore the official title. This man, the blind instrument of his father-in-law, naturally ratified everything required of him by Hanan. The Sanhedrim was assembled at his house. The inquiry commenced; and several witnesses, well instructed beforehand, according to the inquisitorial process described in the Talmud, appeared before the tribunal. The fatal sentence which Jesus had really uttered, "I am able to destroy the temple of God and to build it in three days," was cited by two witnesses. To blaspheme the temple of God was, according to the Jewish law, equivalent to blaspheming God Himself. Jesus remained silent, and refused to explain the incriminating speech. If we may believe one version, the high priest then adjured him to say if he were the Messiah; Jesus confessed it, and proclaimed before the assembly the near approach of his heavenly reign. The courage of Jesus, who had resolved to die, did not require this. It is more probable that here, as when before Hanan, he remained silent. This was in general, during his last moments, his rule of conduct. The sentence was determined on; and they only sought for pretexts. Jesus perceived this, and did not undertake a useless defence. From the orthodox Judaism point of view, he was truly a blasphemer, a destroyer of the established worship, and these crimes were punishable by the law with death. With one voice, the assembly declared him guilty of a capital crime. The members of the council, who had a secret penchant for him, were absent or did not vote. The usual frivolity of old-established aristocracies did not permit the judges to reflect long upon the consequences of the sentence they had rendered. Human life was at that time very lightly sacrificed; the members of the Sanhedrim could not, of course, dream that their sons would have to render account to an angry posterity for the sentence pronounced with such flippant disdain.

The Sanhedrim had not the right to execute a sentence of death. But in the confusion of powers which then prevailed in Judæa, Jesus was, from that moment, none the less condemned. He remained the rest of the night exposed to the wicked treatment of an infamous pack of servants, who spared him no affront.

In the morning the chief priests and the elders again assembled. The question was, how to get Pilate to ratify the condemnation pronounced by the Sanhedrim, whose powers, since the occupation of the Romans, were no longer sufficient. The procurator was not invested, like the imperial legate, with the power of life and death. But Jesus was not a Roman citizen: it only required the authorisation of the governor in order that the sentence pronounced against him should take its course. As always happens when a political people subjects a nation amongst which the civil and the religious laws are confounded, the Romans had been led to give to the Jewish law a sort of official support. The Roman law was not applicable to Jews. The latter remained under the canonical law which we find recorded in the Talmud, just as the Arabs in Algeria are still governed by the code of Islamism. Although neutral in religion, the Romans thus very often sanctioned penalties inflicted for religious faults. The situation was nearly that of the sacred cities of India under the English dominion, or rather that which would be the state of Damascus if to-morrow Syria were conquered by a European nation. Josephus pretends, though the assertion may be doubted, that if a Roman ventured beyond the pillars which bore inscriptions forbidding Pagans to advance, the Romans themselves would have delivered him to the Jews to be put to death.

The agents of the priests therefore bound Jesus and led him to the judgment-hall, which was the former palace of Herod, adjoining the Tower of Antonia. It was the morning of the day on which the Paschal lamb was to be eaten (Friday the 14th of Nisan, our 3rd of April). The Jews would have been defiled by entering the judgment-hall, and would not have been able to share in the sacred feast, and therefore remained without. Pilate, apprised of their presence, ascended the bima or tribunal, situated in the open air, at the place named Gabbatha, or in Greek, Lithostrotos, on account of the pavement which covered the ground.

Hardly had he been informed of the accusation before he manifested his annoyance at being mixed up in the affair. He then shut himself up in the judgment-hall with Jesus. There a conversation took place, the precise details of which are lost, no witness having been able to repeat it to the disciples, but the tenor of which appears to have been happily conjectured by the fourth Evangelist. His narrative, at least, is in perfect accord with what history teaches us of the respective positions of the two interlocutors.

The procurator, Pontius, surnamed Pilate, doubtless on account of the pilum or javelin of honour with which he or one of his ancestors was decorated, had hitherto had no relation with the new sect. Indifferent to the internal quarrels of the Jews, he only saw in all these sectarian movements the effects of a diseased imagination and disordered brain. In general, he did not like the Jews. The Jews, on their part, detested him still more. They considered him harsh, scornful, and passionate, and accused him of improbable crimes. Jerusalem, the centre of a great national fermentation, was a very seditious city, and an insupportable abode for a foreigner. The enthusiasts pretended that it was a fixed design of the new procurator to abolish the Jewish law. Their narrow fanaticism, their religious hatreds, shocked that broad sentiment of justice and of civil government which the humblest Roman carried everywhere with him. All the acts of Pilate which are known to us attest him to have been a good administrator. In the earlier period of the exercise of his charge, he had had difficulties with those subject to him which he had solved in a very brutal manner; but it seems that on the whole he was right. The Jews must have appeared to him a very backward people; he doubtless judged them as a liberal prefect formerly judged the Bas-Bretons, who rebelled for such a simple matter as a new road, or the establishment of a school. In his best projects for the good of the country, notably in those relating to public works, he had encountered an impassable obstacle in the Law. The Law narrowed life to such a point that it was opposed to all change and to all amelioration. The Roman structures, even the most useful ones, were, on the part of zealous Jews, objects of great antipathy. Two votive escutcheons with inscriptions, which Pilate had set up at his residence, which was near the sacred precincts, provoked a still more violent storm. Pilate at first cared little for these susceptibilities; and he thus was soon seen engaged in sanguinary repressions, which afterwards culminated in his removal. The experience of so many conflicts had rendered him very prudent in his relations with an intractable people, who avenged themselves upon their governors by compelling the latter to use towards them rigorous severities. The procurator, with extreme displeasure, saw himself led to play a cruel part in this new affair, by a law he hated. He knew that religious fanaticism, when it has obtained some power from civil governments, is afterwards the first to throw the responsibility upon the latter, almost accusing them of being the author of their own excesses. What could be more unjust? for the true culprit is, in such cases, the instigator!

Pilate, then, would have liked to save Jesus. Perhaps the calm and dignified attitude of the accused made an impression upon him. According to a tradition, Jesus found a supporter in the procurator's own wife. She may have seen the gentle Galilean from some window of the palace, which overlooked the courts of the temple. Perhaps she had seen him again in her dreams; and the blood of this beautiful young man, which was about to be spilt, had given her nightmare. Certain it is that Jesus found Pilate prepossessed in his favour. The governor questioned him kindly, with the desire of finding out by what means he could send him away pardoned.

The title of "King of the Jews," which Jesus had never taken upon himself, but which his enemies represented as the sum and substance of his acts and pretensions, was naturally that by which they might be able to excite the suspicions of the Roman authority. He was accused of sedition, and of being guilty of treason against the government. Nothing could be more unjust; for Jesus had always recognised the Roman empire as the established power. But conservative religious bodies are not accustomed to shrink from calumny. In spite of all his explanations they drew certain conclusions from his teaching; they made him out to be a disciple of Judas the Gaulonite; they pretended that he forbade the payment of tribute to Cæsar. Pilate asked him if he was really the King of the Jews. Jesus did not dissimulate his belief. But the great ambiguity of speech which had been the source of his strength, and which, after his death, was to establish his kingship, did not serve him on this occasion. An idealist, that is to say, not distinguishing the spirit from the substance, Jesus, whose words, to use the image of the Apocalypse, were as a two-edged sword, never completely satisfied the powers of earth. If we may believe John, he did avow his royalty, but coupled it with this profound sentence: "My kingdom is not of this world." Then he explained the nature of his kingdom, which consisted entirely in the possession and proclamation of truth. Pilate knew nothing of this grand idealism. Jesus doubtless appeared to him as being an inoffensive dreamer. The total absence of religious and philosophical proselytism among the Romans of this epoch made them regard devotion to truth as a chimera. Such discussions annoyed them, and appeared to them devoid of meaning. Not perceiving the element of danger to the empire that lay hidden in these new speculations, they had no reason to employ violence against them. All their displeasure fell upon those who asked them to inflict punishment for vain subtleties. Twenty years after, Gallio still followed the same course towards the Jews. Until the fall of Jerusalem, the rule which the Romans adopted in administration was to remain completely indifferent to the quarrels those sectarians had among themselves.

An expedient suggested itself to the mind of the governor by which he could reconcile his own feelings with the demands of the fanatical people, whose resentment he had already so often felt. It was the custom to deliver a prisoner to the people at the time of the Passover. Pilate, knowing that Jesus had only been arrested in consequence of the jealousy of the priests, tried to obtain for him the benefit of this custom. He appeared again upon the bima, and proposed to the multitude to release the "King of the Jews." The proposition, made in these terms, though ironical, was characterised by a degree of liberality. The priests saw the danger of it. They acted promptly, and, in order to combat the proposition of Pilate, they suggested to the crowd the name of a prisoner who enjoyed great popularity in Jerusalem. By a singular coincidence he also was called Jesus, and bore the surname of Bar-Abba, or Bar-Rabban. He was a well-known personage, and had been arrested for being mixed up in a disturbance which had been accompanied by murder. A general clamour was raised, "Not this man; but Jesus Bar-Rabban;" and Pilate was obliged to release Jesus Bar-Rabban.

His embarrassment increased. He feared that too much indulgence to a prisoner, to whom was given the title of "King of the Jews," might compromise him. Fanaticism, moreover, constrains all powers to make terms with it. Pilate felt himself obliged to make some concession; but still hesitating to shed blood, in order to satisfy men whom he detested, wished to turn the thing into a jest. Affecting to laugh at the pompous title they had given to Jesus, he caused him to be scourged. Flagellation was the usual preliminary of crucifixion. Perhaps Pilate wished it to be believed that this sentence had already been pronounced, hoping that the preliminary would suffice. Then took place, according to all the narratives, a revolting scene. The soldiers put a scarlet robe on the back of Jesus, a crown of thorny branches upon his head, and a reed in his hand. Thus attired, he was led to the tribunal in front of the people. The soldiers defiled before him, striking him in turn, and knelt to him, saying, "Hail! King of the Jews," Others, it is said, spit upon him, and bruised his head with the reed. It is difficult to understand that Roman dignity could lend itself to acts so shameful. True, Pilate, in the capacity of procurator, had scarcely any but auxiliary troops under his command. Roman citizens, as the legionaries were, would not have stooped to such indignities.

Did Pilate think by this display to shield himself from responsibility? Did he hope to turn aside the blow which threatened Jesus by conceding something to the hatred of the Jews, and by substituting for the tragic denouement a grotesque termination, whence would seem to follow that the affair merited no other issue? If such were his idea, it did not succeed. The tumult increased, and became an actual riot. The cry "Crucify him! Crucify him!" resounded on all sides. The priests, assuming a tone of more and more urgency, declared the law to be in peril if the corrupter were not punished with death. Pilate saw clearly that in order to save Jesus he would have to put down a furious riot. He still tried, however, to gain time. He returned to the judgment-hall, and ascertained from what country Jesus came, seeking a pretext to free him from adjudicating. According to one tradition, he even sent Jesus to Antipas, who it is said was then at Jerusalem. Jesus encouraged but little these benevolent efforts; he maintained, as he had done at the house of Kaïapha, a grave and dignified silence which astonished Pilate. The cries from without became more and more menacing. The people had already begun to denounce the lack of zeal of the functionary who shielded an enemy of Cæsar. The greatest adversaries of the Roman rule were found to be transformed into loyal subjects of Tiberius, so as to have the right of accusing the too tolerant procurator of treason. "We have no king," said they, "but Cæsar. If thou let this man go thou art not Cæsar's friend: whosoever maketh himself a king speaketh against Caesar." The feeble Pilate yielded; he foresaw the report that his enemies would send to Rome, in which they would accuse him of having favoured a rival of Tiberius. Already the Jews, in the matter of the votive escutcheons, had written to the emperor, and their action had been approved. He feared for his office. By a condescension, which was to hold up his name to the lash of history, he yielded, throwing, it is said, all the responsibility of what was about to happen upon the Jews. The latter, according to the Christians, fully accepted it by exclaiming, "His blood be on us and on our children!"

Were these words really uttered? It is open to doubt. They nevertheless are the expression of a profound historical truth. Considering the attitude which the Romans had taken up in Judæa, Pilate could scarcely have acted otherwise than he did. How many sentences of death dictated by religious intolerance have forced the hand of the civil power! The king of Spain, who, in order to please a fanatical clergy, delivered hundreds of his subjects to the stake, was more blamable than Pilate, for he was the representative of a more absolute power than were the Romans at Jerusalem. When the civil power becomes persecuting or meddlesome at the solicitation of the priesthood, it demonstrates its weakness. But let the government that is without sin in this respect throw the first stone at Pilate. The "secular arm," behind which clerical cruelty shelters itself, is not the culprit. No one is justified in saying that he has a horror of blood when he causes it to be shed by his servants.

It was, then, neither Tiberius nor Pilate who condemned Jesus. It was the old Jewish party; it was the Mosaic Law. According to our modern ideas, there is no transmission of moral demerit from father to son; each one has to account to human or divine justice for that which he himself has done. Consequently, every Jew who suffers to-day for the murder of Jesus has a right to complain, for he might have been a Simon the Cyrenean, or at least not have been one of those who cried "Crucify him!" But nations, like individuals, have their responsibilities. Now, if ever a crime was the crime of a nation, it was the death of Jesus. This death was "legal" in the sense that it was primarily caused by a law which was the very soul of the nation. The Mosaic Law, it is true, in its modern yet accepted form, pronounced the penalty of death against all attempts to change the established worship. Now, there is no doubt that Jesus attacked this worship, and hoped to destroy it. The Jews expressed this to Pilate with truthful simplicity: "We have a law, and by our law he ought to die; because he has made himself the Son of God." The law was detestable, but it was the law of ancient ferocity; and the hero who attempted to abrogate it had first of all to endure its penalty.

Alas! it has taken more than eighteen hundred years for the blood that he shed to bear its fruits. For ages tortures and death have been inflicted in the name of Jesus on thinkers as noble as himself. Even to-day, in countries which call themselves Christian, penalties are pronounced for religious derelictions. Jesus is not responsible for these errors. He could not foresee that people with mistaken ideas would one day imagine him to be a frightful Moloch, greedy of burnt victims. Christianity has been intolerant, but intolerance is not essentially a Christian monopoly. It is Jewish, in the sense that it was Judaism which first raised the theory of the absolute in religion, and laid down the principle that every innovator, even if he brings miracles in support of his doctrine, ought without trial to be stoned. The Pagan world has as undoubtedly also had its religious violences. But if it had had this law, how would it have become Christian? The Pentateuch has thus been in the world the first code of religious terrorism. Judaism has given the example of an immutable dogma armed with the sword. If, instead of pursuing the Jews with a blind hatred, Christianity had abolished the order of things which killed its founder, how much more consistent would it not have been--how much better would it not have deserved of the human race!

CHAPTER XXV

DEATH OF JESUS

Although the real motive for the death of Jesus was entirely religious, his enemies had succeeded, in the judgment-hall, in representing him as guilty of treason against the state; they could not have obtained from the sceptical Pilate a condemnation simply on the ground of heterodoxy. Following up this idea, the priests demanded, through the people, the crucifixion of Jesus. This mode of punishment was not of Jewish origin. If the condemnation of Jesus had been purely Mosaic, he would have been stoned. Crucifixion was a Roman punishment. reserved for slaves, and for cases in which it was wished to add to death the aggravation of ignominy. In applying it to Jesus, they treated him as they treated highway robbers, brigands, bandits, or those enemies of inferior rank to whom the Romans did not grant the honour of death by the sword. It was the chimerical "King of the Jews," not the heterodox dogmatist, who was punished. Following out the same idea, the execution was left to the Romans. At this epoch we know that, amongst the Romans, the soldiers performed, at least in cases of political condemnations, the office of executioners. Jesus was therefore delivered to a cohort of auxiliary troops commanded by a centurion, and all the odious accessories connected with executions, introduced by the cruel customs of the new conquerors, were practised upon him. It was about noon. They re-clothed him with the garments which they had removed on arraigning him before the tribunal, and, as the cohort had already in reserve two thieves who were to be executed, the three convicts were placed together, and the procession set out for the place of execution.

This was a locality called Golgotha, situated outside Jerusalem, but near the walls of the city. The name Golgotha signifies a skull; it seems to correspond to our word Chaumont, and probably designated a bare hill, having the form of a bald skulL Where this hill was situated is not exactly known. Certainly it was on the north or north-west of the city, on the high irregular plain which extends between the walls and the two valleys of Kedron and Hinnom--a rather unattractive region, and rendered still more repulsive by the objectionable circumstances that always characterise the neighbourhood of a great city. It is difficult to identify Golgotha with the spot that, since Constantine, has been venerated by all Christendom. This spot is too near the interior of the city, and we are led to believe that, in the time of Jesus, it was comprised within the circuit of the walls.

Any one condemned to the cross was forced himself to carry the instrument of his execution. But Jesus, physically weaker than his two companions, was not able to carry his. The troop met a certain Simon of Cyrene, who was returning from the country, and the soldiers, with the offhand procedure of foreign garrisons, compelled him to carry the fatal tree. In so doing they perhaps exercised a recognised right to enforce labour, the Romans not being allowed to carry the infamous wood. It seems that Simon was afterwards of the Christian community. His two sons, Alexander and Rufus, were well known in it. He related perhaps more than one circumstance of which he had been witness. No disciple was at this moment near Jesus.

The place of execution was at length reached. According to Jewish usage, the victims were offered a strong aromatic wine, an intoxicating drink, which, from a feeling of pity, was given to the condemned to stupefy him. It appears that the women of Jerusalem often brought this kind of stupefying wine to the unfortunates who were being led to execution; when there was none presented by the latter, it was purchased at the expense of the public treasury. Jesus, after having touched the rim of the cup with his lips, refused to drink. This sad consolation of common sufferers did not accord with his exalted nature. He preferred to quit life with perfect clearness of mind, and to await in full consciousness the death he had willed and brought upon himself. He was then divested of his garments, and fastened to the cross. The cross was composed of two beams, tied in the form of the letter T. It was so little raised that the feet of the condemned almost touched the earth. They commenced by securing it; they next fastened the sufferer to it by driving nails into his hands; the feet were often nailed, occasionally only bound with cords. A piece of wood was fastened to the shaft of the cross, near the centre, and passed between the legs of the condemned, who rested on it. Failing this, the hands would have been torn, and the body would have sunk down. At other times a small horizontal rest was fixed at the elevation of the feet, and supported them.

Jesus experienced these horrors in all their atrocity. A burning thirst, one of the tortures of crucifixion, consumed him. He asked to drink. Near him there was a cup full of the ordinary drink of the Roman soldiers, a mixture of vinegar and water, called posca. The soldiers had to carry with them their posca on all their expeditions, amongst which executions were reckoned. A soldier dipped a sponge in this mixture, put it on the end of a reed, and raised it to the lips of Jesus, who sucked it. Two thieves were crucified, one on each side. The executioners, to whom were usually left the small effects of the victims, drew lots for his garments, and, sitting at the foot of the cross, guarded him. According to one tradition, Jesus uttered this sentence, which was in his heart, if not upon his lips: "Father, forgive them, for they know not what they do."

According to the Roman custom, a writing was affixed to the head of the cross, bearing in three languages -- Hebrew, Greek, and Latin -- the words: "THE KING OF THE JEWS." There was in this inscription something painful and insulting to the nation. Those who passed by and read it were offended. The priests complained to Pilate that he ought to have made use of an inscription which implied simply that Jesus had called himself King of the Jews. But Pilate, already tired of the whole affair, refused to change what had been written.

The disciples of Jesus had fled. John, nevertheless, declares himself to have been present, and to have remained standing at the foot of the cross during the whole time. It may be affirmed, with more certainty, that the devoted women of Galilee, who had followed Jesus to Jerusalem and continued to tend him, did not abandon him. Mary Cleophas, Mary Magdalen, Joanna, wife of Khouza, Salome, and others, stood off at a certain distance, never losing sight of him. If we must believe John, Mary, the mother of Jesus, was also at the foot of the cross, and Jesus, seeing his mother and his beloved disciple together, said to the one, "Behold my mother!" and to the other, "Behold thy son!" But we do not understand how the synoptics, who name the other women, should have omitted her whose presence was so striking a feature. Perhaps even the extreme elevation of the character of Jesus does not render such personal emotion probable, at the moment when, solely preoccupied by his work, he no longer existed except for humanity.

Apart from this small group of women, whose presence consoled him, Jesus had before him only the spectacle of the baseness or stupidity of humanity. The passers-by insulted him. He heard around him foolish scoffs, and his greatest cries of pain turned into odious jests: "He trusted in God; let him deliver him now, if he will have him: for he said, I am the Son of God." "He saved others," they said again; "himself he cannot save. If he be the king of Israel, let him now come down from the cross, and we will believe him! Ah, thou that destroyest the temple, and buildest it in three days, save thyself." Some, vaguely acquainted with his apocalyptic ideas, thought they heard him call Elias, and said, "Let us see whether Elias will come to save him." It appears that the two crucified thieves at his side also insulted him. The sky was dark; and the earth, as in all the environs of Jerusalem, dry and gloomy. For a moment, according to certain narratives, his heart failed him; a cloud hid from him the face of his Father; he experienced an agony of despair a thousand times more acute than all his tortures. He saw only the ingratitude of men. Repenting perhaps in suffering for a vile race, he exclaimed: "My God, my God, why hast thou forsaken me?" But his divine instinct still sustained him. In proportion as the life of the body eked out, his soul became clear, returning by degrees to its celestial origin. The object of his mission returned: he saw in his death the salvation of the world; he lost sight of the hideous spectacle spread at his feet, and, irrevocably united to his Father, he began upon the gibbet the divine life which was to enter into the heart of humanity for all eternity.

The peculiar atrocity of crucifixion was that one could live three or four days in this horrible state upon the instrument of torture. The bleeding from the hands soon stopped, and was not fatal. The real cause of death was the unnatural position of the body, which brought on a frightful disturbance of the circulation, terrible pains in the head and heart, and, finally, rigidity of the limbs. Victims with strong constitutions died simply of hunger. The original idea of this cruel punishment was not directly to kill the culprit by positive injuries, but to expose the slave, nailed by the hand of which he had neglected to make good use, and to let him rot on the wood. The delicate organisation of Jesus preserved him from this slow agony. Everything tends to show that the instantaneous rupture of a vessel in the heart killed him, at the end of three hours. A few moments before giving up the ghost his voice was still strong. Suddenly he uttered a terrible cry, which some heard as, "Father, into thy hands I commend my spirit!" but which others, more intent on the accomplishment of prophecies, render, "It is finished!" His head fell upon his breast, and he expired.

Rest now in thy glory, noble founder. Thy work is completed; thy divinity is established. Fear no more to see the edifice of thy efforts crumble through a flaw. Henceforth, stripped of all frailty, thou shalt aid, by the exaltation of thy divine peace, the infinite fruits of thy acts. At the cost of a few hours of suffering, which have not even tinged thy great soul, thou hast purchased the most complete immortality. During thousands of years, the world will extol thee. Ensign of our contradictions, thou wilt be the standard around which will be fought the fiercest battles. A thousand times more living, a thousand times more loved, since thy death than during the days of thy pilgrimage here below, thou wilt become so completely the corner-stone of humanity that to tear thy name from this world would be to shake it to its foundations. Between thee and God, men will no longer distinguish. Complete vanquisher of death, take possession of thy kingdom, whither shall follow thee, by the royal road thou hast traced, ages of adorers.

CHAPTER XXVI

JESUS IN THE TOMB

It was about three o'clock in the afternoon, according to our custom of reckoning, when Jesus expired. A Jewish law forbade a corpse suspended on the cross to be left beyond the evening of the day of the execution. It is not probable that in the executions performed by the Romans this rule was observed. But as the next day was the Sabbath, and a Sabbath of peculiar solemnity, the Jews expressed to the Roman authorities their desire that this holy day should not be profaned by such a spectacle. Their request was granted; orders were given to hasten the death of the three condemned ones, and to remove them from the cross. The soldiers executed this order by applying to the two thieves a second punishment much more speedy than that of the cross, the crurifragium, breaking of the legs, the usual punishment of slaves and of prisoners of war. As to Jesus, they found him dead, and did not think it necessary to break his legs. But one of them, to remove all doubt as to the real death of the third victim, and to complete it, if any breath remained in him, pierced his side with a spear. They thought they saw water and blood flow, which was regarded as a sign of the cessation of life.

The fourth Evangelist, who here represents the Apostle John as having been an eye-witness, insists strongly on this detail. It is evident, in fact, that doubts arose as to the reality of the death of Jesus. A few hours of suspension on the cross appeared to persons accustomed to see crucifixions as entirely insufficient to lead to such a result. They cited many instances of persons crucified, who, removed in time, had been brought to life again by energetic treatment. Origen, later on, thought it needful to invoke miracle in order to explain so sudden an end. The same astonishment is discovered in the narrative of Mark. To speak truly, the best guarantee that the historian possesses upon a point of this nature is the suspicious hatred of the enemies of Jesus. It is very doubtful whether the Jews were at that time preoccupied with the fear that Jesus might be thought to be resuscitated; but, in any case, they must have made sure that he was really dead. Whatever may have been, at certain periods, the neglect of the ancients in all that appertained to legal proof and the strict conduct of affairs, we cannot but believe that for once those interested had taken, on so important a point to them, some precautions in this respect.

According to the Roman custom, the corpse of Jesus ought to have remained suspended in order to become the prey of birds. According to the Jewish law, it would, being removed in the evening, have been deposited in the place of infamy set apart for the burial of those who were executed. If Jesus' disciples had consisted only of his poor Galileans, timid and without influence, the second course would have been adopted. But we have seen that, in spite of his small success at Jerusalem, Jesus had gained the sympathy of some people of consideration who expected the kingdom of God, and who, without avowing themselves his disciples, had for him a strong attachment. One of these, Joseph, of the small town of Arimathea (Ha-ramathaim), went in the evening to ask the body from the procurator. Joseph was a man rich, honourable, and a member of the Sanhedrim. Roman law, at this period, commanded, moreover, the delivering up of the body of the person executed to those who claimed it. Pilate, who was ignorant of the circumstance of the crurifragium, was astonished that Jesus was so soon dead, and summoned the centurion who had superintended the execution to know how this was. Pilate granted to Joseph the object of his request. The body probably had already been removed from the cross. They delivered it to Joseph, that he might do with it as he pleased.

Another secret friend, Nicodemus, whom we have already seen employing his influence more than once in favour of Jesus, came forward at this moment. He arrived bearing an ample provision of the materials necessary for embalming. Joseph and Nicodemus interred Jesus according to the Jewish custom--that is to say, they wrapped him in a sheet with myrrh and aloes. The Galilean women were present, and no doubt accompanied the scene with piercing cries and tears.

It was late, and all this was done in great haste. The place had not yet been chosen where the body would be finally deposited. The carrying of the body, moreover, might have been delayed to a late hour, and have involved a violation of the Sabbath; the disciples still conscientiously observed the prescriptions of the Jewish law. A temporary interment was hence decided upon. There was near at hand, in the garden, a tomb recently dug out in the rock, which had never been used. It belonged, probably, to one of the believers. The funeral caves, when they were destined for a single body, were composed of a small chamber, at the bottom of which the place for the body was marked by a trough or couch let into the wall, and surmounted by an arch. As these caves were dug out of the sides of sloping rocks, they were entered by the floor; the door was shut by a stone very difficult to move. Jesus was deposited in the cave, and the stone was rolled to the door, as it was intended to return in order to give him a more complete burial. But, the next day being a solemn Sabbath, the labour was postponed till the day following.

The women retired after having carefully noticed how the body was laid. They employed the hours of the evening which remained to them in making new preparations for the embalming. On the Saturday all rested.

On the Sunday morning, the women, Mary Magdalen the first, came very early to the tomb. The stone was displaced from the opening, and the body was no longer in the place where they had put it. At the same time, the strangest rumours were spread in the Christian community. The cry, "He is risen!" spread amongst the disciples like lightning. Love caused it to find ready credence everywhere. What had taken place? In treating of the history of the apostles we shall have to examine this point and to investigate the origin of the legends as touching the resurrection. For the historian, the life of Jesus finishes with his last sigh. But such was the impression he had left in the hearts of his disciples and of a few devoted females, that during some weeks more it was as if he were living and consoling them. Had his body been taken away? Did enthusiasm, always credulous in certain circumstances, create afterwards the group of narratives by which it was sought to establish faith in the resurrection? In the absence of opposing documents this can never be ascertained. Let us say, however, that the strong imagination of Mary Magdalen played in this circumstance an important part. Divine power of love! Sacred moments in which the passion of one possessed gave to the world a resuscitated God!

CHAPTER XXVII

FATE OF THE ENEMIES OF JESUS

According to the calculation which we have adopted, the death of Jesus took place in the year 33 of our era. It could not, at all events, be either anterior to the year 29, the preaching of John and Jesus having commenced in the year 28, or posterior to the year 35, as in the year 36, and probably before the Passover, Pilate and Kaïapha both lost their offices. The death of Jesus, moreover, had no connexion whatever with these two removals. In his retirement., Pilate probably never dreamt for a moment of the forgotten episode which was to transmit his pitiful renown to the most distant posterity. As to Kaïapha, he was succeeded by Jonathan, his brother-in-law, son of the same Hanan who had played the principal part in the trial of Jesus. The Sadducean family of Hanan retained the pontificate a long time, and, more powerful than ever, continued to wage against the disciples and the family of Jesus the implacable war which they had commenced against the Founder. Christianity, which owed to him the definitive act of its foundation, owed to him also its first martyrs. Hanan was looked upon as one of the happiest men of his age. The actual person guilty of the death of Jesus ended his life overwhelmed with honours and consideration, without ever doubting for an instant that he had rendered a great service to the nation. His sons continued to reign around the temple, and, kept down with difficulty by the procurators, they ofttimes dispensed with the consent of the latter in order to gratify their haughty and violent instincts. Antipas and Herodias soon disappeared also from the political arena. Herod Agrippa having been raised to the dignity of king by Caligula, the jealous Herodias swore that she too would be queen. Pressed incessantly by this ambitious woman, who treated him as a coward, because he suffered a superior in his family, Antipas overcame his natural indolence, and went to Rome in order to solicit the title which his nephew had just obtained (the year 39 of our era). But the affair turned out very badly. Injured in the eyes of the emperor by Herod Agrippa, Antipas was removed, and spent the rest of his life in exile at Lyons and in Spain. Herodias followed him in his misfortunes. A hundred years, at least, were to elapse before the name of their obscure subject (who had become God) should appear in these remote countries to inscribe upon their tombs the murder of John the Baptist.

As to the wretched Judas of Kerioth, terrible legends were current about his death. It was maintained that he had bought a field in the neighbourhood of Jerusalem with the price of his perfidy. There was, indeed, on the south of Mount Zion, a place named Hakeldama (the field of blood). It was alleged that this was the property acquired by the traitor. According to one tradition he killed himself. According to another, he had a fall in his field, which caused his bowels to gush out. According to others, he died of a kind of dropsy, which, being accompanied by repulsive circumstances, was regarded as a chastisement of heaven. The desire of making out Judas to be another Absalom, and of showing in him the accomplishment of the menaces which the Psalmist pronounces against the perfidious friend, may have given rise to these legends. Perhaps, in the retirement of his field of Hakeldama, Judas led a quiet and obscure life; while his former friends prepared the conquest of the world, and spread the report of his infamy. Perhaps, also, the terrible hatred which was concentrated on his head drove him to violent acts, in which were seen the finger of heaven.

The time of the great Christian revenge was, moreover, far distant. The new sect had nothing to do with the catastrophe which Judaism was soon to experience. The synagogue did not understand till much later to what it exposed itself in practising laws of intolerance. The empire was certainly still further from suspecting that its future destroyer had been born. For nearly three hundred years it pursued its path without suspecting that in its bosom principles were growing which were destined to subject humanity to a complete transformation. At once theocratic and democratic, the idea thrown by Jesus into the world was, together with the invasion of the Germans, the most active cause of the dissolution of the work of the Cæsars. On the one hand, the right of all men to participate in the kingdom of God was proclaimed. On the other, religion was henceforth separated in principle from the state. The rights of conscience, outside of political law, resulted in the constitution of a new power,--the "spiritual power." This power has more than once belied its origin. For ages the bishops have been princes, and the Pope has been a king. The pretended empire of souls has shown itself at various conjunctures as a frightful tyranny, employing the rack and the stake in order to maintain itself. But the day will come when the separation will bear its fruits, when the domain of things spiritual will cease to be called a "power," and will be denominated a "liberty." Proceeding from the bold affirmation of a man of the people, formed in the presence of the people, beloved and admired first by the people, Christianity was stamped by an original character which will never be effaced. It was the first triumph of revolution, the victory of the popular sentiment, the advent of the simple in heart, the inauguration of the beautiful as understood by the people. Jesus thus, in the aristocratic societies of antiquity, opened the breach through which all will pass.

The civil power, in fact, although innocent of the death of Jesus (it only countersigned the sentence, and even in spite of itself), ought to bear a great share of the responsibility. In presiding at the scene of Calvary, the state gave itself a serious blow. A legend full of all kinds of irreverence prevailed, and became known to everybody--a legend in which the constituted authorities played a hateful part, in which it was the accused that was right, and in which the judges and the guards were leagued against the truth. Seditious in the highest degree, the history of the Passion, spread by a thousand popular images, represented the Roman eagles as sanctioning the most iniquitous of executions, soldiers executing it, and a prefect commanding it. What a blow for all established powers! They have never entirely recovered from it. How can they assume infallibility in respect to poor men, when they have on their conscience the great contumely of Gethsemane?

CHAPTER XXVIII

ESSENTIAL CHARACTER OF THE WORK OF JESUS

Jesus, it is seen, never extended his action beyond the Jewish circle. Although his sympathy for outcasts of heterodoxy led him to admit Pagans into the kingdom of God, although he had more than once resided in a Pagan country, and although once or twice we surprise him in kindly relations with unbelievers, it may be said that his life was passed entirely in the small world in which he was born. In Greek or Roman countries he was never heard of; his name only appears in profane authors of a hundred years later, and then in an indirect manner, in connection with seditious movements provoked by his doctrine, or persecutions of which his disciples were the object. Even on the heart of Judaism Jesus made no very durable impression. Philo, who died about the year 50, knew nothing of him Josephus, born in the year 37, and writing at the close of the century, mentions his execution in a few lines, as an event of secondary importance, while in the enumeration of the sects of his time he omits the Christians altogether. Even the Mishna affords no trace of the new school. The passages in the two Gemaras in which the founder of Christianity is named, do not carry us back beyond the fourth or fifth century. The essential work of Jesus was to form around him a circle of disciples, whom he inspired with boundless affection, and in whose breasts he deposited the germ of his doctrine. To have made himself beloved, "to the extent that after his death they ceased not to love him," was the great work of Jesus, and that which most struck his contemporaries. His doctrine was a thing so little dogmatic that he neither thought of writing it nor of having it written. Men did not become his disciples by believing this or that, but by attaching themselves to his person and by loving him. A few sentences easily revoked from the memory, and especially his type of character, and the impression it had left, were what remained of him. Jesus was not a founder of dogmas, or a deviser of symbols; he introduced into the world a new spirit. The least Christianised of men were, on the one hand, the doctors of the Greek Church, who, from the fourth century, began to entangle Christianity in a labyrinth of puerile metaphysical discussions, and, on the other, the scholastics of the Latin Middle Ages, who wished to draw from the Gospel the thousands of articles of a colossal system. To adhere to Jesus with the kingdom of God in prospect was what at first entitled one to be called a Christian.

It will now be understood why, by an exceptional destiny, pure Christianity still presents, after eighteen centuries, the character of a universal and eternal religion. In truth it is because the religion of Jesus is, in some respects, the final religion. The product of a perfectly spontaneous movement of souls, disengaged at its birth from all dogmatic restraints, having struggled three hundred years for liberty of conscience, Christianity, in spite of the catastrophes which have followed it, reaps still the fruits of its excellent origin. To renew itself it has only to return to the Gospel. The kingdom of God, such as we conceive it, differs materially from the supernatural apparition that early Christians hoped to see appear in the clouds. But the sentiment which Jesus introduced into the world is really ours. His perfect idealism is the highest rule of a pure and virtuous life. He created a heaven of pure souls, where are to be found what we seek in vain for on earth,--the perfect nobility of the children of God, absolute holiness, total abstraction from the pollutions of the world; in fine, liberty, which society eschews as an impossibility, and which can only find full scope in the domain of mind. The great Master of those who take refuge in this ideal kingdom of God is still Jesus. He was the first to proclaim the sovereignty of the mind; the first to say, at least through his acts, "My kingdom is not of this world." The foundation of true religion is verily his work. Since him, it only remains to fructify and develop it.

"Christianity" has thus become almost synonymous with "religion." All that one may attempt, outside this grand and noble Christian tradition, is futile. Jesus founded the religion of humanity, just as Socrates founded philosophy, and Aristotle science. There was philosophy before Socrates, and science before Aristotle. But since the times of Socrates and Aristotle philosophy and science have made immense progress; yet it has all been reared upon the foundations they laid down. Similarly, before Jesus religion had passed through many revolutions; since Jesus it has achieved great conquests; yet we have not advanced, and never will improve upon the essential principle Jesus created; he fixed for ever the idea of pure worship. The religion of Jesus in this sense is not limited. The Church has had its epochs and its phases; it has enveloped itself in creeds which have lasted and can only last for a time: Jesus, on the other hand, has founded absolute religion, which excludes nothing, determines nothing unless it be sentiment. His creeds are not fixed dogmas, but ideas susceptible of indefinite interpretations. We should seek in vain for a theological proposition in the Gospel. All professions of faith are travesties of the idea of Jesus, just as the scholasticism of the Middle Ages, in proclaiming Aristotle the only master of a completed science, perverted the teachings of Aristotle. Aristotle, if he had taken part in the debates of the schools, would have repudiated this narrow doctrine; he would have allied himself to the party of progressive science as against the routine which shielded itself under his authority; he would have applauded his opponents. Similarly, if Jesus were to return among us, he would recognise as disciples, not those who pretend to embody his teachings in a few catechismal phrases, but those who labour as he laboured. The eternal glory in all great things is to lay the first stone. It may be that in modern "Physics" and "Meteorology" we may not discover a word of the treatises of Aristotle which bear these titles; but Aristotle remains no less the founder of natural science. Whatever may be the transformations of dogma, Jesus will ever be the creator of the pure spirit of religion; the Sermon on the Mount will never be surpassed. No matter what revolution takes place, nothing will prevent us attaching ourselves in religion to the grand intellectual and moral line at the head of which is enshrined the name of Jesus. In this sense we are Christians, even when we separate ourselves on almost all points from the Christian tradition which has preceded us.

And this great foundation was indeed the personal work of Jesus. To make himself adored to this degree, he must have been adorable. Love is only kindled by an object worthy of it, and we should know nothing of Jesus if it were not for the passion he inspired in those around him, which obliges us still to affirm that he was great and pure. The faith, the enthusiasm, the constancy of the first Christian generation is only explicable on the supposition that at its inception there existed a man of transcendent greatness. In view of the marvellous creations of the ages of faith two equally fatal impressions to good historical criticism spring up in the mind. In one view we are led to regard these creations as too impersonal; we impute to collective action that which has often been the work of a single powerful will. In another, we refuse to see men like ourselves in the authors of these extraordinary movements which have decided the fate of humanity. Let us take a broader view of the powers which nature conceals in her bosom. Our civilisations, governed by minute restrictions, cannot give us any idea of the power of man at periods in which the originality of each one had a far freer development. Let us imagine a recluse, dwelling in the mountains near our capital, coming out from time to time in order to present himself at the palaces of sovereigns, brushing the sentinels aside, and, with an imperious tone, announcing to kings the approach of revolutions of which he had been the promoter. The bare idea provokes a smile. Yet such was Elisha; Elisha the Tishbite, in our days, would not be able to pass the gate of the Tuileries. The preaching of Jesus, and his free activity in Galilee, do not deviate less completely from the social conditions to which we are accustomed. Free from our polished conventionalities, exempt from the uniform education which refines us, but which so greatly dwarfs our individuality, these mighty souls carried a surprising energy into action. They appear to us like the giants of a heroic age, who could not have been real. This is a profound error! These men were our brothers; they were of our stature, felt and thought as we do. But the breath of God was free in them; with us, it is restrained by the iron bonds of a mean society, and condemned to an irremediable mediocrity.

Let us place, then, at the highest summit of human greatness the person of Jesus. Let us not be led astray by sneers in the presence of a legend which keeps us always in a superhuman world. The life of Francis d'Assisi is, too, only a tissue of miracles. Has any one ever doubted, though, of his existence, and of the part he played? Let us say no more that the glory of founding Christianity must be attributed to the multitude of the first Christians, and not to him whom legend has deified. The inequality of men is much more marked in the East than with us. It is no rarity to see spring up there, in the midst of a general atmosphere of wickedness, characters whose greatness astonishes us. So far from Jesus having been made by his disciples, he appeared in everything superior to them. The latter, St. Paul and St. John excepted, were men without invention or genius. St. Paul himself bears no comparison with Jesus, and as to St. John, he has done little more in his Apocalypse than to breathe the poetry of Jesus. Hence the immense superiority of the Gospels among the writings of the New Testament. Hence the painful lowering of sentiment we experience in passing from the history of Jesus to that of the apostles. The evangelists themselves, who have transmitted to us the image of Jesus, are so much beneath him of whom they speak that they constantly disfigure him, not being able to attain to his height. Their writings are full of errors and contradictions. We feel in each line a discourse of divine beauty, told by narrators who do not understand it, and who substitute their own ideas for those they have only half grasped. On the whole, the character of Jesus, far from having been embellished by his biographers, has been marred by them. Criticism, in order to find what he was, needs to discard a series of errors, which prove the mediocre minds of the disciples. The latter painted him as they understood him, and often, in thinking to exalt him, they have debased him.

I know that our modern ideas have been offended more than once in this legend, conceived by another race, under another sky, and in the midst of other social wants. There are virtues which, in some respects, are more conformable to our taste. The upright and gentle Marcus Aurelius, the humble and tender Spinoza, not having believed in miracles, were exempt from some errors that Jesus shared. Spinoza, in his profound obscurity, had an advantage which Jesus did not seek. By our extreme delicacy in the use of means of conviction, by our absolute sincerity and our disinterested love of the pure idea, we have founded--all we, who have devoted our lives to science--a new ideal of morality. But the judgment of general history ought not to be restricted to considerations of personal merit. Marcus Aurelius and his noble masters have left no durable impress on the world. Marcus Aurelius left behind him delightful books, an execrable son, and a decaying nation. Jesus remains an inexhaustible principle of moral regeneration for humanity. Philosophy does not suffice for the multitude. They must have sanctity. An Apollonius of Tyana with his miraculous legend, is therefore more successful than a Socrates with his cold reason. "Socrates," it was said, "leaves men on the earth, Apollonius transports them to heaven; Socrates is but a sage, Apollonius is a god." Religion, so far, has not existed without a share of asceticism, of piety, and of the marvellous. When it was wished, after the Antonines, to make a religion of philosophy, it was requisite to transform the philosophers into saints, to write the "Edifying Life" of Pythagoras and of Plotinus, to attribute to them a legend, virtues of abstinence, contemplation and supernatural powers, without which neither credence nor authority were found in that age.

Preserve us, then, from mutilating history in order to satisfy our petty susceptibilities! Which of us, pigmies as we are, could do what the extravagant Francis d'Assisi, or the hysterical Saint Theresa, has done? Let medicine have names to express these grand errors of human nature; let it maintain that genius is a disease of the brain; let it see in a certain delicacy of morality the commencement of consumption; let it class enthusiasm and love amongst the nervous accidents--it matters little. The terms healthy and diseased are entirely relative. Who would not prefer to be diseased like Pascal, rather than healthy like the common herd? The narrow ideas which are spread in our times respecting madness, mislead our historical judgments in the most serious manner in questions of this kind. A state in which a man says things of which he is not conscious, in which thought is produced without the summons and control of the will, exposes him to being confined as a lunatic. Formerly this was called prophecy and inspiration. The most beautiful things in the world are done in a state of fever; every great creation involves a breach of equilibrium; child-birth is, by a law of nature, a violent process.

We acknowledge, indeed, that Christianity is too complex to have been the work of a single man. In one sense, entire humanity has co-operated therein. There is no one so shut in as not to receive some influence from without. History is full of singular synchronisms, which cause, without any communication with each other, very remote portions of the human species to arrive at the same time at almost identical ideas and imaginations. In the thirteenth century, the Latins, the Greeks, the Syrians, the Jews, and the Mussulmans adopted scholasticism, and very nearly the same scholasticism prevailed from York to Samarcand; in the fourteenth century every one in Italy, Persia, and India yielded to the taste for mystical allegory; in the sixteenth, art was developed in a very similar manner in Italy, and at the court of the Great Moguls, without St. Thomas, Barhebræus, the Rabbis of Narbonne, or the Motécallémin of Bagdad having known each other, without Dante and Petrarch having seen any sofi, without any pupil of the schools of Perouse or of Florence having been at Delhi. We should say there are great moral influences running through the world like epidemics, without distinction of frontier and of race. The interchange of ideas in the human species does not take place only by books or by direct instruction. Jesus was ignorant of the very name of Buddha, of Zoroaster, and of Plato; he had read no Greek book, no Buddhist Soutra, nevertheless there was in him more than one element, which, without his suspecting it, came from Buddhism, Parseeism, or from the Greek wisdom. All this was done through secret channels and by that kind of sympathy which exists among the various portions of humanity. The great man, on the one hand, receives everything from his age; on the other, he governs his age. To show that the religion founded by Jesus was the natural consequence of that which had preceded does not diminish its excellence, but only proves that it had a reason for its existence, that it was legitimate--that is to say, conformable to the instinct and wants of the heart in a given age.

Is it more just to say that Jesus was wholly indebted to Judaism, and that his greatness is only that of the Jewish people? No one is more disposed than myself to place high this unrivalled people, whose particular heritage seems to have been to contain amongst them the extremes of good and evil. Jesus doubtless sprang from Judaism; but he proceeded from it as Socrates did from the schools of the Sophists, as Luther proceeded from the Middle Ages, as Lamennais from Catholicism, as Rousseau from the eighteenth century. A man belongs to his age and race even when he reacts against his age and race. Far from continuing Judaism, Jesus represents the rupture with the Jewish spirit. The supposition that his idea in this respect could lead to equivocation is disproved by the general direction of Christianity after him. The general tendency of Christianity has been to separate itself more and more from Judaism. Its perfection depends on its returning to Jesus, but certainly not in returning to Judaism. The great originality of the founder remains then unchallenged; his glory does not admit any legitimate sharer.

Doubtless, circumstances much aided the success of this marvellous revolution; but circumstances only second endeavours as to what is just and true. Each branch of the development of humanity, art, poetry, religion, encounters, in crossing the ages, a privileged epoch, in which it attains perfection by a sort of spontaneous instinct, and without effort. No labour of reflection would succeed in producing afterwards the masterpieces which nature creates at those moments by inspired geniuses. What the golden age of Greece was for art and profane literature, the age of Jesus was for religion. Jewish society exhibited the most extraordinary moral and intellectual state which the human species has ever passed through. It was truly one of those divine hours in which the sublime is produced by combinations of a thousand hidden forces, in which great souls find a flood of admiration and sympathy to sustain them. The world, delivered from the very narrow tyranny of small municipal republics, enjoyed great liberty. Roman despotism did not make itself felt in a disastrous manner until much later, and it was, moreover, always less oppressive in those distant provinces than in the centre of the empire. Our petty preventive interferences (far more destructive than death to spiritual things) did not exist. Jesus, during three years, could lead a life which, in our societies, would have brought him twenty times before the magistrates. Our laws upon the illegal exercise of medicine would alone have sufficed to cut short his career. The unbelieving dynasty of the Herods, on the other hand, occupied itself little with religious movements; under the Asmoneans, Jesus would probably have been arrested at his first step. An innovator, in such a state of society, only risked death, and death is a gain to those who labour for the future. Imagine Jesus reduced to bear the burden of his divinity until his sixtieth or seventieth year, losing his celestial fire, wearing out little by little under the burden of an unparalleled mission! Everything favours those who have a special destiny; they become glorious by a sort of invincible impulse and command of fate.

This sublime person, who each day still presides over the destiny of the world, may be called divine, not in the sense that Jesus has absorbed all the divine, but in the sense that Jesus is the person who has impelled his fellow-men to make the greatest step towards the divine. Humanity in its totality presents an assemblage of low beings, selfish, superior to the animal only in the single particular that its selfishness is more reflective. Still, from the midst of this uniform depravity, pillars rise towards the sky, and testify to a nobler destiny. Jesus is the highest of these pillars that show to man whence he comes, and whither he ought to tend. In him was concentrated all that is good and elevated in our nature. He was not without sin; he had to conquer the same passions that we have to combat; no angel of God comforted him, except it was his good conscience; no Satan tempted him, more than each one bears in his heart. In the same way that many of his great qualities are lost to us, in consequence of the lack of intelligence of his disciples, it is also probable that many of his faults have been concealed. But never has any one made the interests of humanity predominate to the same extent in his life over the littlenesses of self-love. Unreservedly devoted to his idea, he subordinated everything to it to such a degree that, towards the end of his life, the universe existed no longer for him. It was by this transport of heroic will that he conquered heaven. There never was a man--Sakya Mouni alone excepted--who so completely trampled under foot family, the pleasures of this world, and all temporal care. He lived only for his Father and the divine mission with which he believed himself charged.

As to us, eternal children, condemned to impotence, who labour without reaping, and who will never witness the fruit of that which we have sown, let us bow before these demi-gods. They did that which we cannot do--create, affirm, act. Will great originality be borne again, or will the world henceforth content itself by following the paths opened by the bold original minds of antiquity? We do not know. In any case, Jesus will not be surpassed. His worship will constantly renew itself, his history will provoke endless pious tears, his sufferings will subdue the stoutest hearts; all ages will proclaim that, among the sons of men, no one has been born who is greater than Jesus.

END OF THE LIFE OF JESUS.

APPENDIX

OF THE USE IT IS PROPER TO MAKE OF THE FOURTH GOSPEL IN WRITING THE LIFE OF JESUS

The greatest difficulty which presents itself to the historian of Jesus is the value of the sources upon which such a history rests. On the one hand, what is the value of the Gospels called synoptic? On the other, what use is to be made of the fourth Gospel in writing the life of Jesus? On the first point all those who occupy themselves with these studies, according to the critical method, are thoroughly in accord. The synoptics represent the tradition, often legendary, of the two or three first Christian generations in regard to the person of Jesus. This permits of much uncertainty in the application, and necessitates the continual employment in the narrative of the formulas: "Some have said this," "Others have related that," &c. But that suffices to inform us as to the general character of the founder, the charm and the principal features of his teaching, and even as regards the most important circumstances of his life. The writers of the life of Jesus, who confine themselves to the employment of the synoptics, do not differ more from one another than the narrators of the life of Mahomet who have made use of the hadith. The biographers of the Arab prophet may take different views of the value of such and such a document. But, on the whole, they are all agreed as to the value of the hadith. They all, according to their manner, class them along with those legendary and traditional documents, but not as precise documents of history properly speaking.

Upon the second point, I desire to say, in regard to the employment it is fitting to make of the fourth Gospel, that there is disagreement. I have, with many reserves and precautions, made use of this document. In the opinion of excellent judges, I ought not to have made any use of it, with the exception of chapters xvii. and xix., which contain the narrative of the Passion. Almost all the enlightened criticisms which I have received apropos of my work are in accord on that point. I am not surprised at this: for I could not be ignorant of the somewhat contrary opinion as to the historic value of the fourth Gospel which obtains in the liberal schools of theology. Objections coming from men so eminent rendered it imperative that I should submit my opinion to the test of a new examination. Putting to one side the question as to knowing who wrote the fourth Gospel, I set myself to follow that Gospel through, paragraph by paragraph, as if it had come to me as a manuscript newly discovered, without the name of the author. Let us divest ourselves of every preconceived idea, and let us endeavour to render an account of the impressions produced on us by that singular writing.

§ 1. The opening verses (i. 1-14) raise within us at once the gravest suspicions. This introduction transports us into the very heart of apostolic theology, presents no resemblance to the synoptics, puts forth ideas assuredly very different from those of Jesus and of his true disciples. At the outset this prologue warns as that the work in question cannot be a simple history, transparent and impersonal like the narrative of Mark, for example; that the author has a theology; that he wishes to prove a thesis, to wit, that Jesus is the divine logos. We are hence admonished to take great precautions. Is it necessary, nevertheless, in regard to this first page, to reject the book in its entirety, and to perceive an imposture in the 14th verse, in which the author declares he has been a witness of the events which compose the life of Jesus?

That would be, in my opinion, a premature conclusion. A work full of theological ideas may embrace valuable historical information. Were not the synoptics written with the constant preoccupation of demonstrating that Jesus realised all the Messianic prophecies? Because of this, are we to give up searching in their accounts for a historical basis? The theory of the logos, which is so strongly developed in our Gospel, is not a reason for rejecting it at the middle or close of the second century. The belief that Jesus was the logos of the Alexandrian theology must have been early put forward, and that in a most logical manner. Happily, the founder of Christianity had no idea of that kind. But, from the year 68, it was already called "The Word of God." Apollos, who was from Alexandria, and who appears to have resembled Philo, passes already (about the year 57) for a new preacher, holding peculiar doctrines. These ideas are in perfect accord with the state of mind in which the Christian community found itself, when people despaired of seeing Jesus appear soon in the clouds as the Son of Man. A change of the same kind appears to have been wrought in the opinions of St. Paul. We knew the difference there is between the first epistles of that Apostle and the last. The hope, for example, of the immediate coming of Christ, which pervades the two epistles to the Thessalonians, disappears towards the end of the life of St. Paul. The Apostle then turns his attention towards another order of invention. The doctrine of the epistle to the Colossians has a great resemblance to that of the fourth Gospel, Jesus being represented in the said epistle as the image of the in, visible God, the first-born of every creature, by whom every-thing has been created, who was before all things, and through whom everything subsists, in whom the plenitude of the Divinity corporeally dwells. Is there not here the "Word" of Philo? I know there are those who reject the authenticity of the epistle to the Colossians, but for reasons, in my opinion, altogether insufficient. These changes of theories, or rather of style, amongst the men of those times, men who were filled with ardent passion, are, within certain limits, matters quite admissible. Why should not the crisis which was produced in the soul of St. Paul not be produced in other apostles, men in the last years of the first century? When the "kingdom of God," as it is described in the synoptics and the apocalypse, had become a chimera, people took refuge in metaphysics. The theory of the logos was the consequence of the disappointment of the first Christian generation. People carried into the ideal that which they hoped to see realised in the order of things. Each delay that was put on the coming of Jesus was one step more towards his deification; and this is so true that it was exactly at the hour when the last Millenarian dream vanished that the divinity of Jesus was proclaimed in an absolute manner.

§ 2. Let us return to our subject. According to consecrated usage the evangelist commences his narrative with the mission of John the Baptist. That which he says of the relations of John with Jesus is similar in many points to the tradition of the synoptics; in other points the divergence is considerable. The theory, soon held so dear by all the Christians, according to which John proclaimed the divine mission of Jesus, is greatly exaggerated by our author. Things are better managed in the synoptics, where John entertains to the end doubts as to the character of Jesus, and sends to him messengers to question him. The narrative of the fourth Gospel implies a perfectly prearranged plan, and confirms us in the idea that we have divined the prologue, to wit, that the author sought rather to prove than to record. We shall discover presently, however, that the author, though differing much from the synoptics, possesses many traditions in common with them. He cites the same prophecies; like them he believes in a dove which should descend upon the head of Jesus immediately after baptism. But his narrative is less ingenuous, more advanced, more ripe, if I may so speak. One single detail staggers me; this is v. 28, which fixes the place with precision. Admit that the designation Bethania is inexact (Bethania was not known along those coasts, and the Greek interpreters have arbitrarily substituted Bethabara for it), what does it matter? A theologian having nothing Jewish about him, nor possessing any recollections direct or indirect of Palestine, a pure theorist like him who composed the prologue, would not have put in that detail. What did this topographical detail matter to a sectary of Asia Minor or of Alexandria? If the author inserted it, it was because he had a substantial reason for so doing, either in the documents he possessed or in some recollections. Already, then, we are led to think that our theologian is indeed able to inform us of things in regard to the life of Jesus of which the synoptics knew nothing. Nothing, certainly, proves ocular testimony. But it must at least be supposed that the author had other sources of information from those which we have, and that to us it may well have the value of an original.

§ 3. Beginning with v. 35 we read about a series of conversions of apostles, associated together in a manner not very natural, and which do not correspond with the accounts of the synoptics. Can it be maintained that the accounts of these last have here a historical superiority? No. The conversions of the apostles recorded in the synoptics are all cast in the same mould; one perceives that a legendary and idyllic type is being indistinctly applied to all narratives of this species. The short narratives of the fourth Gospel have more character and angles less polished. They much resemble badly edited recollections of one of the apostles. I know that the narratives of simple-minded people and of children always enter much into details. I do not insist upon the minutiæ of v. 39. But wherefore that idea of connecting the first conversion of disciples with the sojourn of Jesus near John the Baptist? Whence come these so precise particulars about Philip, about the father of Andrew and Peter, and, above all, about Nathaniel? This latter personage belongs to our Gospel. I cannot hold the latter as inventions which were concocted a hundred years after Jesus and far away from Palestine, together with the so precise details which are reported of him. If he is a symbolical personage, why are we troubled with being told that he was of Cana of Galilee, a city that our evangelist appeared to be particularly well acquainted with? Why should anyone have invented all this? There is no dogmatic intention implied, if it be not in v. 51, which is put in the mouth of Jesus. Above all, there is no symbolical intention. I believe in intentions of this kind when they are indicated, and, if I might say so, underlined by the author. I do not believe in them when the mystic allusion is not self-indicative. The allegorical exegete does not speak in half sentences; he presents his argument and insists upon it with complacency. I say as much also of the sacramental numbers. The adversaries of the fourth Gospel have remarked that the miracles it records are seven in number. If the author himself had selected this number it would be a serious matter, and would prove his motives. The author did not count them; he must only have taken them up at random.

The discussion on this point is somewhat favourable to our text. Verses 35 to 51 have a more historic turn than the corresponding passages in the synoptics. It seems that the fourth evangelist was better acquainted than the other narrators of the life of Jesus with that which concerned the vocation of the apostle; I admit that it was the school of John the Baptist from which Jesus attached to himself the first disciples, whose names remain celebrated; I opine that the principal apostles were disciples of John the Baptist before they became disciples of Jesus, and this affirms the importance which the whole of the first Christian generation accorded to John the Baptist. If this importance, as is argued by the learned Hollandic school, was in part factitious, and conceived almost wholly to sustain the rôle of Jesus as respects an incontestable authority, why was John the Baptist chosen, a man who was not held in great repute except by the Christian family? The truth, in my opinion, is, that John the Baptist was not only for the disciples of Jesus a simple guarantee, but was also for them a first master, with whom they indissolubly connected the recollection of the very beginnings of the mission of Jesus. A fact of greater importance is that the baptism conserved by Christianity as the necessary introduction to a new life is a mark of the origin which still attests, in a visible fashion, that Christianity was at first a detached branch of the school of John the Baptist.

The fourth Gospel should then be limited to the first chapter, which must be defined as "a fragment made up of traditions or of recollections hastily written, and occupied with a theology far removed from the primitive Christian spirit; a chapter of legendary biography, in which the author permits the introduction of traditional data, which he often transforms, but invents nothing." If the question is one of à priori biography, it is indeed rather in the synoptics that I find a biography of that sort. It is the synoptics which make Jesus to be born at Bethlehem, which make him go into Egypt, which lead the Magi to him, &c., for the necessities of the cause. It is Luke who creates or admits personages who perhaps never existed. The Messianic prophets, in particular, prepossessed our author less than the synoptics, and occasioned in him fewer fabulous recitals. In other terms, we already reach, in that which concerns the fourth Gospel, the distinction between the narrative basis and the doctrinal basis. In the first, Jesus appears to us as a powerful being, superior in certain points to the Jesus of the synoptics; but the second is a great distance from the actual discourses of Jesus, such as the synoptics, particularly Matthew, have preserved to us.

A circumstance, moreover, strikes us from this moment. The author wishes it to be accepted that the two first disciples of Jesus were Andrew and another disciple. Andrew very soon attracts Peter, his brother, who thus finds himself put a little into the shade. The second disciple is not named. But, in comparing this passage with others we encounter later on, we are induced to think that the other unnamed disciple is none other than the author of the Gospel, or at least one who wishes to pass himself off for the author. In the last chapters of the book, in fact, we shall see the author speaking with a certain mystery of himself, and, what is most remarkable, affecting always to place himself before Peter, even when recognising the hierarchical superiority of the latter. Let us observe also that in the synoptics the vocation of John is closely associated with that of Peter; but in the Acts John is continually represented as the companion of Peter. A double difficulty is hence presented to us. For, if the unnamed disciple is really John, the son of Zebedee, one is led to think that John, the son of Zebedee, is the author of our Gospel. To suppose that an impostor, in wishing to make believe that the author is John, had had the intention of not naming John and of designating him in an enigmatical fashion, would be to impute to him a ridiculous artifice. On the other hand, are we to understand that, if the real author of our Gospel commenced by being a disciple of John the Baptist, he speaks of the latter in a fashion so little historical, that the synoptic Gospels on this point are superior to his narrative?

§ 4. Paragraph ii. 1-12 is a miraculous recital like so many others to be found in the synoptics. There is in the structure of the narrative a little more of mise-en-scène, something less ingenuous; nevertheless, there is nothing in the groundwork which departs from the general colouring of the tradition. The synoptics do not speak of this miracle; but it is quite natural that, in the rich marvellous legend which circulated, some were acquainted with one detail, others with another. The allegorical explanation, based principally upon verse 10, and according to which water and wine were to be the old and the new alliance, imputes to the author, in my opinion, a thought which he did not possess. Verse 11 proves that, in the eyes of the latter, the whole narrative has but one aim--to manifest the power of Jesus. The mention of the little town of Cana, and of the sojourn the mother of Jesus made there, is not forgotten. If the miracle of the water being changed into wine had been invented by the author of the fourth Gospel, as is supposed by the adversaries of the historic value of the said Gospel, why introduce this detail? Verses 11 and 12 furnish a connected train of facts. What importance would such topographical circumstances have to Hellenist Christians of the second century? The apocryphal Gospels do not proceed in this manner. They are vague, destitute of local colouring, constructed by people who had no regard for Palestine. Let us add, moreover, that our evangelist always speaks of Cana of Galilee, a wholly obscure small town. How was it possible to create with an after-stroke a celebrity for that small borough, of which assuredly the semignostic Christians of Asia Minor had but faint recollections?

§ 5. That which follows verse 13 is of high interest, and constitutes a decisive triumph for our Gospel. According to the synoptics, Jesus, from the commencement of his public life, only made one visit to Jerusalem. The sojourn of Jesus in that city lasted only a few days, at the end of which he was put to death. That admits of enormous difficulties which I do not repeat here, having touched on them in the "Life of Jesus." A few weeks (if we suppose that the intention of the synoptics goes the length of attributing this stay to the interval which supervened between his triumphal entry and his death) would not have sufficed for all that Jesus ought to do at Jerusalem. Many circumstances placed by the synoptics in Galilee, above all the wranglings with the Pharisees, have but little meaning outside of Jerusalem. All the events which follow the death of Jesus go to prove that his sect had taken deep root at Jerusalem. If the things took place there which Matthew and Mark would have us believe did, Christianity was in an especial manner developed in Galilee. Mere sojourners for a few days would not have chosen Jerusalem for their capital. St. Paul entertains not one souvenir of Galilee: for him the new religion was born at Jerusalem. The fourth Gospel, which admits that Jesus made many journeys to and long sojourns in the capital, appears then much nearer the truth. Luke, in this instance, seems to be in secret harmony with our author, or rather gravitates between the two opposing systems. This is very important, for we shall reveal soon other circumstances where Luke sails along with the author of the fourth Gospel, and seems to have had a knowledge of the same traditions.

But there is yet something more striking. The first circumstance of the sojourns of Jesus at Jerusalem reported by our evangelist is likewise reported by the synoptics, and placed by them almost on the eve of the death of Jesus; this is the driving of the merchants out of the temple. Is it to a Galilean that, on the morrow of his arrival at Jerusalem, we can attribute with any show of likelihood such an act, which, however, might have had some reality, since it is reported in each of the four texts ? In the chronological arrangement of the narrative, the advantage belongs entirely to our author. It is evident that the synoptics accumulated during the last days circumstances which were furnished to them by tradition, and that they did not know where to place them.

We must now touch upon a question which it is time to clear up. We have already found that our evangelist possessed many traditions in common with the synoptics (the part played by John the Baptist, the dove at the baptism, the etymology of the name Cephas, the names of at least three of the apostles, the merchants who were driven from the temple). Does our evangelist imbibe this from the synoptics? No: for he presents these same circumstances with two important differences. Whence, then, did he get these narratives in common? Evidently from tradition, or from recollections. But what does this import, except that the author has sketched for us an original version of the life of Jesus, that this life ought to be put at the very outset upon the same footing as the other biographies of Jesus, but afterwards to be decided in detail by motives of preference? An inventor à priori of a life of Jesus would have nothing in common with the synoptics, or would paraphrase them as is done in the apocrypha. The symbolical and dogmatic intention would have been in that case much more sensible. In the whole of his writings there would then have been reason and intention. There would not have been that sort of indifferent and disinterested circumstances which abound in our narrative. There is nothing which resembles the biography of an æon; it is not thus that the Hindoo writes his lives of Krishna, or recounts the incarnations of Vishnu. An example of this species of composition, in the first centuries of our era, is the Pista Sophia attributed to Valentinus. In the latter there is nothing real: all is truly symbolical and ideal. The same remark applies to "The Gospel of Nicodemus," which is an artificial composition, founded entirely on metaphors. In our text, which possesses similar amplification, there is a lacuna, and, if it were imperative to find analogous amplifications amongst the canonical Gospels, it would be in the synoptics rather than in our Gospel that we should have to seek for them.

§ 6. There follows another incident, the relation of which to the synoptics is no less remarkable. The latter, or at least Matthew and Mark, report, apropos of the proceedings of Jesus and of his agony on Golgotha, a phrase that Jesus would have given expression to, and which would have been one of the principal causes of his condemnation: "Destroy this temple and I will build it up again in three days." The synoptics do not say that Jesus had uttered these words: on the contrary, they treat that as false testimony. Our evangelist records that Jesus did in fact give utterance to this incriminating expression. Did he take this sentence from the synoptics? It is hardly probable: for he gives a different version of it, and even an allegorical explanation of which the synoptics are not cognisant. It seems, then, that here he adhered to an original tradition, one more original even than that of the synoptics, since the latter do not cite directly the expression of Jesus, and only report an echo of it. True it is that, in placing this sentence two years before the death of Jesus, the compiler of the fourth Gospel yields to an idea which does not seem to be the most happy.

Observe the Jewish historical characteristic in v. 20; it is a good enough counterfeit and accords sufficiently well with Josephus.

§ 7. The verses ii. 23-25 are rather unfavourable to our text; they are sluggish, cold and tiresome; they smell of the apologist and the polemic. They prove a premeditated compilation, and are much posterior to that of the synoptics.

§ 8. Let us look now at the episode of Nicodemus (iii. 1-21). I naturally sacrifice the whole of the conversation of Jesus with that Pharisee. It is a fragment of apostolic, not evangelic, theology. Such a conversation could only have been reported by Jesus or Nicodemus. Both hypotheses are equally improbable. Moreover, on leaving v. 12 the author forgets the personage he has introduced into the scene, and launches into a general explanation which is addressed exclusively to the Jews. It is here that we detect one of the essential characteristics of our author: his liking for theological conversations, his tendency to attach to such conversations, incidents more or less historic. Fragments of this sort teach us nothing more regarding the doctrine of Jesus than the dialogues of Plato do regarding the thoughts of Socrates. They are imaginary, not traditional compositions. We can only compare them with the harangues that the ancient historians make no scruple of imputing to their heroes. These discourses are far removed both from the style and the ideas of Jesus; on the contrary, they present a similitude corresponding exactly with the theology of the prologue (i. 1-14), where the author speaks in his own name. Is the circumstance to which the author attaches this conversation historical, or is it his own invention? It is difficult to say. I incline, however, to the former; for the fact is reported further on (xix. 39), and Nicodemus is mentioned elsewhere (vii. 50 and following). I am constrained to believe that Jesus in reality had relations with a person of consideration of that name, and that the author of our Gospel, who knew that, has chosen Nicodemus, like as Plato has chosen Phaeton or Alcibiades as interlocutors in one of his great theoretical dialogues.

§ 9. The v. 22 and following up to v. 2 of chapter iv., transport us, in my opinion, into real history. They show us anew Jesus near John the Baptist, but on this occasion surrounded with a group of disciples. Jesus, like John, baptizes, attracts the multitude more than the latter, and has greater success than he. The disciples, like their master, baptize, and a jealousy, to which the chiefs of the sect rise superior, is kindled between the two schools. This is most remarkable; for the synoptics contain nothing of the kind. As for me, I regard this episode as exceedingly probable. What in certain details it possesses of the inexplicable is far from invalidating the historical value of the ensemble. It contains things which we can only half understand, but which fit in well with the hypothesis of writings of personal recollections, intended for a limited circle. Such obscurities, on the contrary, are not to be explained in a work composed with the single aim of making certain ideas prevail. Those ideas enter everywhere. There could not have been so many singular incidents and without apparent signification. The topography, moreover, is here most precise (v. 22, 23). We do not know, it is true, where Latim was, but ænon is a significant hint. It is the word Ænawan, the Chaldean plural of Aïn or Æn, "fountain." How can you account for some Hellenic sectaries being able to divine this? They could not be the name of any locality, or they would have stood for one which was well known, or they would have coined an impossible word in its relationship to the Semitic etymology.

The sentiment of v. 24 has likewise justness and precision. The connection between v. 25 and that which precedes and follows, which is not very apparent, dispels the idea of a fictitious composition. We should say that here we have notes which have been badly edited, old recollsctions loosely put together, yet at times possessing great lucidity. What could be more artless than the thought at v. 26, and repeated at v. 1 of chapter iv.? Verses 27-36 are quite of another character. The author trips again in his discourse, to which it is impossible to attribute any claim to authenticity. But verse 1 of chapter iv. possesses anew rare transparency, while as to verse v. 2 it is important. The author, in a sort of repenting himself of what he has written, and believing that no evil consequences will be deduced from his narrative, instead of erasing it, inserts a parenthesis which is in flagrant contradiction with that which precedes. He no longer assumes that Jesus has baptized; he pretends that it was only his disciples who baptized. We hold that v. 2 was added later. The fact will always remain that the passage iii. 22 and following is in no wise a fragment of à priori theology, since, on the contrary, the à priori theologian takes up the pen at v. 2 to contradict this passage and to free it from that which might have proved embarrassing.

§ 10. We now come to the interview of Jesus with the Samaritan woman and the mission to the Samaritans (iv. 1-42). Luke knew of this mission, which probably was real. Here, however, the theory of those who do see in out Gospel only a series of fictions is destined to lead to an exposition of principles worthy of being studied. The details of the dialogue are evidently fictitious. On the other hand, the topography of v. 3-6 is satisfactory. Only a Palestine Jew who had often passed the entrance to the Valley of Sichem could have written that. Verses 5, 6 are not exact, but the tradition which is there mentioned may have come from Gen. xxxiii. 19; xlviii. 22; Josh. xxiv. 32. The author seems to make a play on words (Sichar for Sichem), by which the Jews believed they cast bitter raillery upon the Samaritans. I do not think that people were so very solicitous at Ephesus about the hatred which divided the Jews from the Samaritans, and of the mutual interdict which existed between them (v. 9). The allusions which people pretend to see in the verses 16-18 to the religious history of Samaria appears to me to be forced, and v. 22 is important. It cuts asunder the admirable sentence, "Woman, believe me, the time is come . . ." and expresses a wholly opposed sentiment. It would seem that there is here an analogous correction at v. 2 of the same chapter, where either the author or one of his disciples corrects an idea which he found dangerous or too bold. In any case, this verse is profoundly imbued with Jewish prejudices. It is beyond my comprehension, if it was written about the year 130 or 150 in the circle of Christianity the most removed from Judaism. V. 35 is exactly in the style of the synoptics and is the actual words of Jesus. The sentence is a splendid relic (v. 21-23, when 22 is omitted). There is no rigorous authenticity for such sentences. How is it to be admitted that Jesus or the Samaritan woman related the conversation they had had together? The Oriental manner of narration is essentially anecdotic, everything with them resolves itself into precise and palpable facts. General phrases, with us expressing a tendency or general state, are to them unknown. There is thus here an anecdote which we can no more admit than all the other anecdotes of history. But the anecdote often contains a truth. If Jesus never pronounced that Divine sentence, the sentence is none the less his--the sentence would not have existed apart from him. I am aware that in the synoptics there often occur principles wholly opposed to one another, circumstances in which Jesus treats the Jews with great severity. But there are likewise some others in which the broad spirit that pervades this chapter of John is to be found. Discrimination is imperative. It is in these last passages that I discover the true thought of Jesus. The others are, in my opinion, blemishes and lapses, proceeding from disciples only moderately capable of comprehending their master and of extracting his thought.

§ 11. Verses 43-45 of chapter iv. contain something which astonishes. The author pretends that it was at Jerusalem, at the time of the feasts, that Jesus made his great demonstrations. It seems that there, this was a habit of his. But that which proves that such a habit, although erroneous, was connected with recollections is that it is supported (v. 44) by a saying of Jesus which is also reported in the synoptics and which has a high character of authenticity.

§ 12. Ver. 46 of ch. iv., which recalls the small town of Cana, is not to be explained in a composition fictitious and uniquely dogmatic. Thus (v. 46-54) there is a miracle of healing, strongly resembling those which abound in the synoptics and which with some variations respond to the one which is recorded at Matt. viii. 5 and following, and at Luke vii. 1 and following. This is very remarkable, for it proves that the author does not invent his miracles to please, and that in recounting them he follows a tradition. To sum up, in regard to the seven miracles mentioned there are only two the marriage feast at Cana and the resurrection of Lazarus) of which there is no trace in the synoptics. The five others are to be found there with some differences of detail.

§ 13. Chapter v. constitutes a fragment apart. Here the processes of the author are nakedly exhibited. He recounts a miracle which is attested to have taken place at Jerusalem with some dramatic details calculated to render the prodigy more striking, and he seizes this occasion for making a long and dogmatic discourse against the Jews. Does the author invent the miracle or does he take it from tradition? If he invents it, we must admit that he had lived at Jerusalem, for he knows the city well (v. 2 and following). It is not a question of Bethesda; yet, to have invented this name and the circumstances relating to it, the author of the fourth Gospel must have known Hebrew, which is a thing the adversaries of our Gospel do not admit. It is more probable that he made the tradition the basis of his account. This account presents, in fact, notable parallelisms to Mark. A part of the Christian community then attributed miracles to Jesus which were attested to have taken place at Jerusalem. This is a very serious matter. That Jesus had acquired great renown in thaumaturgy in a country simple, rustic, and favourably disposed like Galilee, is quite natural. Even had he not in a single instance connived at the execution of marvellous acts, these acts would have taken place in spite of him. His thaumaturgic reputation would have spread independently of all co-operation on his part and of his knowledge. The miracle explains itself before a benevolent public; in such a case it is in reality the public which creates it. But before an evil-disposed public the matter is wholly different. The latter has been clearly seen in the recrudescence of miracles which took place in Italy five or six years ago. The miracles which were produced in the Roman States succeeded; those, on the other hand, which ventured to make their appearance in the Italian provinces were immediately subjected to an inquest and quickly arrested. Those whom it was pretended had been cured avowed that they had never been sick. The thaumaturgists themselves, on being interrogated, declared that they knew nothing of them, but, seeing that the rumours of their miracles were so widespread, they believed they were able to work them. In other words, for a miracle to succeed there is need of a little complaisance. The bystanders not assisting in them, it was necessary for the participants to lend a hand. In like manner, if Jesus performed miracles at Jerusalem we arrive at suppositions which are to us very shocking. Let us reserve our judgment, for we shall soon have to treat of a Jerusalemitish miracle, in other respects more important than the one now in question, and much more intimately connected with the essential events in the life of Jesus

§ 14. Chapter vi. 1-14. The Galilean miracle, moreover, is still nevertheless identical with one of those which are reported by the synoptics; we refer to the multiplication of loaves. It is clear that this is one of those miracles which was attributed to him in his lifetime. It is a miracle to which a real circumstance gives colour. There is nothing more easy than to instil such an illusion into consciences at once credulous, artless, and sympathetic. "While we were with him, we had neither hunger nor thirst:" this very simple utterance becomes a marvellous fact, which is retold with all sorts of additions. The narrative in our text, as always, aims at a little more effect than in the synoptics. In this sense it is of an inferior quality. But the part which the Apostle Philip plays in it is to be noted. Philip is particularly acquainted with the author of our Gospel (compare i. 43 and following: xii. 21, and following). Now, Philip resided at Hierapolis, in Asia Minor, where Papias knew his sons. All this may be readily enough reconciled. We can assume that the author took this miracle from the synoptics, or from an analogous source, and appropriated it in his own way. But why does the detail which he has added to it harmonise so well with that which we have from other sources, if this detail did not come from a direct tradition?

§ 15. By means of evidently artificial connections, which prove clearly that all these recollections (if recollection it be) were written afterwards, the author introduces a strange series of miracles and visions (vi. 16, and following). During a tempest, Jesus appeared on the waves, seeming to be walking on the sea: the barque itself is miraculously transported. This miracle is also found in the synoptics. Here, then, we are yet dealing with tradition, and not with individual fantasy. Verse 23 fixes the localities, establishes a connection between this miracle and that of the multiplication of the loaves, and seems to prove that these miraculous accounts ought to be put in the class of miracles which have a historical basis. The prodigy which we are now discussing probably corresponds with some hallucination which the companions of Jesus entertained in regard to the lake, and in virtue of which they, in a moment of danger, believed they saw their master come to their rescue. The idea into which they had easily drifted, that his body was impalpable like that of a spirit, gave credence to this. We shall soon find (chap. xxi.) another tradition which is founded on analogous fancies.

§ 16. The two miracles which precede serve to lead up to a most important sermon, which Jesus is alleged to have delivered in the synagogue of Capernaum. This sermon was evidently related to a collection of symbols which were very familiar to the oldest Christian community--symbols in which Christ was presented as the bread of believers. I have already said that, in our Gospel, the discourses of Christ are almost all fictitious works, and the one in question may certainly be one of the number. I would, if put to it, own that this fragment possesses more importance in regard to the history of the eucharistic ideas of the first century than the statement even of the sentiments of Jesus. Nevertheless, I believe that our Gospel furnishes us here again with a gleam of light. According to the synoptics, the institution of the eucharist does not ascend beyond the last soiree of Jesus. It is clear that very far back this was believed in, whilst it was the doctrine of St. Paul. But to admit this to be true, it is necessary to suppose that Jesus knew absolutely the day when he would die, a supposition which we cannot accept. The usages which gave rise to the eucharist ascend, then, beyond the last supper, and I believe that our Gospel is completely within the truth, in omitting the sacramental account of the soiree of the Friday, and in disseminating eucharistic ideas in the course even of the life of Jesus. That which is essential in the eucharistic account is at bottom only the reproduction of what took place at every Jewish repast. It was not once, but a hundred times, that Jesus had blessed the bread, broken and distributed it, and also blessed the cup. I by no means pretend that the words which are attributed to Jesus are textual. But the precise details furnished by verses 60, and following, 68, 70-71, have an original character. Later on we will again take notice of the personal hatred entertained by our author against Judas of Kerioth. The synoptics, certainly, have no affection for the latter. But the hatred of the fourth narrator is more premeditated, more personal; it comes out in two or three places previous to the account of the betrayal: it seeks to accumulate upon the head of the culprit wrongs of which the other evangelists make no mention.

§ 17. Ver. 1-10 of ch. vii. are a small historical treasure. The wicked sulky humour of the brothers of Jesus, the precautions which the latter is obliged to take, are therein expressed with admirable ingenuousness. It is here that the dogmatic and symbolical explanation is completely at fault. What a dogmatic or symbolic intention to find in that short passage, which is calculated rather to give rise to the objection that has served the requirements of the apologetic Christian! Why should an author whose unique device had been Scribitur ad probandum have imagined such a fantastic detail? No, no, here we can say boldly, Scribitur ad narrandum. It is hence an original souvenir, come whence it might and from whose pen soever it had proceeded. Why say after this that the personages of our Gospel are certain types, certain characters, and not historic beings of flesh and bones? In fact, it is rather the synoptics which have an idyllic and a legendary turn; compared with them the fourth Gospel possesses the requisites of history, and a narrative which aims at being correct.

§ 18. Now comes a dispute (vii. 11, and following) between Jesus and the Jews, to which I attach little value. Scenes of this description are hence very numerous. Our author's species of imagination imposes itself very strongly on all that he recounts; with him such pictures must be moderately true in the colouring. The discourses put in the mouth of Jesus are conformable with the ordinary style of our author. The intervention of Nicodemus (v. 50 and following) may alone in all this possess a historic value. Verse 52 is open to objections. This verse, they say, contains an error which neither John nor even a Jew could have committed. Could the author be ignorant of the fact that Jonas and Nahum were born in Galilee? Yes, certainly, he might not know it, or, at least, he might not think of it. The historical and exegetical knowledge of the evangelists, and in general the authors of the New Testament, Saint

Paul excepted, was very incomplete. In any case they wrote from memory, and were not careful as to being exact.

§ 19. The account of the woman taken in adultery gives room for great critical doubts. This passage is wanting in the best manuscripts; I believe, however, that it constituted part of the primitive text. The topographical data of verses 1 and 2 are correct. There is nothing in the fragment which harmonises with the style of the fourth Gospel. I think it is by reason of a misplaced scruple which originated in the minds of some false rigorists as to the apparent moral laxity of the episode, that would make one cut away these lines which, in view of their beauty, might be saved by attaching them to other parts of the gospel texts. In any case, if the detail of the adulterous woman did not at first form a part of the fourth Gospel, it is surely of evangelical tradition. Luke was acquainted with it, though in a different form. Papias seems to have read a similar account in the Gospel according to the Hebrews. The sentence "Let anyone amongst you who is without sin" . . . is so perfectly in accord with the spirit of Jesus, corresponds so well with other sentiments of the synoptics, that we are quite entitled to consider it as being authentic to the same extent as sentences of the synoptics. At all events, we can much more readily comprehend why such a passage may have been abridged instead of added to.

§ 20. The theological disputes which fill up the rest of chap. viii. are without any value in the life of Jesus. The author evidently attributed his own ideas to Jesus, without either supporting them by any proof, or by any direct hearsay. How, it might be said, could an immediate disciple or a traditionist directly associated with an apostle, thus alter the words of the master? But Plato was an immediate disciple of Socrates, and he, nevertheless, made no scruple of attributing to him fictitious discourses. The "Phædon" contains historical information of the strictest verity, and discourses which have no authenticity. The tradition of facts is much easier preserved than that of discourses. An active Christian school, pervading rapidly the circle of ideas, succeeded in fifty or sixty years in totally modifying the image which had been made of Jesus, whilst it was much better able than all the others to recall certain peculiarities and the general contexture of the biographies of the reformer. The simple and gentle Christian families of Batanea, amongst whom was formed the collection of Δόγια,--small committees, which were very pure and very honest, of ebionine (the poor of God), remained most faithful to the teachings of Jesus, having piously guarded the depôt of his words, forming a little world in which there was little movement of ideas--could have at once very well preserved the timbre of the master's voice, and be very bad authorities as to the biographical circumstances for which they cared little. The distinction which we here indicate is reproduced, moreover, in that which concerns the first Gospel. This evangelist is surely the one who gives us the best rendering of the discourses of Jesus, and yet is, as to facts, more inexact than the second. It is in vain that unity of authorship is alleged by some for the fourth Gospel. This unity I indeed recognise: but a composition compiled by a single hand may yet embrace data of very unequal value. The life of Mahomet, by Ibn-Hescham, is perfectly uniform, and yet this Life contains things which we can admit, others which we cannot.

§ 21. Chapters ix. and x. up to verse 21 of the latter form a paragraph commencing with a new Jerusalem miracle, that of the man being born blind, where the intention of heightening the demonstrative force of the prodigy is made to be felt in a more fatiguing manner than in anywhere else. We nevertheless discern a somewhat precise knowledge of the topography of Jerusalem (v. 7): the explanation of ευλοως is rather good. It is impossible to pretend that this miracle was evolved from the symbolical imagination of our author; for it is also found in Mark (viii. 22, and following), with a coincidence which bears a minute and bizarre characteristic (comp. John ix. 6 and Mark viii. 23). In the discussions and discourses which follow, I acknowledge that it would be dangerous to seek an echo in the mind of Jesus. An essential characteristic of our author, which is henceforward conspicuous, is his habit of taking a miracle as a point of departure for long demonstrations. His miracles are reasoned and explained miracles. This is not the case with the synoptics. The theurgy of the latter is perfectly artless: they never retrace their steps in order to draw marvellous conclusions upon what they have related. The theurgy of the fourth Gospel, on the contrary, is reflective, set forth with all the artifices of exposition whose aim is conviction, and exploited in favour of certain sermons in which the author makes the account of his prodigies to follow. If our Gospel was limited to such fragments, the opinion which sees in it a simple thesis of theology would be perfectly established.

§ 22. But it is far from being limited to this. Beginning with verse 22 of chap. x. we enter into topographical details of rigorous precision, which are hardly applicable if it is maintained that in no degree does our Gospel embrace the Palestinian tradition. I sacrifice the whole of the dispute contained in verses 24-39. The journey to Perea indicated at verse 40 appears, on the contrary, to be historical. The synoptics are cognisant of this journey, to which they attach the divers incidents of Jericho.

§ 23. We reach now a most important passage (xi. 1-45). It relates to a miracle, but a miracle which trenches upon others, and is produced under circumstances entirely different. All the other miracles are represented as having been attended with some éclat and as wrought upon obscure individuals who never again figure in evangelical history. In this instance the miracle takes place in the centre of a well-known family, and in which the author of our Gospel in particular, if he is sincere, appears to have participated. The other miracles are little aside gyrations, designed to prove by their number the divine mission of the master, but, taken by themselves, of no consequence, since in no single case are we told what took place; nor does one amongst them form an integral part of the life of Jesus. They can be treated en bloc, as I have done in my work, without shaking the edifice or breaking the continuity of events. The miracle in question here, on the contrary, is deeply concerned in the account of the last weeks of Jesus, such as we find them in our Gospel. Now we shall see that it is precisely on account of that record of these last weeks that our text possesses an incontestable superiority. This miracle makes then by itself a class apart; at first glance it seems as if it ought to be reckoned among the events in the life of Jesus. It is not the minute detail of the account which strikes me. The two other Jerusalem miracles of Jesus, of which the author of the fourth Gospel speaks, are recounted in similar fashion. If the whole of the circumstances of the resurrection of Lazarus had been the product of the imagination of the narrator, it would have proved that all these circumstances had been combined with the view (a constant habit that we have remarked in our author) that the principal fact should not remain less exceptional in evangelical history.

The miracle of Bethany is to the Galilean miracles what the stigmata of Francis d'Assisi were to the miracles of the same saint. M. Karl Hase has composed an exquisite Life of Christ in the shades, without insisting particularly upon any of these latter; but he saw clearly that it would not have been a sincere biography if he had not descanted upon the stigmata; he has devoted to these a long chapter, giving place to all sorts of conjectures and suppositions.

Amongst the miracles which are spread over the four compilations of the Life of Jesus, a distinction makes itself felt. Some are pure and simple legendary creations. There is nothing in the real life of Jesus which has a place in them. They are the fruit of that labour of imagination which is produced around all popular celebrities. Others have had actual facts for their foundation. Legend has not arbitrarily attributed to Jesus the healing of those possessed of devils. Doubtless, Jesus more than once was believed to make such cures. The multiplication of loaves, many cures of sickness, perhaps certain apparitions, ought to be put in the same category. These are not miracles hatched out of pure imagination, they are miracles conceived àpropos of real incidents, exaggerated and transformed. Let us absolutely discard an idea which is very widespread, that no eye-witness reports miracles. The author of the last chapter of the Acts is surely an ocular witness of the life of St. Paul. Now this writer records miracles which have taken place before him. But what am I saying? St. Paul himself speaks to us of his miracles and founds upon them the truth of his preaching. Certain miracles were permanent in the Church, and were in some sort common property. "Why," said they, "challenge ocular testimony when people recount things which have never been heard or seen?" But then the tres socii did not know of Francis d'Assisi, for they record a multitude of things which they could not have seen or heard.

In what category must we place the miracle which we are now discussing? Did some actual fact, which had been exaggerated and embellished, give rise to it? Or, again, does it possess reality of any sort? Is it a pure legend, an invention of the narrator? What complicates the difficulty is that the third Gospel, that of Luke, presents to us here consonances which are most peculiar. Luke, in fact, knew Martha and Mary; he knew at the same time they did not hail from Galilee; in fine, he knew them in a light which was strongly analogous to that under which these two personages figure in the fourth Gospel. Martha, in the latter text, plays the rôle of a servant, διηχόνει, Mary, the rôle of a forward, ardent personage. We know the admirable little episode which Luke has extracted thence. But, if we compare the passages in Luke and in the fourth Gospel, it is clearly the fourth Gospel which plays here the original part; not that Luke, or whoever the author of the third Gospel may be, may have read the fourth, but in the sense in which we find in the fourth Gospel the data which explain the legendary anecdote of the third. Was the third Gospel also cognisant of Lazarus? After having for a long time refused to admit this, I have arrived at the belief that this is very probable. Yes, I now think that the Lazarus of the parable of the rich man is but a transformation of our resurgent one. Let it not be said that in thus being metamorphosed it has been much changed in the process. In this respect everything is possible, since the repast of Martha, Mary, and Lazarus, who play a great part in the fourth Gospel and who are placed by the synoptics in the house of Simon the Leper, becomes in the third Gospel a repast at the house of Simon the Pharisee, where there figures a fisherwoman who, like Mary in our Gospel, anoints the feet of Jesus and wipes them with her hair. What thread holds together this inextricable labyrinth of broken and patched-up legends? For my part, I admit the family of Bethany to have had a real existence, and to have given rise in certain branches of the Christian tradition to a cycle of legends One of these données legendaires was that Jesus had called back to life the head even of the family. Certainly, such an "on dit" may have originated after the death of Jesus. I do not, however, regard as impossible that one real fact in his life may not have given it birth. The silence of the synoptics in regard to the Bethany episode does not greatly astonish me. The synoptics were very badly informed as to all that which immediately preceded the last weeks of Jesus. It was not only the Bethany incident which was lacking to them, but also the whole period of the life of Jesus to which this incident relates. We are here brought back once more to that fundamental point, that of knowing which of the two accounts is the true one, the one which makes Galilee the theatre of all the activity of Jesus, or the one which makes Jesus pass a part of his life at Jerusalem.

I know what has been attempted here by means of symbolical explanation. The miracle of Bethany, according to the learned and profound defenders of this system, signifies that Jesus is to believers in a spiritual sense the resurrection and the life. Lazarus is the poor man, the ebion resurrected by Christ from his state of spiritual death. It was on account of this, the sense of a popular reawakening which came to perplex them, that the official classes decided on making Jesus perish. This is the theory upon which the best theologians that the Church has possessed in our days repose. In my opinion it is an erroneous one. That our Gospel is dogmatic I recognise, but it is by no means allegorical. The really allegorical writings of the first centuries, the Apocalypse, the Pastor of Hermas, the Pista Sophia, possess quite a different charm. At bottom of all this symbolism is the companion of the mysticism of M. Strauss; the expedients of theologians at their wit's end, seeking by means of allegory, mysticism, and symbolism to escape from their dilemma. For us, who are seeking only for pure historic truth without a shade of either theological or political arrière pensée, we have more scope. For us, all this is not mythical, all this is not symbolical, all this is sectarian and popular history. It must necessarily provoke grave distrust, but no party offers fitting explanations.

Divers examples are pleaded. The Alexandrian school, such as we know it through the writings of Philo, exercised unquestionably a strong influence upon the theology of the apostolic century. Now, do we not see this school press its taste for symbolism to the verge of folly? The whole of the Old Testament became in its hands only a pretext for subtle allegories. Are not the Talmud and the Midraschim full of pretended historical teachings which have been stripped of all truth, and which can only be explained by religious tenets or by the desire of originating arguments in support of a thesis? But this is not the case with the fourth Gospel. The principles of criticism which it is proper to apply to the Talmud and the Midraschim, cannot be transferred to a composition altogether at variance with the likings of the Palestinian Jews. Philo discerns allegories in the ancient texts; he does not invent allegorical texts. An old sacred book exists; the plain interpretation of this text embarrasses or is insufficient; we seek in it its hidden and mysterious meaning; examples such as these abound. But when we write an extended historical narrative with the arrière pensée of concealing in it symbolical finesse which was only to be discovered seventeen hundred years later, this is what is but seldom seen. It is the partisans of the allegorical explanation who, in this case, play the part of Alexandrians. It is they who, embarrassed by the fourth Gospel, treat it just as Philo treated Genesis, just as the Jewish and Christian tradition has treated the Canticle of Canticles. For us simple historians who admit first of all (1) That the question here is only one of legends, in parts true, in parts false, like all legends; (2) that the reality which served as a basis for these legends was beautiful, splendid, touching and delicious, but, like all things human, greatly marred by weaknesses which would disgust us if we saw them--for us, I say, there are no difficulties of this kind. There are texts, and the question is to extract the largest amount of historic truth possible, that is all.

Another very delicate question presents itself here. In the miracles of the second class, in those which owe their origin to a real fact in the life of Jesus, is there not mixed up with these sometimes a little complaisance? I believe so, or at least I declare that if this were not so, nascent Christianity has been an event absolutely without parallel. This event has been the greatest and the most beautiful amongst facts of the same species; but it has not escaped the common laws which must govern the facts of religious history. There does not exist a single great religious creation which does not embrace a little of that which would now be denominated--fraud. The ancient religions were full of it. Few of the institutions of the past have a greater right to be recognised by us than the oracle of Delphi, seeing that that oracle eminently contributed to save Greece, the mother of all science and of all art. The enlightened patriotism of Pythia was not more than once or twice found at fault She was ever the mouthpiece of the sages who were endowed with the justest sentiment of Greek interests. These sages, who have founded civilisation, made no scruple about consulting this virgin, who was reputed to be inspired by the gods. Moses, if the traditions we have regarding him contain anything historical, made use of natural events, such as tempests and fortuitous plagues, to further his designs and his policy. All the ancient legislators gave their laws as if inspired by a god. All the prophets, without any scruple, made it appear as if their sublime invectives were prompted by the Eternal. Buddhism, which is full of such high religious sentiment, saw permanent miracles, which could not be produced of themselves. The most artless country of Europe, the Tyrol, is the country of the stigmatics, the fashion of which is only possible by means of a little trickery. The history of the Church, so respectable in its way, is full of false relics and false miracles. Was there ever a religious movement more ingenuous than that of Francis d'Assisi? And yet the whole history of the stigmata is inexplicable without some connivance on the part of the intimate companions of the saint.

"People do not prepare," I have been told, "sophistical miracles, when people believe they everywhere are truth." This is an error. It is when people believe in miracles that they are drawn away, without doubting in them, to augment their number. We can with difficulty, with our consciences clear and precise, figure to ourselves the bizarre illusions by which these obscure but powerful consciences, playing with the supernatural, if I might say so, would glide incessantly from credulity to complaisance, and from complaisance to credulity. What can be more striking than the mania spread at certain epochs of attributing to the ancient sages the apocryphal books? The apocrypha of the Old Testament, the writings of the hermetic cycle, the innumerable pseudo-epigraphic productions of India, responded to a great elevation of religious sentiments. People believed they were doing honour to the old sages in attributing to them these productions; people became their collaborators without thinking that the day would come when that would be denominated a fraud. The authors of the Middle Age legends, magnifying in cold blood upon their desks the miracles of their saints, would also be surprised in hearing themselves called impostors.

The eighteenth century would describe all religious history as imposture. The critic of our times has totally discarded that explanation. The term is certainly improper; but to what extent have the most beautiful souls of the past not aided in their own illusions, or in those of which they have been the object, is what a reflective age can no longer comprehend. For one to understand this thoroughly one must have been in the East. In the East passion is the soul of everything and credulity has no limits. We can never get at the bottom of the mind of an Oriental; because this bottom often does not exist for himself. Passion on one side, credulity on the other, make imposture. So no great movement is produced in this country without some fraud. We no longer know how to desire or to hate; cunning finds no longer a place in our society, for she has no longer an object. But exaltation is a passion which does not accommodate itself to this reserve, this indifference to consequences which is the basis of our sincerity. When absolute natures will embrace a thesis after the Oriental manner, they are no longer restrainable, and nothing, the day even when illusion becomes necessary, is too dear to them. Is that the fault of sincerity? Not at all; it is because conviction is most keenly felt by such spirits, because they are incapable of returning upon themselves, that they have few scruples. To call this deceit is inexact; it is precisely the force with which they embrace their idea which extinguishes in them every other thought, for the end appears so absolutely good to them that everything which can serve it seems in their view legitimate. Fanaticism is always sincere in respect of its thesis, but an impostor in respect of the choice of methods of demonstration. If the public do not at first accept the reason which it believes to be good, that is to say, its affirmations, it has recourse to reasons which it knows to be bad. With it to believe is everything: the motives which induce belief are of but little importance. Who among us would accept the responsibility for all the arguments through which was wrought the conversion of the barbarians? In our days people only employ fraudulent devices when they are aware of the falsity of that which is maintained. Formerly, the employment of these means presupposed a profound conviction, and was allied to the highest moral elevation. Our method of criticism is different. It professes to expose falsehood and to discover the truth through the network of deceptions and illusions of every sort which envelop history; while in face of such facts we experience a sentiment of repugnance. But do not let us impose our delicate scruples upon those whose duty it has been to direct poor humanity. Between the general truth of a principle and the truth of a meagre fact the man of faith never hesitates. We had, at the time of the coronation of Charles X., the most authentic proofs of the destruction of the ampulla. The ampulla was found again, inasmuch as it was necessary. On the one side, there was the salvation of royalty, so at least it was believed; on the other, the question of the authenticity of some drops of oil; no good royalist hesitated.

To summarise amongst the miracles which the Gospels attribute to Jesus, there are some purely legendary. But there were probably some of them in which he consented to play a part. Let us put to one side the fourth Gospel. The Gospel of Mark, the most original of the synoptics, is the life of an exorcist and thaumaturgist. Some details, as in Luke viii. 45, 46, are not less sad than those which, in the episode of Lazarus, lead the theologians to exclaim in a loud voice against the myths and symbols. I do not hold to the reality of the miracle in question. The hypothesis which I propose in the present edition reduces everything to a misapprehension. I desire solely to show that this fantastic episode of the fourth Gospel is not a decisive objection against the historic value of the said Gospel. In each part of the "Life of Jesus," on which we are now about to enter, the fourth Gospel contains many special points of information, which are infinitely superior to any in the synoptics. Now it is singular that the account of the resurrection of Lazarus is joined to these last pages by hooks so slender that, if we were to reject it as being imaginary, the whole edifice of the last weeks of the "Life of Jesus," which are so solid in our Gospel, would crumble at a stroke.

§ 24. Verses 46-54 of chapter xi. introduce us to a first secret council held by the Jews, in order to put Jesus to death, as a direct consequence of the miracle of Bethany. People might say that this bond was an artificial one. Bat why? Does not our narrator more nearly approach probability than the synoptics, which make the conspiracy against Jesus begin only two or three days before his death? The whole account we have just examined is otherwise very natural; it is terminated by a circumstance which was not surely invented--the flight of Jesus to Ephraim or Ephron. What allegorical meaning is to be found in that? Is it not evident that our author possessed data totally unknown to the synoptics, which latter, caring little about composing a regular biography, compressed into a few days the last six months of the life of Jesus? Verses 55, 56 present a chronological arrangement which is very satisfactory.

§ 25. Again (xii. 1 and following) is an episode common to all the narratives, except to Luke, who has, in this instance, arranged his facts in a wholly different fashion; we mean the feast of Bethany. We have seen in the "six days" of verse xii. 1 a symbolical reason. I mean the intention of making the day of the unction coincide with the 10th of Nisan, the day on which the paschal lambs should have been selected (Exodus xii. 3, 6) The latter is much less clearly indicated. At chapter xix. v. 36, where we can penetrate the design of assimilating Jesus to the paschal lamb, the author is much more explicit. As regards the incidents of the feast, is it from pure fancy that our author here enters into details which were unknown to Matthew and to Mark? I do not think so. It is that he was better acquainted with them. The woman who is not named in the synoptics is Mary of Bethany. The disciple who makes the observation is Judas, and the name of this disciple immediately leads the narrator into lively personal abuse (v. 6). This v. 6 breathes strongly the hatred of two co-disciples who have lived long together, who are deeply embittered against one another, and who have followed opposite paths. And this Μάρθα διηκόνει explains so fully an episode of Luke! And the hair used to wipe the feet of Jesus, is it not also found in Luke! All leads to the belief that we here hit upon an original source, which serves as a key to the other less skilfully constructed narratives. I do not deny the strangeness of verses 1, 2, 9-11, 17, 18, which return three times to the resurrection of Lazarus and improve upon xi. 45 and following. On the contrary, I see nothing at all unlikely in the design imputed to the family of Bethany of awakening the indifference of the Jerusalemites by exterior demonstrations which were unknown to the simple Galilean. It must not be said such and such suppositions are false, because they are shocking and pitiful. If people were to see the obverse of the greatest events which take place in this world, of those which enchant us, of those amidst which we live, nothing would be accomplished. Let us remark, moreover, that the actors here are women who have imbibed that unequalled love which Jesus knew how to inspire around him; women who believed they were living in the bosom of the marvellous, who felt convinced that Jesus had done innumerable prodigies, and who were placed face to face with incredulous people, who railed at him whom they loved. If a scruple could have arisen in their soul, the recollection of other miracles of Jesus would have silenced it. Suppose that a legitimist dame was reduced to the extremity of assisting heaven to save Joas? Would she hesitate? Passion imputes always to God anger and selfishness; it enters into the councils of God, makes him speak, urges him to act. People are sure of being in the right; they make use of God in advocating their cause, in supplementing the zeal which he does not evince.

§ 26. The account of the triumphal entry of Jesus into Jerusalem (xii. 12 and following) is conformable with the synoptics. Yet that which astonishes us here is the imperturbable appeal to the miracle of Bethany (v. 17, 18). It was on account of that miracle that the Pharisees decided on the death of Jesus; it was that miracle which made the Jerusalemites think; it was that miracle which was the cause of the triumph of Bethphage. I should like to put the whole of this to the account of an author of the year 150, who was ignorant of the real character and the artless innocence of the Galilean movement. But first let us guard against believing that innocence and conscientious illusion were likewise excluded. It is in the fugitive sensations of the soul of the woman of the East that we must here seek for analogies. Passion, ingenuousness, abandon, tenderness, perfidy, poetry and crime, frivolity and depth, sincerity and deceit, alternate in these sorts of natures, and baffle any absolute estimation. The critic ought in such circumstances to steer clear of every exclusive system. The mythical explanation is often true; but for all that the historical explanation ought not to be banished. Now look at verses xii. 20 and following, which contain an undoubted historical secret. First, it is the obscure and isolated episode of the Hellenes which is addressed to Philip. Remark the part played by this apostle; our Gospel is the only one which knows anything of it. Remark, especially, how the whole of this passage is exempt from any dogmatical or symbolical design. To say that these Greeks are reasonable beings, like Nicodemus and the Samaritan woman, is most gratuitous. The discourses which they hold (v. 23 et seq.) have no relation to them.

The aphorism in v. 25 is again met with in the synoptics; it is evidently authentic. Our author does not copy it from the synoptics. Again, even when he makes Jesus speak, the author of the fourth Gospel now and then follows a tradition.

§ 27. Verses 27 et seq. possess much importance; Jesus is troubled. He prays his Father "to deliver him from this hour." Then he resigns himself. A voice makes itself heard from heaven, or better, according to other accounts, an angel speaks to Jesus. What does this episode import? There is no doubt that it is the parallel of the agony of Gethsemane, which, to be sure, is omitted by our author at the place where it should have been found--after the Last Supper. Remark the incident of the apparition of an angel, which Luke alone knew of. There is one more feature to add to the series of those agreements between the third Gospel and the fourth, which constitute for evangelical criticism a fact of so great importance. But the existence of two versions so different from an incident which happened during the last days of Jesus, which is certainly historic, constitute a fact much more decisive still. Which merits here the preference? The fourth Gospel, in my opinion. First, the narrative of this Gospel is less dramatic, less skilfully adjusted and constructed, less beautiful, I admit. In the second place, the moment where the fourth Gospel introduces the episode in question is much more convenient. The synoptics report the scene of Gethsemane, along with other solemn circumstances, as taking place on the last evening of Jesus, in consequence of the tendency we have of accumulating our recollections upon the last hours of a beloved person. These circumstances placed thus have, moreover, more effect. But, to admit the order of the synoptics, we must suppose that Jesus knew with certainty the day on which he should die. We thus generally find the synoptics yielding oftentimes to the desire for an arrangement which shall proceed with a certain art. Art divine, whence has emerged the most beautiful popular poem that has ever been written--the Passion But undoubtedly in such a case the historical critic will always prefer the version which is least dramatic. It is this principle which makes us place Matthew after Mark, and Luke after Matthew, when the question is one of determining the historical value of a synoptical account.

§ 28. We have now reached the last evening (chapter xiii). The farewell repast is recounted, as in the synoptics, at great length. But the surprising thing is that the capital circumstance of this repast, as reported in the synoptics, is omitted. There is not a word about the establishment of the Lord's Supper, which holds such an important position in the preoccupations of our author (chap. vi.). And this is as though the narration took here a reflective turn (v. 1), as though the author insists upon the tender and mystic signification of the last feast. What does that silence mean? Here, as in the episode of Gethsemane, I see in such an omission an idea of superiority on the part of the fourth Gospel. To pretend that Jesus reserved for the Friday evening so important a ritual institution is to believe in a sort of miracle, to suppose that he was certain to die the next day. Although Jesus (it is permissible to believe) might have presentiments, we cannot, apart from the supernatural, admit such distinctness in his previsions. I hence think that it was by means of a displacement, very easy to explain, that the disciples centred all their eucharistic remembrances upon the Last Supper. Jesus on this occasion, as he had done many times before, practised the habitual Jewish rite at table, in attaching to it the mystical sense when it was convenient, and, as the last supper could be better recalled to mind than others, people fell into accord in referring to it this fundamental usage. The authority of St. Paul, which is here in accord with the synoptics, possesses no preeminence, seeing that he had not been present at the repast; it proves only that which no one can doubt, that a great part of tradition fixed the establishment of the sacred memorial on the eve of his death. This tradition answers to the generally accepted tradition that on the said evening Jesus substituted a new Eastern for the Jewish Passover; it supports another opinion of the synoptics, which is contradicted by the fourth Gospel, to wit, that Jesus made with his disciples the paschal feast, and died, consequently, on the morrow of the day when people eat the paschal lamb.

What is very remarkable is, that the fourth Gospel, in place of the eucharist, gives another rite, the washing of feet, as having been the proper institution of the last supper. Doubtless, our evangelist has for once yielded to the natural tendency of reporting on the last evening the solemn acts in the life of Jesus. The hatred of our author against Judas unmasks itself more and more, because of a strong prepossession which made him speak of this unhappy man, even when he is not directly in evidence (verses 2, 10, 11, 18). In the account of the announcement that Jesus had committed treason, the great superiority of our text again reveals itself. The same anecdote is to be found in the synoptics, but is presented in an improbable and contradictory manner. In the synoptics Jesus is represented as designating the traitor in indirect language, and yet the expressions he makes use of become known to all. Our fourth Gospel explains clearly this little misapprehension. According to it, Jesus privately confided his presentiment to a disciple who lay upon his bosom, who, in turn, communicated to Peter what Jesus had said to him. In regard to the others present, Jesus shrouds himself in mystery, and no one has any suspicion of what has passed between him and Judas. The little details of the account, the broken bread, the glimpse which verse 29 gives us of the inner life of the sect, are also characterised by justness, and when we see the author saying quite clearly, "I was there," one is inclined to think that he speaks the truth. Allegory is essentially cold and stiff. The persons in it are of brass, and are moved simultaneously. It is not so with our author. That which is striking in his narrative is its life, its realism. We perceive a passionate man, who is jealous because he loves much, and susceptible, a man who resembles the Orientals of our days. Fictitious compositions never possess this personal trait; there is something vague and awkward which always betrays their origin.

§ 29. Now follow long discourses which possess a certain beauty, but which, there can be no doubt, contain nothing traditional. These are fragments of theology and rhetoric, having no analogy to the discourses of Jesus in the synoptic Gospels, and to which we must not attribute any more historical reality than to the discourses which Plato puts into the mouth of his master at the moment of dying. Nothing must be concluded hence as to the value of the context. The discourses inserted by Sallust and Titus Livy in their histories are assuredly fictions; but are we to conclude from this that the basis of these histories is fictitious) It is probable, moreover, that in these homilies attributed to Jesus there is one feature which is of historic value, Thus, the promise of the Holy Spirit (xiv. 16 et seq. 26; xv. 26; xvi. 7, 13), which Mark and Matthew do not give in a direct form, are found in Luke (xxiv. 49), and correspond with a statement in Acts (ii.) which must have had some reality. In any case, this idea of a spirit which Jesus will send from the bosom of his Father, when he shall have quitted the earth, is another instance of agreement with Luke (Acts i. and ii.). The idea of the Holy Spirit concerned as Mediator (Paraclete) is also found, especially in Luke (xii. 11, 12; comp. Matthew x. 20; Mark xiii. 11). The scheme of the Ascension, explained by Luke, finds its obscure germ in our author (xvi. 7).

§ 30. After the Supper our evangelist, like the synoptics, conducts Jesus to the Garden of Gethsemane (chap. xviii.). The topography of v. 1 is exact. Τὸνχέδρον may be an inadvertence of the copyist, or, if we might say so, of the editor, of him who prepared the narrative for the public. The same error is to be found in the Septuagint (2 Sam. xv. 23). The Codex Sinaïticus bears τοῦχέδρου. The true reading τοῦχέδρου would appear strange to people who did not know Greek. I have elsewhere already explained the omission of the agony at this particular moment, an omission in which I see an argument in favour of the account of the fourth Gospel. The arrest of Jesus is also much better told. The incident of the kissing of Judas, so touching, so beautiful, but which has a legendary odour, is passed over in silence. Jesus names himself and frees himself. This is, indeed, a very useless miracle (v. 6); but the incident of Jesus requesting of them to let the disciples go away which acompanied it (v. 8) is plausible. It is quite possible that the latter may have been at first arrested with their master. Faithful to his habits of precision--whether real or apparent--our author knew the names of the two persons who were for the moment engaged in a struggle, from which resulted a slight effusion of blood.

But here follows the proof the most sensible which our author possesses on the Passion--evidence much more original than that of the other evangelists. He alone causes Jesus to be conducted to Annas or Hanan, the father-in-law of Kaïaphas. Josephus confirms the correctness of this account, and Luke seems here again to gather a sort of echo of our Gospel. Hanan had for a long time been deposed from the Pontificate; but, during the remainder of his long life, he in reality retained the power, which he exercised under the names of his son and sons-in-law, who were successively raised to the sacerdotal sovereignty. This circumstance, which the two first synoptics, very poorly informed as to matters at Jerusalem, cast no doubt upon, is a trait de lumière. How could a sectary of the second century, writing in Egypt or Asia Minor, have known this? The too oft repeated opinion that our author knew nothing of Jerusalem or of matters Jewish appears to me to be utterly destitute of foundation.

§ 32. The recital of the denials of Peter possesses the same superiority. The whole episode, in our author, is more circumstantial and better explained. The details of v. 16 contain a marvellous amount of truth. Far from seeing in them an improbability, I discover in them a mark of simplicity, resembling that of a provincial who boasts of having influence in a minister's office because he is acquainted with a doorkeeper or a domestic. Will it also be maintained that there is here some mystic allegory? A rhetorician coming a long time after the events, and composing his work from accepted texts, would not have written like that. Look at the synoptics: everything is ingeniously combined for the sake of effect. Certainly a multitude of the details of the fourth Gospel smell also of an artificial arrangement, but others seem indeed only to be there because they are true, being so many accidents and sharp angles.

§ 33. We come now to Pilate. The incident of v. 28 has all the appearance of truth. Our author is at variance with the synoptics as to the day on which Jesus died. According to him it was on the day on which the paschal lamb was eaten, the 14th of Nisan; according to the synoptics it was the day following. The error in the synoptics might be quite naturally explained by the desire which people had to make of the last supper the paschal feast, so as to give it more solemnity and to furnish a motive for the celebration of the Jewish Passover. True, it may also be said that the fourth Gospel has placed the death on the day on which the paschal lamb was eaten, so as to inculcate the idea that Jesus himself was the veritable paschal lamb, an idea which he in one place avows (xix. 36), and which, perhaps, is to be met with in other passages (xii. 1, xix. 29). That which, however, clearly proves that the synoptics here do violence to historical reality is that they add a circumstance drawn from the ordinary ceremony of the Passover, and not certainly from a positive tradition. I refer to the singing of psalms. Certain incidents reported by the synoptics--the fact, for example, of Simon of Cyrene returning from his labours in the fields--presuppose thus that the crucifixion took place before the commencement of the sacred period. Finally, it cannot be conceived that the Jews should provoke an execution, or even that the Romans should bring about one, on a day so solemn.

§ 34. I abandon the conversations of Pilate and Jesus, composed evidently from mere conjecture, yet with an exact enough sentiment as regards the situation of the two persons. The question in v. 9 has, however, its echo in Luke, and, as usual, that insignificant detail becomes in the third Gospel wholly legendary. The topography and the Hebrew are good counterfeits. The whole scene presents great historical exactness, even though the language imputed to the personages is in the narrator's style. What concerns Barabbas, however, is, in the synoptics, more satisfactory. Our author doubtless is mistaken in making of this man a thief. The synoptics are much nearer probability in representing him to be a personage beloved by the people and arrested for causing a riot. As regards the flagellation, Mark and

Matthew contain also a little shade more of information. In their account we see better that flagellation was a simple preliminary of crucifixion, ordained by common law. The author of the fourth Gospel does not seem to doubt that flagellation presupposed an irrevocable condemnation. Once more, he proceeds in perfect accord with Luke (xxiii. 16), and like the latter seeks in everything which concerns Pilate to exculpate the Roman authority and to inculpate the Jews.

§ 35. The minute details of the seamless coat furnish also an argument against our author. It might be said that his false conception of it arose from his having eagerly seized the parallelism of the passage in Psalm xxii. which he cites. We have an example of the same kind of error in Matt. xxi. 2-5. Perhaps also the seamless vestment of the high priest (Josephus, Ant. III. vii. 4) has something to do with all this. We touch now upon the greatest objection against the veracity of our author. Matthew and Mark make only the Galilean women, the inseparable companions of Jesus, assist at the crucifixion. Luke adds to those women all the people of the acquaintance of Jesus (pant es oignostoi auto), an addition which is at variance with the two first Gospels, and with what Justin tells us of the defection amongst the disciples (oi gnori moiautou pantes) after the crucifixion. At all events, in the three first Gospels, this group of the faithful kept at a distance from the cross, and did not hold converse with Jesus. Our Gospel adds three essential details. 1st. Mary, the mother of Jesus, assisted at the crucifixion. 2nd. John also assisted at it. 3rd. They all stood at the foot of the cross; Jesus conversed with them, and confided the care of his mother to his favourite disciple. This is most singular. "The mother of the sons of Zebedee," or Salome, whom Matthew and Mark place amongst the faithful women, is deprived of these honours in the recital which is alleged to have been written by her son. The attributing of the name of Mary to the sister of Mary, the mother of Jesus, is also a most singular thing. Here I am wholly with the synoptics. "That the knowledge of the touching presence of Mary near the cross, and the filial functions which Jesus entrusted to John," says M. Strauss, "should be forgotten, is that which is indeed less easy of comprehension than it is to comprehend why all this should have been invented by the circle from which the fourth Gospel emanated. Is it to be thought that it was a circle in which the Apostle John enjoyed especial veneration, the proof of which we see in the care with which our Gospel chooses him from amongst the three most esteemed confidants of Jesus, in order to make of him the one apostle well-beloved? henceforth, is it possible to find anything which puts the seal to this predilection in a more striking manner than the solemn declaration of Jesus, who, by a last act of his will, bequeaths to John his mother, as the most precious legacy, substituted him thus in his place, and made him Vicar of Christ,' without thinking whether it was natural to ask this, both in respect of Mary and of the apostle well-beloved, and whether it was possible when they were far removed from the side of Jesus at that supreme moment?"

This is very happily put. It completely proves that our author had more than one arrière pensée, that he had not the sincerity and the absolute naïvete of Matthew and Mark. But it is, at the same time, the most apparent indication of the origin of the work we are discussing. In comparing this passage with others where the privileges "of the disciple whom Jesus loved" are mentioned, there can be no doubt as to the Christian family whence this book originated. This does not prove, however, that an immediate disciple of Jesus wrote it; yet it proves that he who held the pen believed, or wished it to be believed, that he recorded the recollections of an immediate disciple of Jesus, and that his intention was to exalt the prerogative of that disciple, and show that he had been what neither James nor Peter had been--a true brother, a spiritual brother of Jesus.

In any case, this new accord which we have found between our text and the Gospel is very remarkable. The words of Luke, in fact (xxiii. 49), do not exactly exclude Mary from the foot of the cross, and the author of the Acts, who is in truth the same person as the author of the third Gospel, places Mary amongst the disciples at Jerusalem a few days after the death of Jesus. But this is of small historical value, for the author of the third Gospel and of the Acts (at least of the first chapters of the latter work) is the least authoritative traditionist of all the New Testament. Still, it establishes more and more this fact, in my eyes a very serious one, that the Johannine tradition was not an isolated accident in the primitive Church, that many traditions belonging to the school of John had become known or were common to other Christian churches, even before the compilation of the fourth Gospel, or at least independently of it. For to suppose that the author of the fourth Gospel had the Gospel of Luke under his eyes when composing his work, is what appears to me most improbable.

§ 37. Our text recovers its superiority in that which concerns the potion offered on the cross. This circumstance, with respect to which Matthew and Mark express themselves with obscurity, which in Luke is entirely transformed (xxiii. 36), finds here its true explanation. It is Jesus himself who, burning with thirst, asks for something to drink. A soldier offers him, on a sponge, a little acidulated water. This is very natural and most consistent with ancient usage. It's presented neither in derision nor to aggravate his sufferings, as the synoptics would have us believe. It is a humane action on the part of the soldier.

§ 38. Our Gospel omits the earthquake and the phenomena which the most widely circulated legend would have it believed accompanied the last supper of Jesus.

§ 39. The episode of the crurifragium (the breaking of Jesus' legs) and the lance thrust, which are peculiar to our Gospel, is certainly possible. The ancient Jewish and Roman customs, contained in v. 31, are exact. The crurifragium was indeed a Roman punishment. As to the medicine spoken of in v. 34, it is attributable to several sources. But, even though our author should give proof here of an imperfect physiology, no inference can be drawn from this. I am aware that the lance thrust may have been invented to accord with Zechariah xii. 10, comp. Apoc. i. 7. I recognise that the à priori symbolical explanation was very well adapted to the circumstance that Jesus was not subjected to the crurifragium. The author wishes to assimilate Jesus to the paschal lamb, and it suits his thesis very well indeed that the bones of Jesus were not broken. Nor was he perhaps displeased that a little hyssop should have been introduced. As for the water and the blood which flowed from his side, it is equally easy to discover their dogmatic value. Is it to be said that the author of the fourth Gospel invented these details? I can very well understand people who reason thus: Jesus, as Messiah, was to be born at Bethlehem; the writings, most improbable in other respects, which make his parents go to Bethlehem on the eve of his birth, belong to fiction. But can it also be said that it was written beforehand that not a bone of Jesus was to be broken, and that water and blood should flow from his side? Is it not admissible that such circumstances really happened, circumstances that the subtle mind of the disciples would instantly remark, and whence appeared profound providential combinations? I know of nothing more instructive in this respect than in the comparison of that which concerns the potion offered to Jesus before the crucifixion in Mark (xv. 23) and in Matthew (xxvii. 34). Mark here, as almost always, is the most original. According to his account, Jesus is offered, as was customary, an aromatic wine, to render him insensible. There is nothing Messiani about that. According to Matthew, the aromatic wine was compounded of gall and vinegar. In this manner was brought about a pretended fulfilment of the 22nd verse of Psalm lxix. Here then is one instance where we can attach to a fact a process of transformation. If we had only the narrative of Matthew, we would be authorised in believing that that circumstance was of pure invention, that it was created to obtain the realisation of a passage alleged to have reference to the Messiah. But the account of Mark indeed proves that there was in this instance an actual fact, and that it has been warped to suit the requirements of the Messianic interpretation.

§ 40. At the burial, Nicodemus, a personage peculiar to our Gospel, reappears. It must be observed that this personage plays no part in the early apostolic history. Moreover, as regards the Twelve Apostles, seven or eight of them disappeared completely after the death of Jesus. It seems that there were near Jesus groups which looked upon him in very different lights, and some of which do not figure in the history of the Church. The author of the teachings which form the basis of our Gospel has been able to recognise friends of Jesus who are not mentioned in the synoptics, who lived in a less extended world. The evangelical personnel was very different in the different Christian families. James, brother of the Lord, a man in St. Paul's eyes of the first importance, plays only a very secondary part in the eyes of the synoptics and of our author. Mary Magdalene, who, according to the four texts, played a capital part in the resurrection, is not included by St. Paul in the number of the persons to whom Jesus showed himself, and after that solemn hour she is no more heard of It was the same in the case of Babism. In the accounts which we possess of the origins of that religion, and which are in complete accord, the personnel differs quite sensibly. Each witness has observed the fact from his own point of view, and has attributed a special importance to such of the founders as were known to him.

Observe a new textual coincidence between Luke (xx3 53) and John (xix. 41).

§ 41. An important fact arises from the discussion which have just instituted. Our Gospel, disagreeing very considerably with the synoptics up to the last week of Jesus, is throughout the whole account of the Passion in general accord with them. We cannot say, however, that it has borrowed from them, for, on the contrary, it sails perfectly clear of them, it has not copied any of their expressions. If the author of the fourth Gospel had read some account of the synoptic tradition, which is very possible, it must at least be said that he did not have it before him when he wrote. What is to be concluded hence? That he had a tradition of his own, a tradition similar to that of the synoptics, although between the two we have only intrinsic reasons to guide us in forming a decision. A fictitious narrative, a sort of à priori gospel, written in the second century, would not have had that character. Like as with the apocryphas, the author has copied the synoptics, but has amplified them to suit his own tastes. The position of the Johannine writer is that of an author who was not ignorant of what had already been written on the subject he was treating, who approved many of the things which had been said, but who believed himself to be possessed of superior information, and advanced the latter without disturbing himself about others. This may be compared to what we know of the Gospel of Marcion. Marcion wrote a gospel under similar conditions to those which had been attributed to the author of the fourth Gospel. But observe the difference: Marcion had a sort of agreement or had an extract made setting forth certain views. A composition of the same description as that imputed to the author of our gospel, if that author lived in the second century and wrote with the end in view that is alleged of him, is absolutely without precedent. That is neither the eclectic method and conciliation of Tatian and of Marcion, nor the amplification pasticcio of the apocryphal Gospels, nor the wholly arbitrary reverie, without historical basis, of the Pista Sophia. To get rid of certain dogmatic difficulties, one falls into verbal historical difficulties which are destitute of meaning.

§ 42. The agreement of our Gospel with the synoptics, which strikes one in the narrative of the Passion, is hardly discernible, at least in Matthew, in that of the resurrection and what follows. But here again I think our author much more near the truth. According to it, Mary Magdalene alone goes first to the tomb; alone, she is the first messenger of the resurrection, which accords with the finale of the Gospel of Mark (xvi. 9, et seq.). On the news brought by Mary Magdalene, Peter and John go to the tomb; another most remarkable consonance, even in the expression and the little details, with Luke (xxiv. 1, 2, 12, 24) and with the finale of Mark, preserved in the manuscript L and in the margin of the Philoxenian version. The two first evangelists do not speak of a visit of the apostles to the tomb. A decisive authority gives here the advantage to the tradition of Luke and of the Johannine writer; we refer to St. Paul. According to the first epistle to the Corinthians, he writes about the year 57, and surely a good while before the Gospels of Luke and John the first apparition of the resurrected Jesus was seen by Cephas. True, this assertion of Paul coincides better with the account of Luke, who does not mention Peter, than with the account of the fourth Gospel, according to which the well-beloved apostle should have accompanied Peter. But the first chapters of the Acts constantly present Peter and John to us as inseparable companions. It is probable that at this decisive moment they were together, that they were together when they were informed of the event, and that they ran together. The finale of Mark in the manuscript L makes use of a more vague formula: oi peri ton Petrou.

The ingenuous personal characteristics which are presented here in the narrative of our author are almost sign-manuals. The determined adversaries of the authenticity of the fourth Gospel impose on themselves a difficult task in forcing themselves to see in these characteristics the artifices of a forger. The design of the author to place himself alongside or before Peter in important circumstances (i. 35, et seq.; xiii. 23, et seq.; xviii. 15, et seq.) is altogether remarkable. If one would give to it the meaning desired, one would say that the compilation of these passages could be but little posterior to the death of John. The account of the first goings and comings of Sunday morning, which are somewhat confused in the synoptics, is in our author perfectly distinct. Yes, here the tradition is original, the disjointed members of which have been arranged in the three synoptics in three different manners, but wholly inferior, in point of likelihood, to the scheme of the fourth Gospel. Remark, that at the decisive moment on Sunday morning, the disciple alleged to be the author does not attribute to himself any particular vision. A forger, writing without regard to tradition for the purpose of creating the chief of a school, would not have committed the blunder, in the midst of a rolling fire of apparitions, with which latter every tradition of these first days was full, of attributing it to a favourite disciple, just as it has been done in the case of James.

Note again a coincidence between Luke (xxiv. 4) and John (xx. 12, 13). Matthew and Mark have only an angel at this moment. Verse v. 9 is un trait de lumiere. The synoptics are here destitute of all credulity, when they pretend that Jesus had predicted his resurrection.

§ 43. The apparition which follows, in our author--we mean the one which takes place before the apostles assemble on Sunday evening--coincides well with the account of Paul. But it is with Luke that the agreements here become striking and decisive. Not only does the apparition take place on the same date in presence of the same people, but also the words pronounced by Jesus are the same; the circumstance of Jesus showing his feet and his hands is lightly transposed, but it is recognisable as a part of the other, whilst it is wanting in the two first synoptics. The Gospel of the Hebrews marches here in accord with the third and fourth Gospels. "But why," it might be said, "hold to the narrative of an eyewitness, a narrative which embraces manifest impossibilities? He who does not admit the miracle, and admits the authenticity of the fourth Gospel, is he not forced to regard as an imposture the so formal assurance of verses 30, 31?" Certainly not. St. Paul also affirms that he saw Jesus, and yet we do not reject either the authenticity of the first chapter to the Corinthians or the veracity of St. Paul.

§ 44. A peculiarity of our Gospel is that the inspiration of the Holy Spirit occurs on the very evening of the resurrection (xx. 22). Luke (Acts ii. et seq.) places this event after the ascension. It is nevertheless remarkable that the verse John xx. 22 has its parallel in Luke xxiv. 49. Only the contour of the passage in Luke is made to be undecided, so as not to contradict the account of the Acts (ii. 1 et seq.). Here again, the third and fourth Gospels communicate with one another through a kind of secret channel.

§ 45. Like all critics, I make the compilation of the fourth Gospel terminate at the end of chapter xx. Chapter xxi. is an addition, but an addition nearly contemporaneous, either by the author himself or by one of his disciples. The chapter contains the account of a new apparition of the resurrected Jesus. Here again important coincidences with the third Gospel are to be remarked (comp. John xxi. 12, 13 with Luke xxiv. 41-43), not to mention certain resemblances to the Gospel to the Hebrews.

46. Details somewhat obscure follow (15 et seq.), in which we have a more lively sensation than anywhere else of the imprint of the school of John. The perpetual preoccupation of the relations of John and Peter reappear. The aim of all this resembles a series of private letters which are only understood by him who has written them or by the initiated. The allusion to the death of Peter, the amicable and

fraternal sentiment of rivalry between the two apostles, the belief, emitted with reserve, that John should not die before seeing the apparition of Jesus--all this appears sincere. The exaggeration of bad style, in v. 25, is not felt to be inconsistent in a composition so inferior, in the literary sense, to the synoptics. This verse is lacking, moreover, in the Codex Sinaïticus. Verse 24, finally, seems a signature. The words, "And we know that his witness is true," are an addition of the disciples, or rather induce the belief that the last editors utilised notes or recollections of the apostle. These protestations of veracity are found in almost similar terms in two writings which are by the same hand as our Gospel.

§ 47. So, in the account of the life beyond the tomb of Jesus, the fourth Gospel retains its superiority. This superiority is to be especially recognised in portions taken generally. In the Gospels of Luke and Mark (xvi. 9-20) the life of Jesus resurrected has the appearance of enduring only for a day. In Matthew it seems to have been short. In the Acts (chapter i.) it endures forty days. In the three synoptics and in the Acts it terminates by an adieu or by an ascension to Heaven. Matters are arranged in a less convenient form in the fourth Gospel. The life beyond the tomb has no fixed limits; it is prolonged somehow indefinitely. Elsewhere I have demonstrated the superiority of this system. It suffices for the present to remember that it responds much better to the important passage of St. Paul, 1 Cor. xv. 5-8.

What is the result of this long analysis? Firstly, that considered by itself the narrative of the material circumstances of the life of Jesus, as furnished by the fourth Gospel, is superior in point of probability to the narrative of the synoptics. Secondly, that, on the other hand, the discourses which the fourth Gospel impute to Jesus have in general no character of authenticity. Thirdly, that the author has a tradition of the life of Jesus very different from that of the synoptics, except as concerns the last days. Fourthly, that this tradition, however, was pretty well spread; for Luke, who does not belong to the school whence emerged our Gospel, has an idea more or less vague of many of the facts which were known to our author, and of which Matthew and Mark knew nothing. Fifthly, that the work is less beautiful than the synoptic Gospels, Matthew and Mark being the masterpieces of spontaneous art, Luke presenting an admirable combination of ingenuous art and of reflection, whilst the fourth Gospel presents only a series of notes, very badly arranged, in which legend and tradition, reflection and naïveté se fondent mal. Sixthly, that the author of the fourth Gospel, whoever he may be, has written to raise the authority of one of the apostles, in order to show that this apostle had played a part, in circumstances where he is not mentioned in the other narratives, in order to prove that he knew things which the other disciples knew not. Seventhly, that the author of the fourth Gospel wrote at a time when Christianity was more advanced than the synoptics, and with a more exalted idea of the divine rôle of Jesus, the figure of Jesus being with him more rugged, more heretical, like that of an Æon or a divine hypostasis who operates through his own will. Eighthly, that if the material teachings are more exact than those of the synoptics, its historic colouring is much less so, insomuch that, in order to seize the general physiognomy of Jesus, the synoptic Gospels, despite their lacunes and their errors, are still the veritable guides.

Naturally, these reasons in favour of the fourth Gospel would be singularly confirmed if it could be established that the author of this Gospel is the apostle John, son of Zebedee. But the present is a research of a different order. Our aim has been to examine the fourth Gospel by itself, independently of its author. This question of the authorship of the fourth Gospel is assuredly the most singular that there is in literary history. I know of no question of criticism in which contrary appearances are so evenly balanced and which hold the mind more completely in suspense.

It is clear at first that the author wishes to pass himself off as an ocular witness of evangelical facts (i. 14, xix. 35), and for the friend preferred by Jesus (xiii. 22 et seq., xix. 26 et seq., compared with xxi. 24). It will serve no purpose to say that chap. xxi. is an addition, since this addition is by the author himself or by his school. In two other places, moreover (i. 35 et seq., xviii. 15 et seq.), one sees clearly that the author loves to speak of himself in covered language. One of two things must be true: either the author of the fourth Gospel is a disciple of Jesus, an intimate disciple, and belonging to the oldest epoch; or else the author has employed, in order to give himself authority, an artifice which he has pursued from the commencement of the book to the end, the tendency being to make believe that he was a witness as well situated as it was possible to be to render a true account of the facts.

Who is the disciple whose authority the author thus seeks to make prevail? The title indicates it; it is "John." There is not the least reason to suppose it may have been added in opposition to the intentions of the real author. It was certainly written at the head of our Gospel at the end of the second century. On the other hand, evangelical history only presents, outside of John the Baptist, a single personage of the name of John. It is necessary then to choose between the hypotheses; either we must acknowledge John, son of Zebedee, as the author of the fourth Gospel, or regard that Gospel as an apocryphal writing composed by some individual who wished to pass it off as a work of John, son of Zebedee. The question at issue here is not in fact one of legends, the work of multitudes, for which no person is responsible. A man who, in order to give credence to that which he records, deceives the public not only in regard to his name, but also as to the value of his testimony, is not a writer of legends, he is an impostor. Such a biography as that of Francis d'Assisi, written one or two hundred years posterior to that extraordinary man, may recount shoals of miracles created by tradition, without ceasing, for all that, to be one of the most candid and most innocent men of the world. But if this biography were to say, "I was his companion, he preferred me to any other, everything I am about to tell you is true, for I have seen it," without contradicting the proper qualification, then it is quite another thing.

That fault is not, moreover, the only one which the author may have committed. We have three epistles which in like manner bear the name of John. If there is one thing in the domain of criticism which is probable, it is that the first at least of these epistles is by the same author as the fourth Gospel. One might almost denominate it as a detached chapter. The vocabulary of the two writings is identical. Now the language of the works of the New Testament is so poor in expression and so little varied that such inductions can be drawn with an almost absolute certainty. The author of this epistle, like the author of the Gospel, gives himself out as an eyewitness (1 John i. 1, et seq., iv. 14) of evangelical history. He represents himself as a person well-known, and enjoying high consideration in the Church. At first glance, it seems that the most natural hypothesis is to admit that the whole of these writings are indeed the work of John, son of Zebedee.

Let us hasten to add, nevertheless, that critics of the first order have not without grave reason rejected the authenticity of the fourth Gospel. The work is too rarely cited in the most ancient Christian literature; its authority only commences to be known much later. Nothing could less resemble than this Gospel that which might be expected from John, an old fisher on the Lake of Gennesareth. The Greek in which it is written is not in any sense the Palestinian Greek with which we are acquainted in the other books of the New Testament. The ideas, in particular, are of an entirely different order. Here we are in full Philonian and almost Gnostic metaphysics. The discourses of Jesus as they are reported by this pretended witness, this confidential friend, are false, often flat, nay impossible. In a word, the Apocalypse is also given out as the work of John, not, it is true, in the quality of Apostle, but by one who, in the churches of Asia, arrogates to himself such a preeminence, and who, with but little effort, can be identified with the Apostle John. Now, when we compare the style and the thoughts of the author of the Apocalypse with the style and the thoughts of the author of the fourth Gospel and the first Johannine epistle, we find the most striking discordance. How are we to get out of that labyrinth of singular contradictions and of inextricable difficulties?

For my part I see but one way. It is to hold that the fourth Gospel is, indeed, in a sense χατὰλοάνοην, that it was not written by John himself, that it was for a long time esoteric and secret in one of the schools which adhered to John. To penetrate into the mystery of this school, to learn how the writing in question was put forth, is simply impossible. Can the notes or data left by the Apostle be used as a basis for the text which we have? Has a secretary, nurtured by the reading of Philo, and possessing a style of his own, given to the narratives and letters of his master a turn which without this they could never have had? Have we not here something analogous to the letters of Saint Catherine of Sienna, revised by her secretary, or to those revelations of Catherine Emmerich, of which we can say equally that they are by Catherine, and that they are by Bretano, the ideas of Catherine having traversed the style of Bretano? Have not some purely semi-Gnostics, at the close of the life of the Apostle, seized his pen, and, under the pretext of aiding him in writing his recollections and of assisting him in his correspondence, incorporated their ideas, and favourite expressions, covering themselves with his authority. Who is that Presbyteros Johannes, a sort of double of the Apostle, whose tomb is pointed out by the side of John's? Is he a different personage from the Apostle? Is he the Apostle himself whose long life was for many years the foundation of the hopes of believers? I have elsewhere touched upon these questions. I shall often return to them again. I have had but one aim in this: that in recurring so often in the "Life of Jesus" to the fourth Gospel, in order to establish the thread of my narrative, I have had strong reasons, even in the case of the said Gospel, for not holding it to be the work of the Apostle John.